*"My poor dreams  
Of blissful love,  
You perished at the apogee of joy.  
You were born so proud yet so ill fated  
Like birds in the woods where you died."*

SALVATORE GIULIANO

© Copyright 2000 ARNONE Editore
Administration: Via Filippo Patti 25 - 90133 Palermo - Italy
Tel. 01139-091333461 - Fax 01139-091333484

*All rights reserved. No part of this publication may be reproduced in any form or by any means without the prior permission in writing of the publisher.*

*Layout, graphics and cover:* Saverio Rao
*Translation:* Quid Translation Services - Palermo (Joseph Caliò)
*Printed by:* Officine Grafiche Riunite - Palermo

**ISBN 88-87663-15-7**

Marianna Giuliano - Giuseppe Sciortino Giuliano

# My Brother, Salvatore Giuliano

*The True Story*

Arnone Editore - Palermo

Portrait of Castellammare del Golfo by the painter Gian Battista Di Liberti.

Introduction

*Before starting to write this book, I would like to explain the reasons which led me to undertake such an arduous task.*

*Undoubtedly, for those who do it to earn a living, this statement may seem amusing. Yet, as this the first time for me, this task bears two great difficulties.*

*First, there is the difficulty of writing. I have no experience in this field. The second is the difficulty posed by the complexity of the subject matter, although it is the story of my family.*

*In order to avoid any risk of manipulation, I was forced to improvise. I was the proofreader, I took care of the layout and finally I also became a publisher.*

*I kindly ask all the experts of the field, who may rightly levy criticism, to pardon me.*

*As many already know, much has been written on my Uncle Salvatore Giuliano. There are innumerable books in many languages telling the stories of his love affairs. Some are true, others false. Some are fanciful episodes created by the lively imagination of novelists.*

*Handsome, brawny and generous, my uncle was a real man in flesh and blood.*

*In 1960/61 a movie based only on four episodes taken from the proceedings of the trials was made. They only put on the screen the lies of the "official truth".*

*Up to this day these lies, some of which are so huge and gross, are so entwined with the truth that it is almost impossible to trace a clear-cut line between reality and fantasy.*

*These books and movies, though positively contributing to spread and immortalize the figure of the personage, but little is said or known of Giuliano, the man, of his fascinating personality, and of the political, social and economic situation of the Sicily of his days.*

*So what is the truth about the story of this man who for seven long years eluded every attempt to capture him?*

*Before starting this book, no one had taken the trouble of looking for the real protagonists of this story, of going deeper, below the surface of the "official truth", the truth of the establishment and what was said during the trials.*

*The "official truth", the behavior of petty criminals who used Turiddu's name for their own selfish interests to commit crimes, the superficial behavior of those wearing police uniforms in those days who accused him of unsolved crimes in Western Sicily, the deleterious behavior of some of his men who unfortunately caused infamous incidents such as the notorious episode of the "Portella delle Ginestre" and the turnabout of political leaders who used my uncle as a scapegoat and depicted his exploits as personal initiatives: all these false accusations and the defamation (by calling him a bandit) contributed to ruin the reputation and figure of Salvatore Giuliano, the man. The result is that, instead of shining bright as the sun, "Turiddu" is just a weak blade of moonlight without enough force to cast its light on the sea surrounding the island.*

*This figure, who was above all a Sicilian, a fervent patriot, a generous freedom fighter who in the face of danger risked his own life, contributed substantially to obtain that "autonomy" which his own fellow countrymen still enjoy in part today after 125 years of apparent happiness and freedom afflicted by sorrow.*

*The "Giuliano phenomenon" erupted immediately after the end of WWII when hunger revealed itself in all its cruel reality and when individual freedom fell under the yoke of obscurantist forces.*

*Those who lived during that woeful period know and understand what I am saying. Only by understanding this period of need, terror, revolts and threats can we have a clear view of all these events and understand what actually happened.*

*Over the years I have watched powerless, read and understood that those were days of abuse, of infamy and easy money at the expense of a noble-hearted man with superior values who grew in the midst of poverty and intimidation.*

*He had the courage to rebel against the injustice perpetrated against by his fellow Sicilians who for centuries had been kept in shackles without pride, union or sense of brotherhood.*

*SALVATORE GIULIANO was and will always be the sword of Damocles hanging over the heads of those who are well aware of the slavery of this land and who despite everything continue to portray him as an outlaw.*

*With regard to this latter statement, it is not only the nephew of this man that is speaking, but also a son of this land who feels in* his own blood the fervor for this beloved land, which is offended, abused, humiliated and exploited.

I am writing to launch my battle cry:
- *"Picciotti!":*
*"The moment of Truth has come!"*

After years of research, of questions, and of pressing requests, I have finally succeeded in tearing down the wall of silence, which hides these events like a blanket of fog.

I have collected every single piece and put them all together to form this mosaic.

The merit of this feat is not only mine as I had the advantage of being his nephew. The merit must be shared with all those who helped in this difficult task.

Everything now is clearer and easier to grasp.

I received advice from people who would never have spoken to any other: my dear and unforgettable grandmother, Maria Lombardo (Turiddu's mother) to whom I would listen for hours and hours and who entrusted me a document written by Cosma Acampora, the family's lawyer, and which I jealously cherish. It was a precious source of information for some of the episodes told in this book.

My uncle Peppino Giuliano (his brother), who died about 1 year after his mother, the "Picciotti" who I searched for to obtain their description of their leader and who remembered those days, feats and ideals with great joy.

Very few of those who witnessed those events are still alive and it is my duty to pay homage to all those who sacrificed themselves together with my uncle for Sicily.

Yet the greatest merit of all goes to my mother, MARIANNA GIULIANO, Turiddu's sister who shared his ideals and was at his side in the armed and political battle.

Without my mother, whom recently passed away owing to a terrible illness and has left me to join the other members of our family, I would never have succeeded in my task.

I was just an instrument for writing this book, as she was the one to provide most of its contents. It is as if she was the one to actually write it.

It is my duty here to pay tribute to her.

In order to carry out her specific request, I included a number of episodes, which at first sight a careful observer may deem as repetitive. Yet they have the specific purpose of better highlighting the humanity of the personage.

*Now I will leave the stage to Her, the HISTORY OF SICILY, as our family lawyer, Cosma Acampora, loved to call her, so that she can tell this story as she told it to me and that TRUTH above all else can be revealed. For all those citizens of Montelepre who contributed with their suffering and blood to fight for our Autonomy and for Sicily and to bring to the light the true SALVATORE GIULIANO to attribute him the place that he deserves.*

*I am the voice
Of she who lies
But has no peace,
Because all she has done
Is unknown or
Kept secret by the people.
I will act in her name,
I will shout, ...
Till I remain breathless,
I will run fleet of foot,
I will be like a bird of prey,
I will fight and be ferocious,
I will guide those who are not capable
Until she who lies
Finds peace.*

GIUSEPPE SCIORTINO GIULIANO

*My Brother, Salvatore Giuliano*

Giuseppe Sciortino Giuliano proudly shows a shirt that belonged to his mother.

May all the young know
And may all those who are no longer young remember.

*The Author*

## Chapter 1

# WE WERE PEACEFUL FARMERS

A crown of bare hills, sloping hillsides in some areas colored by green patches of olive trees, to the west a plain dotted with isolated homes and towns and in the background the marvelous Gulf of Castellammare: in the midst of this breathtaking landscape lies MONTELEPRE.

And Montelepre has been the home of my family for generations now.

**"You know son that our family had a clean record till the seventh generation. No one ever had problems with the law.**

**What happened was the consequence of that hurricane called war on our family".**

I'll start telling you this story from when your grandmother was about seventeen years old so that you can better understand our origins.

She had just come back from America and she was walking along one of the town's roads together with her two brothers, Nino and Gioacchino. They were a few steps behind her, each carrying two heavy suitcases. They were a bit tired, the voyage had lasted eight days, but they were anxious to see their parents again.

They had been away for three years, so their return had aroused the curiosity of the women in town as they looked out from behind half-shut doors.

There were soft whispers, nods and comments of the young men at the corner of the road.

Once they entered the little road leading to their house, they saw her face light up with life all of a sudden.

Excited calls followed:

"Comare Rosa!"

"Comare Peppina!"

"Look!"

"Marianna Bono's children are back!"

In a few seconds a small crowd of neighbors fled out to meet them. Hugs here, kisses there and tears of joy everywhere.

At that very moment, after a long day of hard work in the fields, grandfather was coming home on his mule.

Hearing all the chaos and seeing the crowd of people he spurred the mule in that direction and reached the three brothers.

He looked at grandmother with such interest and intensity that she had to turn away as if a mysterious and irresistible force had compelled her to do so.

For a never-ending moment of unspeakable sweetness their eyes met and they both blushed owing to the embarrassing presence of the others. They faintly smiled and feebly waved to each other before returning to their homes.

In the evening the news of the arrival of grandmother and her brothers was the main topic of conversation at Fifì Giacopelli's Café, the only place where you could go if you didn't want to go to bed early and if you were looking for a place where you could break the peaceful monotony of town life.

Grandfather too was there that evening; he listened to the small talk on the news of the day. The more he listened, the more the encounter of a few hours before seemed to be vivid.

He was surprised to find himself gazing more than once towards an unknown point of the café, as his friends uselessly tried to invite him to play cards.

He went home.

With a fixed idea in his mind.

Maria.

He too had recently come back from America. He had worked in Canada. There he managed to save some money, with which he bought a piece of land in the "Buonagrazia" contrada so that he could earn a living without any hardships yet which was far from being well off.

His father, Don Peppino Giuliano, still worked in the fields despite his 65 years of age and was very active.

When he saw him come back early he thought he wasn't feeling very well, but he soon understood that he was afflicted by a malaise, which was not physical in nature.

He was in love.

They started to talk about the girl and her family.

In those days, before getting engaged, a specific ritual had to be followed: first the aspiring fiancée had to find out whether the girl was free from previous commitments and then whether the girl was interested in the suitor.

Then there were cases in which the parents would decide everything without consulting their daughter. It was wrong yet those were the customs.

But that's another story.

Ten days had gone by from the evening when grandmother had come back. They were ten days of anxious waiting. Every evening he would come back from work, get washed and then grandfather would go to walk under Maria's window hoping to see her. While grandmother, unaware of his real intentions, would go to peek through the shutters at the same hour. She was curious to know whether it was the young man she had met at her arrival and who had caught her attention by looking at her in that strange way.

From the moment of her arrival in Montelepre her parents had already received nineteen wedding proposals, but they answered to all nineteen that their daughter was only seventeen and that they did not feel ready to force onto her the burden of a family.

Don Peppino Giuliano and his wife Giuseppina Gaglio, who had already heard of the nineteen refusals from the town folk, had little hope of seeing their proposal accepted especially since they had refused also the proposals of the sons of the town's most respectable families.

They hesitantly knocked at her parents' door. They were welcomed with due respect while grandfather stayed outside to wait under the window according to custom.

After the first moments of mutual embarrassment, grandfather's parents made their proposal. In the meantime, after having peeked outside from behind the curtains and having listened to the usual rite, grandmother looked outside the window to see the new suitor. Her surprise was great when she saw that it was the young man she had longed to meet. She abandoned all hesitation and, forgetting the social conventions of the time, she called him.

Grandfather was overwhelmed with dismay for a few moments and he then ran immediately to her window. They finally had the chance to introduce themselves and to talk together.

In the meantime grandmother's father, Salvatore Lombardo, had refused also the wedding proposal of grandfather's parents and they were about to leave with an expression on their faces which revealed the humiliation they had just suffered, when all of a sudden the door of the room opened and in came grandmother. She asked the guests to stay for a few more minutes and then she called her father into the other room and said to him:

"Father, I want him!"

Salvatore Lombardo was caught by surprise, but he had the joy of his daughter at heart.

They both returned to the room where the guests were waiting.

"Don Peppino, please excuse me, but our children want each other" he started.

"As far as I am concerned, there is no obstacle at all!"

"So I officially declare that my daughter Maria is to marry your son Salvatore!"

Grandfather was invited into the home of his new fiancée. He stayed for about an hour. He could only speak to her from a distance because it was absolutely forbidden to have any physical contacts before the wedding.

For the whole period of their engagement, which lasted six months, there was perfect harmony between both families. The wedding was finally celebrated in the church of Montelepre.

A month after the wedding, hoping to improve his economic situation, my father (now I can call him this way) opened a textile and clothing shop. My mother took care of the shop while he would go to work in the fields.

The months went by monotonously and my father was unsatisfied with how much he was earning because he only had just enough to survive.

He was a restless man who wanted to improve his condition. He decided to leave for America. When he left, my mother was pregnant. The baby that was born was a girl and she was called Giuseppina, like her father's mother. At the time of her birth my father was in Louisiana.

He came back three years after with a nice amount of money, with which he bought a piece of land in the "LO ZUCCO" contrada, at about five kilometers from Montelepre. The soil was good but the work was hard.

A year later another baby was born. He was called Peppino Giuliano, like his father's father. The family continued to grow but not the money. It just never seemed to be enough. The business in the shop, which at the beginning had done well, was slow.

The town folk seldom bought clothing and especially shoes. There were people who had never had a pair of shoes in their life and the best suit they had was full of patches of different colors. Then there were those who would buy on credit and would forget to pay.

The piece of land instead yielded all the necessary for the family's survival without making them suffer hardship. Yet the work in the fields was too much for a just one man with his hoe and a plow pulled by an animal.

My father soon got tired.

A bit for the desire to improve his position, a bit for his inborn spirit of adventure, he left for California. He immediately found a job and he would send all the money he could put aside to my mother.

He was away for four years during which my mother, who had

Maria Lombardo at the age of 17.

managed to put together a substantial amount of money, bought eight hectares of land from the Lupo family. She didn't say anything to my father. When he came back, he found this beautiful surprise and he was so happy that he bought the house right next to the piece of land.

After repairing it, the whole family moved into the new house. The inconvenience was that it was located on the outskirts of town, to the right along the road from Palermo. But otherwise the home and the adjacent piece of land were a true delight. There was a rich variety of fruit trees and plenty of vegetables.

Almost a year after his return, exactly December 13, 1920, I was born. But they registered me at the town hall five days later.

According to the customs of the time I was named Marianna after my mother's mother.

My father was very happy and with a new charge of energy he would work in the fields to provide us with everything we needed. But two years later his restless and adventurous spirit had the best over him. He wasn't satisfied with what he was earning so he decided to go back to America at all costs. He left for California while my mother was pregnant again and very close to giving birth to the child.

The town midwife was very busy and my mother's sister-in-law, the wife of her brother Nino Lombardo, was about to give birth too. The poor woman was forced to rush between the homes of the two women. She was lucky that they lived one in front of the other.

Finally, on November 16, 1922, almost at the same time, both my mother and her sister-in-law gave birth to two boys.

The whole family and all the neighbors were waiting for the moment to come and when it finally arrived news spread quickly.

This was also the result of the fact that a neighbor soon after the event went out onto the balcony and started to shout:

"The baby's born! The baby's born!"

This ostentatious gesture, which was typical of those days, attracted many people. For days people were coming and going from both houses, especially from ours.

Everyone would ask my mother what name she would give the baby and she gave them all the same answer:

"My husband is still on his way to California, so I will have to decide on my own!" "We left my husband's family happy by naming our first-born children after them; my mother too was left happy!" "Now the only one left is my father, so I will call him Salvatore, Salvatore Giuliano, just like his father!"

Chapter II

# THE MAN

I was about two years old when my brother was born. My older sister and brother preferred to play with the other children of their age and I was often left alone.

I had awaited anxiously his birth and from the moment he was born I felt I was finally complete. I would spend hours watching him.

He was beautiful: he had dark skin, a round face, deep black hair, and dark and lively eyes. From early on during our childhood, as we were almost the same age, my brother Salvatore, my cousin Salvatore Lombardo, who was born on the same day as Salvatore, and I formed an inseparable trio.

We were always together: we would play together, share our secrets, joys and fears. But my brother had something special inside him. He was always inventing new games and he knew how to explain them to us clearly and with great confidence.

We were fascinated by him and, although at times there may have been some hesitation, all he needed to do was to look at us with his piercing eyes and with that smile of his traced across his face to dispel our hesitations like fog in the sun.

Unlike me, he was growing healthy and strong and was never ill. He loved everyone, but he was especially close to our father, whom he had little chance of knowing better during the first years of his childhood.

But in those days people were compelled to emigrate. He missed him very much. He would take father's picture, press it against his heart and kiss it.

He was good and kind and animated by a sense of deep sympathy for the suffering of others. This was an innate aspect of his character, which continued to grow in him and manifested itself in many ways.

At the age of seven he started to go to elementary school, where he acquired his first elements of knowledge first from Prof. Francesco Purpura and then from his teacher, Mrs. Campanella. His intelligence was above average and soon made him distinguish himself.

His especially lively and affectionate character fascinated all those who met him. He had a manifest inclination for the humanities and he could learn poems with great ease. He was the best student of his class and the teachers were proud of him.

Salvatore had become the leader of his class thanks to his openness and fairness. His fascinating personality won him the love of his classmates who would follow him in all his feats.

At the age of twelve, he finished elementary school. In that same period my father decided to come back for good from the United States. He was happy because his family was now better off thanks to his work and the money he had saved. With the money he bought six hectares of land in contrada "Ecce Homo" just outside Giardinello, a town located a kilometer away from Montelepre and dedicated himself to farming.

There were no other schools in town and our father couldn't afford to send Salvatore to study in Palermo. So Salvatore too went to work with our father in the fields together with our brother Peppino.

In the evening his back was in pieces when he would come home. But he had no rest. He would quickly change his clothes to go to church and meet Fr. Giuseppe Di Bella. He was happy to spend his time with him. He felt great esteem and respect for him and he envied his culture. He would listen with great interest to his teachings.

He had an innate thirst for knowledge and he finally found a rich well where he could quench it. But he didn't know how to take without giving. In exchange he would take care of the church and he was an altar boy during the Mass.

Salvatore, or "Turiddu" as he was called by friends and relatives, didn't like working in the fields, as he often told me. Besides mother, I was the only one with whom he would open his heart.

He preferred commerce, because it was a lighter profession and more respectable. He would have had the chance of travelling, of meeting over people, of being independent and having greater satisfaction from a personal and economic point of view.

Work in the fields instead not only was wretched and heavy, but it also offered no hopes of a better life in the future.

At the age of thirteen, his personality started to show itself in all its true nature. He nurtured high ideals and feelings: a deep sense of honor and the commitment to keep his word.

I remember one day when I found a letter he wrote to a girl of his age, while I was going through the pockets of his trousers before washing them.

In that letter he revealed to her his burning love, for which, he said, he couldn't find more appropriate words. He concluded by telling her that, if she didn't return his love, he would have avoided meeting her so that he wouldn't have to bear the pain of seeing her.

As soon as I was alone with him, I started to wave the letter under his nose and jokingly I told him:

"So, young man, you've started to fall in love with girls?"

After a first moment of surprise he ordered me to give it back.

"You can forget it," I answered, "I'll show it to everyone!"

He looked at me, he seemed calm, but he suddenly jumped at me. But I avoided him and I started to run around the table.

After his unsuccessful assault, he stopped all of a sudden, his face turned red and told me:

"If you don't give me that letter, I swear to you I'll never, ever look at you again!"

From the tone of his voice I understood he was very angry and irritated because he was jealous of his most intimate feelings. So I stopped fooling around with him and I gave it back to him.

A few months later Salvatore confessed to me that everything was over between the girl and him. He found consolation by spending his time reading.

He borrowed some books from Father Di Bella, from his old teacher and others.

He read epic poems: the story of the French knights, the "Orlando Furioso" and others. He then started to read more difficult books by Manzoni, Verga, and Pascoli and the Gospels and the Bible.

At his return from the fields, after his usual visit to the church or a game of billiards every now and then at the workers' club, he would close the door of his room and dedicate himself to his books.

Day after day, as the work in the fields strengthened his body making him stronger and stronger, his readings nourished his mind and opened new horizons for him.

There weren't many extraordinary episodes during my brother's adolescence. Mother Nature had bestowed onto him more virtues than vices. Our life was monotonous yet peaceful.

In November 1936, two people from a nearby town rented a house in Montelepre in via Milano. They decorated it as best as they could and transformed it into a puppet theater.

During holidays and on the eve of holidays, the "Puppet Opera" would present to the audience a great variety of characters.

The town did not offer many distractions and Turiddu would go together with his inseparable cousin Salvatore to listen to the jokes. They would sit amongst the children, yet also adults would watch the show.

In the middle of the audience there was a man named Sebastiano. He was a poor simpleton who was driven to alcoholism by the pain of having been abandoned by his wife.

The poor man was continuously mocked, pushed and shoved both by the young and the adults.

Turriddu couldn't stand that shameful behavior any longer. Despite his age he already had the build of a man of average height: he had wide shoulders and powerful arms. He rebelled against everyone. He emanated anger and disgust from his whole body. He was red with anger, his eyes were fiery. He jumped onto a desk near the stage and shouted:

"You bunch of cowards!"

"What fun is there?"

"Why don't you try to pick on me, instead of bothering that poor man?"

All of a sudden silence fell over the crowd. They all seemed a bunch of statues, everyone was holding their breath. He was so resolute that he had scared everyone.

He went towards the crowd, which meekly made way as he passed. He went towards poor Sebastiano, he took him by the arm and took him home.

With that gesture he had won the esteem and respect of many. He made many new friends, both male and female.

Every evening many would look for his company. Probably, they too felt that feeling of protection and security that I had when I was with him.

In the meantime, amongst infatuations and sighs, illusions and disappointments, the years of our youth went by quickly.

Turiddu was now eighteen. It was February 1940.

The Funaro company, which worked on behalf of the Telephone Company, was hiring workers. Turiddu decided to accept the job. But after a few days our father complained that he had been left alone to work in the fields. He answered:

"Listen, father. I love you and I have always paid you due respect. But you must understand me!"

"If you have problems with the work, then we can hire some farmhands to help you with a part of my pay. With the rest of the money I'll buy some books and other things I need!"

Our father accepted his offer and Turiddu was happy. A dream had come true. He had found a job that he liked and that gave him the chance of having more free time to dedicate to his studies. Turiddu, the youngest of the workers, soon won the esteem and trust of the engineer.

His way of living had improved and he even managed to buy a bicycle.

In the evening, after studying, he would go out with our cousin and they would then meet with other friends or just stay home to listen to the records he had brought from America. He loved all types of music, but he loved especially Verdi, Rossini, Beethoven and Leoncavallo's "Pagliacci". Music was his passion. He worked hard to learn to play the guitar and the accordion. He managed to do so in no time at all. He would sing as he played and he even wrote songs.

One evening, as he chatted along the way, he rode to Partinico with a friend of his named Pino. They had some biscuits and wine in a tavern. Then, as they continued to talk, they returned home. They were already halfway when he stopped suddenly:

"Did you pay for the biscuits?" he asked.

"No, I thought you did!" replied his friend.

"Damn! Let's go back and pay!"

"Are you crazy? We're almost home!" said Pino.

"Absolutely not! We must go back!" answered firmly Turiddu. "If you don't want to come, you can either wait here or continue on foot!" Once they had paid and apologized, they returned to Montelepre.

During a party at some friends' house my brother met a girl, Mariuccia B. He fell in love with her. She was fifteen, had hair that was blond as gold and blue eyes. She was short and meek and very sensitive. She was studying to become an elementary school teacher.

She was Turiddu's first big love and she had a great influence on his romantic inclination. Turiddu was a handsome man, almost six feet tall. He had everything that could make a girl go crazy: a strong body, courage, generosity without limits, self-confidence and a beautiful voice. Even Mariuccia was crazy for him.

So one evening, after having told me everything, he decided to go dedicate a serenade to the girl.

"Why don't you come too?" he asked.

"Do you really want me come?" I answered.

"Of course!.... So she will hear your voice too and she will come out!"

It seemed unbelievable for me to be part of the group and I accepted with enthusiasm. After dinner, we waited for our parents to go to bed. Around midnight, Turiddu took the guitar and we sneaked out the door.

First he took me to meet some of female friends of his to form a numerous group of girls. He wanted to make Mariuccia jealous, because that day she had ignored him. It didn't take much to convince his friends to come with us, because they were all fond of Turiddu. When they saw that they had his guitar with him, they immediately joined in.

We went into the deserted streets laughing and playing together. To our great surprise, when we reached Mariuccia's house, Turiddu started to sing a song he had written for her. In that silent and moonless night, the notes of his guitar and his beautiful voice raised his call of love:

> Girl of Love,
> If I were a bird
> I would fly to you
> From across the sea
> To be close to you.
> But yet you are far
> with woe
> I send you my salute
> I never lose a minute
> I think always of you.
>
> I would like to kiss you
> But my heart
> Can't bear it
> I wish I could be a bird
> To fly close to you.
> Wait for me
> My dear Maria
> What joy you give me,
> If you don't heed my words
> My heart can't live any longer.
> My dear Mariuccia,
> How I love you!

> I wait for the moment
> When you will exchange my feelings.
> For you, dear Maria,
> I am here to sing,
> I hope that your heart
> Will be filled with love
> For me.
> I wish I could kiss you, etc.

Mariuccia was curious to hear our voices together with my brother's and she looked outside. She covered strangely her forehead with her hand. As soon as she saw the girls, she slammed the window. She was obviously jealous.

Turiddu smiled with satisfaction. He then turned to me and said:
"Now you sing, or else I'll be ruined tomorrow!"

As he played the guitar, I too sang a song that was very popular at the time. But the window didn't open again.

The next day I went to visit Mariuccia. With great surprise I saw a bump on her forehead. She explained to me that the evening before, while we were singing, she tried to reach the window in the dark and she hit her head against the closet.

We couldn't help laughing. I then told what happened to my brother and he too burst in laughter.

By now, all the relatives of both families knew of the love that the young couple had for each other. Turiddu wanted to ask her to marry him. But after the German invasion of Poland, the specter of the imminent war was luring. Everyone in our family told him to wait for better days.

Salvatore Giuliano at the age of 16 (Publifoto).

*My Brother, Salvatore Giuliano*

Salvatore Giuliano Senior and Salvatore Giuliano Junior.

Salvatore Giuliano and his sister Giuseppina.

CHAPTER III

# HUMAN FOLLY PREVAILS. . .
# WAR BREAKS OUT!

What everyone had feared fatally happened.

On June 10, 1940, Mussolini announced on the radio that Italy had declared war on France and England. The consequences were immediate. People rushed to buy everything they could.

Those who had money tried to put together all the supplies they could. It became increasingly difficult to find flour, pasta, bread and sugar. Day after day the situation became worse and worse and hunger afflicted the poor. Some people were actually forced to eat what the farm animals would eat.

The city folk fled their homes and flooded into the nearby villages or rushed to homes in the countryside far away from the larger towns. Montelepre also offered shelter to this wave of displaced people.

The war continued relentlessly. War bulletins exalted the victories of the Italian troops, yet they could barely hide the truth of the great losses suffered. But if the situation on the front was not easy, those at home were no better off. Women of all ages would scour the countryside in search of edible herbs. There were no shoes, clothes or medicine. The number of deaths caused by malnutrition kept growing, especially infants and young children.

Thanks to the industry of our father and of our brothers Peppino and Salvatore, our family was able to avoid the pains of hunger. Our fields produced wheat, pulses, fruit, greens and other vegetables. Our harvest was sufficient to feed us all.

One evening, towards the end of October 1940, my brother Turiddu met Professor Francesco Purpura in the streets of Montelepre. He was very pleased to once again meet the man who had been his teacher at elementary school. In the meantime he (his former teacher) had moved to the city and now taught at a high school. Turiddu asked him if he would be his tutor. The Professor agreed. So he bought more books, ready to face other sacrifices.

When he would come back from work he would eat quickly,

Salvatore Giuliano and his mother.

Peppino Giuliano and his wife.

get his bicycle and ride to Palermo. Every day he would travel about 60 kilometers to go to lessons. While he spent his days studying and working, Sicily, tormented more than any other part of Italy, was abandoned once again to its own destiny. Resentment against the government, responsible like all the previous governments of continuing the age-old conspiracy against the Island, was mounting by the day.

Since 1860 Sicily had never succeeded in keeping up the pace with the northern part of the country. From a certain point of view the situation had actually worsened. As the years went by, the great divide between the two cultures, with their different origins and history, kept growing. They encompassed differing opinions regarding the role of the family, women, land, and the State. The most manifest behavior was that of resentment against any form of public authority.

The government, in the light of the emergency in Italy's Mezzogiorno and especially in Sicily, had ordered the pooling of wheat. Yet for small farmers the harvests were barely sufficient to feed their own families and had nothing to hand over.

The sadly famous "coupons" for the daily ration of 150 gr of flour and 100 gr of pasta per person were not enough to guarantee survival. Life had become a slow and relentless agony. Our family too did not hand over the wheat of its fields, but we could not have it milled because the mills were under surveillance. They were guarded 24 hours a day.

Having wheat and not being able to have it milled was worse than not having it at all. Yet my brother Turiddu managed to solve the problem. After various attempts he succeeded to build a small mill in a corner of our barn. It functioned by pushing a wooden beam that made the hand-sculptured millstones work. It took a lot of time, effort and strength to grind the wheat. But it seemed like a game for my brother. He could work for hours without relent. Yet the flour was never enough. It wasn't only for our family but also for our relatives and other families who didn't have anything and had to feed small children.

Only my brother Turiddu and I knew about it. With the famine hanging over the land, our parents would never have allowed us to. They told us not to tell anyone because they were afraid the authorities would find out. The day came when this finally happened.

At the beginning of 1941 the police came to search our properties. It was a shock for the whole family: for generations no member of the Giuliano family had ever had problems with the law. The town's marshal came together with two "carabinieri". He said that he received an anonymous letter and that he had to search our properties.

"Come in, Marshal!" said my mother.

"We haven't stolen anything and we don't have anything to hide!"

"You're absolutely right, donna Maria!" replied the Marshal. "But with the war we are no longer the owners of our own property!"

It didn't take them too long to find what they were looking for. We were forced to watch powerlessly as they took away the work of a whole year. But that wasn't it. The Marshal was forced to file a report, despite our mother's pleas to understand the situation.

In the month of June of that very year, my brother Peppino was drafted and assigned to a detachment of the Engineer Corps in the port of Palermo. Turiddu, who had continued to work and study, was forced to ask for some time off to help my father in the fields.

It was harvest time. The golden wheat waved in the valleys as it awaited to give its reward to the farm-workers who had grown it with love. Our wheat too was ready to be reaped. Our father took us all into the fields.

On our land there was an old house. While the men worked, the women would do the cooking. At sunset we would sit together on the straw on the threshing floor. After the heat of the day, it was so restoring to enjoy the fresh air and to eat outside.

I had invited some friends of mine, but I was hoping that they would not take up my invitation. But they did. I saw them arriving as they sang along the road. My brother had forgotten his guitar at home, but when my friends suggested to organize a dance on the threshing floor. He said that it was a good idea and that he would go get the guitar.

In just an hour he came back with some friends of his. One of them brought along an accordion, which he could play superbly. We sang and danced till late at night. Around midnight Turiddu asked us to go with him to Mariuccia's house and to sing a song for her. We all accepted enthusiastically. We reached her house singing along the way:

"Oh, Mari! Oh, Mari! Quanto sonno ho già perso per te!"(Oh, Mari! Oh, Mari! How much sleep I have lost for you!). Then with a wave of his hand we started to sing his song on the notes of the famous song "Mamma":

> Maria, I'm so sad,
> To live so far away,
> But my heart says,

> That there isn't any love for me .
> Maria, I'm so sad,
> To live so far away, but why?
> Maria!
> You are the joy of my life,
> Maria!
> I cry for you, but maybe I am mad.
> When I see you
> I think of your eyes full of love,
> And my heart swears
> That I will never leave you anymore.
> Maria!
> You are the joy of my life,
> You are my love,
> And never again in my life will I leave you.
> I see your bright face,
> Surrounded by your golden hair,
> But your heart does not hear
> The agony of my love,
> But if you were here,
> I would press you to my heart.
> Maria! Etc.

Maria slowly opened the window. The pale moon shone in her hair that hung over her shoulders, exalting her beauty. She exchanged very few words with Turiddu and with us and she went back to bed.

Once the harvest was over, Turiddu went back to his job. But he was tormented. Each time the engineer would go away for any reason, the foreman would take advantage of the situation to provoke and humiliate him. He was probably jealous that Turiddu had replaced him in tracing the line with a series of poles.

My brother didn't want to lose his job and was forced to bear with it all. But one day he felt he could take no more and told him clearly to stop or else he would beat him up. The foreman didn't react, but he went to the company offices to report him. Turiddu was called to explain what had happened but the foreman would not let him speak.

Turiddu lost his calm and ended up on the ground with a blackened eye. That was the end of his job with the "Funaro" company. Turiddu went back to work in the fields with our father. But he was firm in his intent to continue his studies.

He was ready to do almost any job to earn the money to pay Professor Purpura. So, every now and then, he would go up into mountains to pick "disa", a fibrous plant that a local factory used for the production of mattress padding. Other times he would work as a laborer for a local contractor.

The report for the wheat hidden at home had now made its course and the hearing was set for February 2, 1942.

That morning, my father and mother went to court in Palermo. As they waited to be called in the courtroom for their "crime", a soldier ordered them to follow him into the courtroom after verifying their identity.

He explained to the judge that during the bombing of Palermo the day before, their son Peppino had been wounded and that his conditions were serious. My parents asked the judge to adjourn the hearing so that they could go to the hospital immediately. The adjournment was granted.

Once they arrived at the military hospital, my parents found Peppino with his head and neck all wrapped with bandages. He was purplish, he had wounds on his face and in various parts of his body. He couldn't speak nor eat owing to his broken jaw. Despite everything, they thanked God because he was still alive. They went back home. Their pain was too great to hide. When my sister, Giuseppina, Turiddu and I asked what happened they broke the news to us. After asking for further details, Turiddu decided to go visit his brother.

"It's late. They won't let you in!" said my father. And he added "Tomorrow we'll all go together!"

But he was inflexible:

"Don't try stopping me! If I don't see my brother tonight, I won't be able to sleep in peace!"

Having said as much, he took his bicycle and left.

For days we would go to and from the hospital. We had feared for the life our brother, but thanks to God his conditions improved until he finally recovered completely. The only sign left was a scar on his face.

He came back home on leave. One month later he was sent to Germany. From there he was sent to join the Italian army on the Russian front. Together with the Italian expedition he reached the outskirts of Stalingrad in September 1942.

For the second time he escaped death during the tragic retreat that cost the life of 100,000 Italian soldiers.

In Sicily the food situation was desperate. The small farmers who had previously managed to survive with the fruit of their land now also felt the grip of hunger. The carabinieri would scour the countryside to confiscate the wheat on the threshing floor. Popular discontent mounted against the government and its emissaries as hunger grew more and more.

While the large landowners who had the possibility of "getting around" the situation were becoming richer and richer by selling their wheat on the black market, the small landowners were no longer in the physical or mental conditions to work and produce as they did before. In order to add something to the poor rations assigned with the "coupons", many were forced to eat bran, barley and carob, food that was used to feed the livestock and other food that was even more repulsing. If there was any.

Those who had some money, making the most of the Sicilian's famous solidarity, would buy wheat from other more fortunate farmers who had managed to avoid confiscation. Others would buy and sell the wheat to have the money to buy other primary products on the black market.

This was called "ILLICIT TRADE" AND IT WAS SEVERELY FORBIDDEN BY THE LAW.

Those who trespassed the law – and there were many that did owing to the great hunger of those days – were punished severely. The situation was made even worse by some German detachments deployed in Sicily. They behaved like a mass of plunderers. They sacked isolated homes, killed anyone who tried to stop them, raped women and set fire to houses. Many mothers who would go out into the fields to look for food for their children would never come back home again. They were found raped and killed. Hate grew in the heart of every Sicilian.

In November 1942, Turiddu was at the home of his teacher in Palermo. He was studying together with a young man from Misilmeri. He too came for private lessons. That evening they were studying the "Carbonari" uprisings, when Turiddu all of a sudden shouted:

"Damn! I've been thinking about it for years. . .!"

"About what?" asked Prof. Purpura.

"If we too had an organization like that, we could rid ourselves of the fascists and Germans!"

The Professor and the other young man glanced at each other.

"Why are you so angry with them? What did they do to you?" asked the Professor.

"Excuse me, but I didn't expect such a question from you!" replied Turiddu with resentment.

"You're asking me what they've done to me? They have deprived me of my bread and they continue to take it away from me. They've declared war against everyone and they don't care about those who they send to be slaughtered or leave to die of hunger. They have opened our doors to a foreign power! That's what they have done!"

The Professor looked at him complacently. He stopped to think for a moment and then he said:

"And what if I told you that there is a secret organization of that kind right here in Palermo? What would you do?"

"What would I do? I would have no hesitation at all. I would do anything to become a part of it!"

"Then you must know that there is one!"

"There is!" exclaimed Turiddu full of surprise.

The Professor went towards him and put his hand on his shoulder and with paternal tone of voice he added:

"If you hadn't said what you did, you would never have known!"

This is how Turiddu became a disciple of Prof. Purpura's teachings. He revealed to him that a series of secret organizations had already been active in Sicily since 1940. The first one was founded by a relative of his, Vincenzo Purpura. It was called "Sicily and Freedom" and it had a statute and a president, Andrea Finocchiaro Aprile.

He also explained that the objective of this association was to fight fascism and the regime, to establish a democratic republic on the Island and to restore the ancient grandeur of the Sicilian people. He spoke to him about Sicilian history, about the "Vespri", Garibaldi, the unity of Italy and how Sicily had been annexed.

Turiddu listened to him enthusiastically. For years he had dreamed of a free Sicily. He was so enthusiastic that he asked to join the association immediately. The professor explained to him that it wasn't possible for the moment, because the members were all intellectuals and belonged to the upper middle class.

But there was a chance. Some members had succeeded in setting up a training camp on Mount Pellegrino, which overlooks Palermo. Amongst them there were many young men.

"So what can I do?" asked Turiddu.

"Have patience and wait! They will need young men like you!"

"I'll help you to join in the exercises at the training camp!"

The whole conversation was so appealing for him and it lasted for quite a while. In Turiddu's heart the hope of a better future started to blossom.

On January 2, 1943, the war was experienced in all its cruelty. Palermo was bombed various times. Anglo-American air raids brought death and destruction to Sicily. On January 5th Palermo was bombed again as were Licata and Lampedusa. On January 13th, Lampedusa again and Sciacca. On the 16th Gela, the 17th Pachino, the 19th Porto Empedocle, the 22nd Gela and Castelvetrano, the 23rd Noto and Pachino, the 24th Castellammare, Ragusa, Licata and Lampedusa. The bombings continued every day untill February 25th.

The many bombings devastated towns and cities causing thousands of deaths. For some time now agents of the Anglo-American secret services were carrying out propaganda throughout the Island. They were preparing the population in view of the oncoming invasion. The people were morally and physically exhausted. Thanks also to the clever propaganda divulged through leaflets, they started to convince themselves that the only way to put an end to the situation and to rid themselves of the Germans and fascists was to hand themselves over to the Anglo-American troops.

The psychological situation was favorable to the invasion, as they made it look like a sort of "Liberation Crusade". Sicily by now was a "ripe fruit", ready for the invasion.

My brother Peppino had come home from the front in May 1943. Our family was in bad physical conditions owing to the widespread dearth. The little wheat we had had been confiscated once again by the Carabinieri and our stocks had finished. After a few days Peppino took Turiddu's bicycle and went to look for someone who could sell him some wheat. He managed to buy about 50 kg from a landowner outside San Giuseppe Jato. When it would finish, he would go back and buy some more.

In June, some Yugoslav rebels camped outside our town had been informed that the American invasion was only a matter of days. They decided to leave before falling into their hands, so they sold all they had to travel as light as possible.

Peppino bought a horse from one of them, while Turiddu exchanged a loaf of bread for a 4-shot Derringer gun. When he came home with the gun, my mother was upset to see it.

"Mamma, don't worry. These days having gun can be a godsend! Have you forgotten? Only recently did they steal the wheat from Peppino. If he could have defended himself, the thieves would have run away!"

In this atmosphere of fear, hunger and uncertainty the end of June came. Turiddu was called for the draft and assigned to the Air Force. He was to leave on July 8th. In the meantime, he doubled his efforts to work and study. He wanted to become a regular officer in the Air Force.

But from the 4$^{th}$ to the 7$^{th}$ of July, Sicily was under a shower of airborne bombs. Almost 5,000 tons of explosives were dropped. The nerves of the population, already tired from the long suffering and the dearth of food, was severely put to the test.

Turiddu didn't leave for the military.

On July 10, 1943, especially along the coastline, air raids were almost continuous. Finally a massive deployment of naval forces appeared at the horizon of the Island's south-eastern coasts. There were approximately 3,000 units of all kinds. The invasion of Sicily on the part of the Anglo-American forces had started. Besides the naval forces, the operation saw the deployment of more than 4,000 planes, 15,000 motor vehicles, 600 tanks and 1,800 cannons.

A few days later, on July 23, 1943, while my brother was near Montelepre, he saw the American troops coming from the plain of Partinico. He remembered the instructions he had received in case of this eventuality.

He started to run through town shouting:

"The Americans! The Americans are coming!"

At the news the town folk was caught by surprise. No one knew what to do.

Some asked: "What are we going to do?"

"We have nothing to defend ourselves with!" said others.

Turiddu managed to impose himself: "Don't put up useless resistance!"

"Gather all the people you can and welcome them!"

He then ran home to tell us the news. He took a white sheet and he tied it to a stick like a flag. He climbed like a cat to the top of the roof of our house, which overlooked the whole town. He put it in a position where it could easily be seen.

When the Americans reached the outskirts of town, seeing the warm welcome, they started to distribute plenty of food: meat, beans, tuna, chocolate, sugar, candies. It was a true blessing for the poor people who had suffered hunger for years.

They slowed down their march for a minutes and then continued towards Palermo. The city didn't welcome them as enemies, but as friends.

The news led the Grand Council of Fascism to oust the Duce who was forced to resign. After more than twenty years of dictatorship, fascism fell.

The news was reason for relief and exaltation throughout the country, especially in Sicily where the separatist and anti-fascist associations, though ignoring their reciprocal existence, had worked secretly for years and now could come to the light.

On July 28th, leaflets written by the Committee for Sicilian Independence spread the following proclamation in all the towns of the Island:

"THE COMMITTEE FOR SICILIAN INDEPENDENCE
convened solemnly in representation of the People of the Island, whose thoughts and feelings it is sure to represent,

SINCE the House of Savoy first received the crown of Sicily in the person of Victor Amedeus II with the Treaty of Utrecht in 1713 and that, having ousted the Bourbons, the Sicilian Parliament offered the crown of Sicily to Prince Ferdinand, the brother of King Victor Emmanuel II;

SINCE the Monarchy has failed to meet its solemn commitments undertaken towards Sicily in 1860 according to which it was to respect its autonomy and dedicate itself to the advancement of its civil and economic life;

SINCE the Savoy dynasty, unmindful of its commitments, on the occasion of the union of Sicily with the Kingdom of Italy failed to attract the attention of the government to the needs of the Sicilian people in order that they be duly addressed, assisting complacently in the meantime to total state of abandonment in which Sicily was left with deplorable moral and economic consequences;

SINCE the King, following the shameful fall of the Fascist party, has deluded himself of being able to bolster his wavering position by establishing a government composed of men who for many years have served under the Fascist regime and who have no authority or prestige, a government, which is mocked by all and destined to complete failure;

SINCE the People of Sicily are ready for a more worthy and higher Destiny and aspire to obtain their freedom and independence;

HEREBY convenes by acclamation
of the PEOPLE OF SICILY

and requests that the Allied Governments give their consent to the constitution of an Interim Sicilian Government to prepare a referendum so as to declare the downfall of the Savoy monarchy, in the person of Victor Emmanuel III and his successors, in Sicily and that

SICILY be recognized as a SOVEREIGN INDEPENDENT STATE WITH A DEMOCRATIC REGIME.
Palermo, July 25, 1943"[1]

The Americans, seeing the separatist movement as the ensign of the fight against fascism, considered it as a powerful ally against the luring threat of Communism. They not only left the separatists do as they pleased but they also ordered their secret services to obtain their cooperation.

On August 8th, after the last German soldier had left the Island, another organization was set up in Catania: the M.I.S. (Movement for the Independence of Sicily).

On August 25th the M.I.S. and the groups belonging to "Sicily and Freedom", the association founded by Vincenzo Purpura and presided by Andrea Finocchiaro Aprile merged.

[1] *Municipal Library of Palermo.*

The massive Anglo-American fleet (Publifoto).

The Anglo-American invade Sicily (Publifoto).

American soldiers hand out food (Publifoto).

Chapter IV

# FOR A HANDFUL OF WHEAT

The wheat that my brother Peppino had managed to buy was about to finish. It was the morning of September 2, 1943 and he was to go to San Giuseppe Jato. We had managed to put together the money to buy another 80 kg.

But that morning Peppino was not feeling very well. He was still affected by the consequences of the wounds he suffered in the war. He asked Turiddu to take his place and he willingly accepted. He jumped onto the horse's saddle and rode off to the destination.

Following his brother's instructions, he easily found the farm. The farmer looked at him suspiciously. He asked him many questions. When he finally was convinced, he gave him the wheat. Turiddu put the two sacks on each side of the horse and he started to ride back to home.

Peppino, who had much more experience, had explained to him how to avoid unpleasant encounters along the way. Turiddu looked around warily as he walked quickly and pulled the horse with its load by the reins.

A few kilometers away from Partinico, as he was crossing the stream in "Quarto Molino", he suddenly heard a voice from behind a cane thicket along the bank:

"To the ground! To the ground!"

He feared they were thieves, so Turiddu froze where he was. His hand slid quickly down his leg to his boot where he had hidden the gun he bartered with the Yugoslav soldier. But they were not thieves. They were a Carabiniere, a corporal and two field guards[1]. At the sight of the guards he felt relieved. But maybe it would have been better if he had met thieves.

The soldiers came towards him:

"Where do you come from? What are you carrying?" asked the corporal.

[1] *The field guards belonged to a special corps specialized in surveilling fields and crops.*

"I'm carrying some wheat to feed my family!" he answered.

"Where did you get it?" asked the Carabiniere.

My brother quickly realized that, if he told the truth, he would have put the farmer in serious trouble. He could not go back to buy some more. For no reason in the world he would have betrayed him.

"I don't know!" he replied. "I traveled for days. No one had any! Then I met a farmer, I told him that my family was dying of hunger and he was moved by my begging! He told me to wait for him. Maybe he didn't want me to follow him, so I stayed where I was. I waited for two hours. He then came back with these two sacks of wheat loaded on a mule. He gave them to me and I paid him!"

"How much did you pay for this wheat?" asked the corporal.

"Seven and half Lire a kilo, at consortium price!"

"Who do you want to fool with your lies?" retorted the soldier. "Take us where you got it!"

"But it's the truth! How can I take you there if I don't know?" replied Turiddu.

"Cut it young man! Either you take us where you got the wheat or we'll take you the American Presidium!"

The American Presidium controlled the whole Island from the day of the invasion and it was composed of a military tribunal. It charged expensive fines for minor misdemeanors and capital punishment for felonies. My brother was aware of this. He did not want to ruin the farmer or go to the Presidium. He feared that if they searched him they would find the gun on him. So he tried to convince the officers to leave him alone:

"Please! Why do you want to ruin me? If you take me to the Presidium they'll arrest me! My father will have to sell everything he owns to pay my bail and the fine! Please, I'm only twenty years old! Don't ruin me!"

He humiliated himself. He dropped to his knees desperately trying to move them.

"What will we get in exchange if we let you go?" said the corporal.

"Take my horse and the wheat!" said Turiddu without hesitating.

"We don't want your horse! Let's take you to the Presidium!"

"But I don't have anything else. I spent everything I had for this wheat!"

At a nod of their colleague, the field guards took the horse by the reins and started off.

"So are you going to talk or do we have to take you to the Presidium?" insisted the corporal.

"Please, let me go! I don't know anything!"

Turiddu started to go through his jacket and pulled out his documents.

"Here are my documents! Do whatever you want, but don't take me to the Presidium!"

"Why? Are you shy? You'll get used to it soon!" answered ironically the corporal.

All of the sudden the officers' attention was attracted by the arrival of four people with mules carrying loads on their backs. They left my brother alone and went towards the group of men. They treated them kindly, almost as if they were old friends.

Turiddu took advantage of the situation to run away. But the Carabinieri noticed him immediately and they shot their rifles against him six times.

Two shots hit him in his side. My brother fell in the middle of the bushes. He was writhing with pain, but he didn't shout.

In those terrible moments all the suffering, hunger and humiliations he had suffered from the outbreak of the war came back to mind. He felt the anger accumulated over the years against the system and its thugs mount inside him. The images of the past were mixed with those of the present. The war was over. Everyone was hoping that tyranny and suffering were a bad dream of the past. He now was on the brink of a dark and deep abyss.

All his dreams, all his hopes were vanishing miserably before his eyes. He was only twenty! Shocked and appalled, he was still trying to understand what was happening. The voice of the corporal made his blood freeze in his veins:

"Go see if he's dead!" ordered the senior officer.

"If he's not, shoot him in the head and let's get out of here!"

Those words awoke in Turiddu his spirit of survival. His hand, stained with blood, moved almost automatically. He reached towards his boot and pulled out the gun. He waited there without moving as he held his breath. His muscles were tense as he fought to suppress his desire to shout:

"Why? Just for some wheat!" He saw the carabiniere move cautiously towards him with his rifle pointed. He waited for him to come within a range of 10 meters. Then the long-suppressed desire of rebellion, the age-old hate against the tyrants and their thugs exploded.

It was him or the officer. He had no choice. Without aiming he shot him. A cry of pain, a thud.

Like a puppet whose threads had broken, the soldier fell to the ground wounded seriously. He rushed away from that place of death with all the energy of his youthful body. No one followed him.

He made way towards home. At each step he made he felt his energy dwindle away. His side was burning like hell. One bullet has passed through his side; the other was stuck in his flesh to torment him.

He saw a mule pasturing in a meadow. He walked up to it cautiously and he grabbed its reins. With a superhuman effort he mounted on its back and he continued his journey.

After about a hundred meters a farmer ran towards him waving his hands. It was the owner of the mule who was shouting to him:

"Hey! Where are you going with my mule?"

Turiddu spurred the mule towards him.

"Friend!" he said to him. "Look at what the cops did to me! I can't walk! I'll send it back to you later!"

In those days with all the thieves infesting the area it was obvious that the man couldn't believe him.

"Trust me, friend! I'm the son of Turi Giuliano, the American!"

The man let him go. Turiddu continued his way towards Montelepre. Near town he met two fellow townsmen. He knew them both, especially one of them. He asked him to take him home with his bicycle. The other took back the mule.

There was no need to beg them. They did as they were told. The road climbed steeply but there was just a short way to go. Curiosity led his friend to ask him what happened, but Turiddu was careful. His instinct told him not to trust anyone and he did not even like that others knew of his own business. He invented a story. He said he had injured himself by falling into a cane thicket.

He finally reached town. His thoughts ran to his mother. He did not want to scare her. Instead of going home, he asked him to take him to the house of his cousin Rosa. When she saw him arrive in those conditions, she almost fainted. But she recovered immediately. Her cold blood won over the fear, the shock and the incredulity. She made him lay down in a room and she took care of him.

She gave him a dose of sedative. She understood how serious the wound was, so she tried to tampon it as best as she could.

Turiddu was shivering from the cold, which was the symptom of the fever that had started to rise. His conditions were worsening. Rosa soon was aware of it and called with a soft voice:

"Turiddu. . . . Turiddu can you hear me?"

He feebly answered:

"Yes. . . . I can hear. What do you want?"

"We need a doctor! You can't be left in these conditions! We have to tell your mother!"

"Don't worry! I'm not dead yet!" he answered.

Rosa replied immediately: "This isn't the time for joking! You've got a bad wound!"

"OK. But try not scare her, find some excuse!"

Rosa pressed his hand in agreement and went out. Her house was just 200 meters away from ours. She ran all the way. When she got there, she was panting. Had my mother seen her panting, she would have understood right away that something was wrong. But Rosa was smart enough to rest a minute before going in. She knocked at the door.

"Aunt Maria! Aunt Maria!" she cried aloud.

The door opened slowly. My mother looked outside. She had not seen her niece for a few days now and was surprised to see her behind the door.

"Aunt Maria!" said Rosa as she cut the greetings short.

"There's someone who urgently needs to talk to you! He's waiting for you at my house!"

"But who is he? Why don't you tell him to come here?"

"If you come to my house, you'll understand!"

My mother hesitantly went back in to get her shawl. She then followed her.

They walked along the road without saying a word. But once she entered Rosa's house, my mother asked her who was the person that wanted to see her.

Her niece took her by the hand and led her to the room where Turiddu was. As soon as she saw her son in those conditions, she started to cry from the pain. But Rosa quickly covered her mouth with a hand:

"Aunt Maria, be quiet! No one must know that Turiddu is here!"

The poor woman was scared to death. Thousands of thoughts flashed through her mind. But she could not find peace. She lovingly bent over her son. She kissed him with all the love that only a mother has.

"Son! Son! What happened? What did they do to you?"

"Mother, it's a miracle if I'm still alive!" answered Turiddu trying to seem as natural as possible.

"Thank God, I had the chance of seeing you again!"

Our mother, with her heart torn by the pain, could not understand what had happened and she did not find the courage to ask her son. Rosa told her what happened.

My mother could not help exclaiming:

"Son! What did you do! You're ruined! You're ruined! Is he dead?"

"Mother, I don't know! I saw him fall and I don't know whether he's alive! I didn't want to shoot him. I even threw away the gun when it was still loaded. I had given them my documents just a few minutes before! I shot to protect myself. He wanted to kill me. If I didn't shoot, I wouldn't be here now!"

"Oh my God! Dear Lord! Don't let him die!" prayed our mother.

But the officer, Giuseppe Mancino, died the day after at the Military Hospital of Palermo.

Once she had overcome the shock of the situation, our mother pulled together all the strength she had:

"We've got to call a doctor now!" she said firmly.

"I'll do it, but we also need some antitetanic to stop the infection!" added Rosa.

Our mother went back home. Her state of agitation was too obvious not to be noticed immediately by my sister Giuseppina and me. We started to ask her insistently what was wrong until she confessed what was tormenting her so much. As soon as my father and my brother Peppino came back from the fields they were informed of the situation.

Our family had always been happy and now it was in silence. We looked at each other with dumbfounded eyes. That evening no one ate.

I was assigned the task of finding the antitetanic. In those days of dearth it was quite difficult. The drug stores did not have any medicine.

Finally, at about 11 o'clock I found someone who sold medicine on the black market. I bought the medicine and paid without protesting on the price and I ran back to my brother Turiddu.

Dr. Cracolice, the town's doctor, was already at his bedside. He injected the antitetanic and examined the wound. He understood that they were caused by a firearm, but he didn't say anything. The bullet was deep in his side. A surgeon was needed. The doctor suggested taking Turiddu to Palermo to avoid regrettable consequences. We unanimously accepted his advice.

My brother Peppino rushed home to go get the bicycle. He returned in a few minutes. He lifted Turiddu and he put him on the bicycle. He slowly started to push it. He knew that his brother's life was in his hands. The road climbed for about 5 kilometers. He panted, sweated and puffed but he never stopped. Finally they reached "Portella Cippi". There started the plain and the road descended. Peppino climbed on the bicycle.

At the first lights of dawn they reached Palermo. They looked for a safe place where no one would notice them. They found it at the feet of Mount Pellegrino. It was a bombed construction just outside of the city surrounded by a lemon orchard. The owners had gone to a nearby town in the province.

At the center of the orchard there was an irrigation tank, while next to the house there was a well supplied by a spring of drinkable water. In better days it surely could have been the ideal place for a vacation.

The next day my brother went home. He came to get everything they needed. To avoid suspects he took his wife along. It was not difficult to find a surgeon by paying him well. The removal of the bullet was long and painful, but the operation was a success.

During the first days Turiddu's conditions worsened. We feared many times that he would die. But he was strong and his body was healthy. He made it through the most difficult moments and he started to improve until he recovered completely. Before going back to home he wanted to see Prof. Purpura and he told him his story hoping to get some advice.

"The situation is serious! Of course, you did it for self-defense, but there are no witnesses! Even if you did, the Carabinieri will always have the upper hand. They caught you while you were carrying wheat! You're a smuggler and you killed one of their men. If you give yourself up, you'll spend the rest of your life in prison in the best of cases. But, as I fear, they'll take you to the American Presidium and there you risk being sentenced to death!"

"I prefer killing myself than letting them kill me!" replied Turiddu. "I prefer going into hiding than spend my life in prison! At least I can help my people!"

In the month that my brother was between life and death many things had happened.

On September 8, 1943, Gen. Badoglio surrendered and he was forced to accept crushing conditions.

The news did not meet with the enthusiasm of the inhabitants of the Island, which was still under the control of the American Military Government.

The population was tired. It was left exhausted and famished by the war. By then it no longer cared about the war. What other parts of Italy were still struggling to obtain, was already a fact of history in Sicily.

Sicily had lost all contacts with the rest of the country and was isolated more than ever. The Prefects and "Podestà", who had not left the Island, were dismissed. They were replaced by new administrators in favor of independence who had the approval of the Allies, who also nominated a new city council in Palermo.

In all that chaos during those terrible days the Separatist Movement consolidated itself and carried out a very active and effective propaganda campaign. Andrea Finocchiaro Aprile, the Movement's leader, swayed the crowds with his eloquence. The people were contaminated by a sort of collective rapture. His words found fertile ground in Sicily after all the devastation and hunger caused by a mad war. They stigmatized complex problems that had afflicted Sicily from the moment of Italian Unity.

The northern part of Italy had been favored by the policies of all the governments that had run the country since Unity and Sicily was just a colonial appendix where industrial products could be sold and where agricultural products or cheap labor could be found.

Soon after Unity the laws of Piedmont (the Albertine Statute) were applied to the whole country. The diversity of customs, traditions, ethnic and historical origins, and of the economic and social conditions of the people were not taken into account.

The Sicilian provinces, like those of the rest of the South, were administered by prefects sent from the north. For centuries Sicily was abandoned to a state of economic stagnation. Its main resource was agriculture and it was based on the large estates, on the great mass of farmhands, and on small landowners who barely managed to survive.

The industries were very few, while illiteracy was widespread. There were areas were more than 90% of the population was illiterate. Misery and illnesses caused by malnutrition were widespread. The hygienic conditions were disastrous.

Garibaldi, during his expedition, had fueled great hope and enthusiasm. Poor farmers and young people joined his famous "Thousand" yearning to free themselves from the reign of the Bourbons. But their dreams were soon shattered.

He handed over the entire South to the Piedmontese government. He gave it all the gold of the glorious Bank of Sicily thus avoiding bankruptcy.

Alliances were established between the governing class of the North (composed of capitalists and merchants) and the large landowners of the South at the expense of the farm workers. The electoral system of the time did not allow poor people to be represented in town councils and in Parliament. Women, poor people, and illiterates had no right to vote.

Only male voters who had reached 25 years of age, who knew how to read and write and who had a certain income were entitled to vote. Therefore, the town councils were composed only of the members of the middle and upper classes and by the large landowners allied with the new rulers.

The new Italian government abolished many religious orders in Sicily, confiscated their properties and they sold them together with the lands of the Bourbon crown for a total of 182 million Lire (equal to 18,5 trillion Lire of today).

It could have been the right opportunity to do something for Sicily and the South as a whole, but poverty was left to spread. The Piedmontese tax system was even heavier than that of the Bourbons. The South, which accounted for only 27% of the country's wealth, paid 32% of the taxes levied in the whole country. Cash assets and taxes were invested to build industries and infrastructures in the North.

All the governments from 1861 to 1943 had one thing in common: the savage exploitation of the Island.

That is why the leader of the separatist movement, with fiery rallies, supported the idea that Sicily had every right to accuse Italy for having exploited it as a colony without maintaining or improving its production capacity.

Therefore, Italy was not worthy of Sicily. "Sicily to the Sicilians". That was the slogan of the separatist movement.

In order to best summarize their ideas, they spread this leaflet across the whole of Sicily:

SICILY WANTS TO BECOME
A FREE AND INDEPENDENT REPUBLIC

1) Because its people wants to be free.
2) Because it was annexed to Italy only after the plot of 1860. So its Italianness is false and has failed after 80 disastrous years of experience.
3) Because it speaks Italian for the same reason why Belgium speaks French, North America speaks English and South America Spanish.
4) Because the natural resources and the labor of its people are such that they can guarantee the prosperity and well being it has never enjoyed.
5) Because Italy has violated all its rights and has hindered that, together with its rich agriculture, a lively Sicilian industry like the one that will develop after the war be born.

6) Because a free Sicily will become the great emporium of the South.

7) Because an independent Sicily will be the guarantor for peace in the Mediterranean.

For all the above reasons, the people of Sicily are firm in their intent to die rather than renounce independence.

THE COMMITTEE FOR SICILIAN INDIPENDENCE

The stream in Quarto Molino (Publifoto).

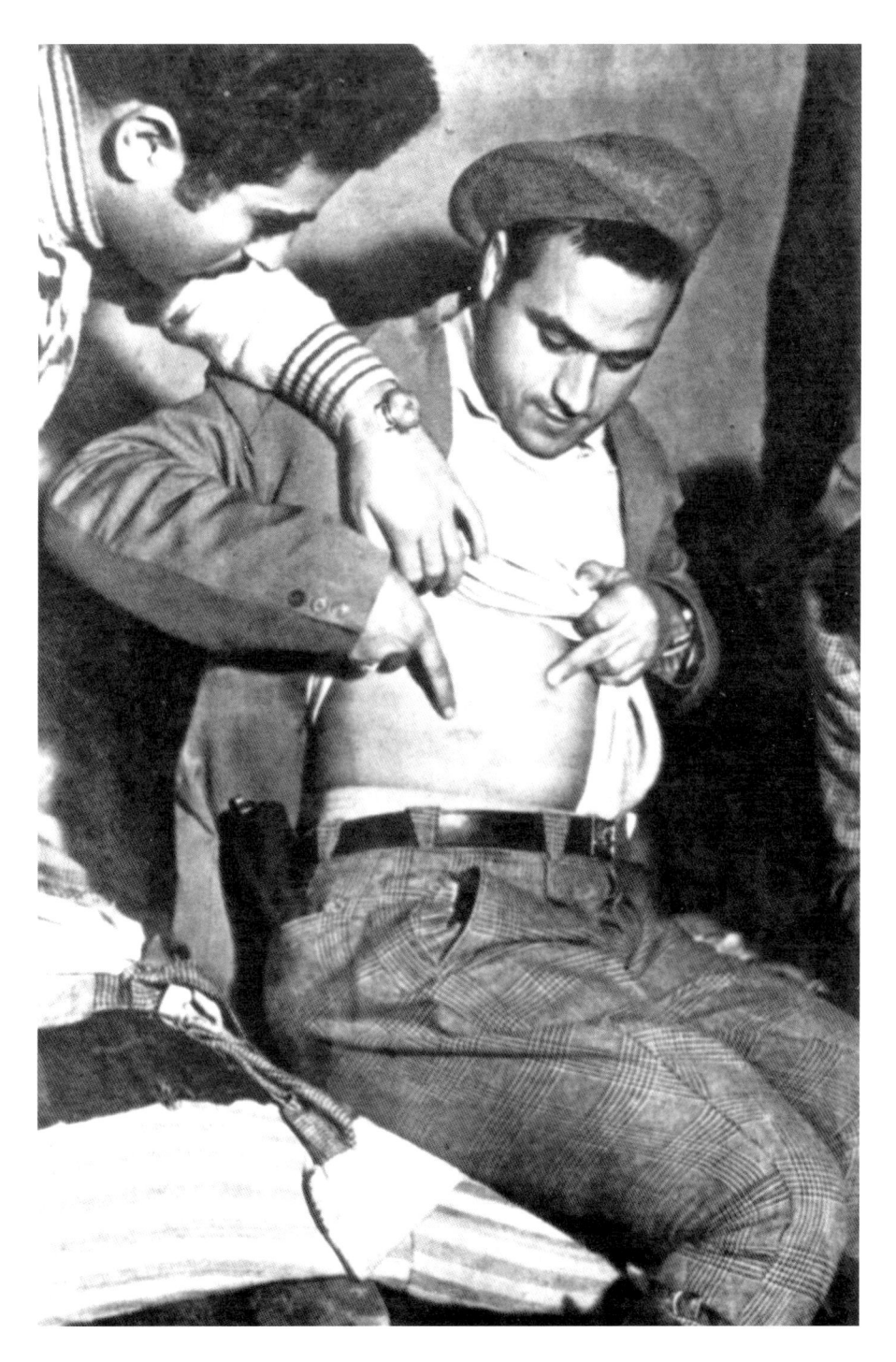

Salvatore Giuliano shows the scars of the wounds suffered at "Quarto Molino" (Foto Mendolesi).

My Brother, Salvatore Giuliano

Marianna Giuliano.

## Chapter V

# RETALIATION

From when he came back home, Turiddu would spend the whole day shut in his room. There was a little door from where he could reach a small terrace. Both sides of the terrace were adjacent to other roofs. He had good chances of escaping from there.

During the day, my mother, my sister and I would take turns at staying on guard, so that he could rest in peace. We could have warned him in case of danger. He would spend his nights all dressed without shutting an eye. He would pass the hours reading and studying. His senses were tense to perceive even the slightest sound coming from the outside. He was always ready to escape.

During those days of idleness he dedicated many hours to training a little dog. It was very smart. He called it Giulia. It soon learned to bark when it saw the police. It could even tell whether there were two or three carabinieri. If they were more than three it would start to howl.

One night Turiddu went to "Piano dell'Occhio" to look through the ruins of an abandoned arms depot. There he found a rifle, a gun and plenty of ammunition. Every now and then, late in the afternoon, he would go to Palermo. He wanted to be kept up-to-date on the news about the separatist movement. He would spend hours with his professor and with a few friends he could trust. Before dawn, after taking the necessary precautions, he would make his way towards home.

The situation in Montelepre was calm. Every now and then a patrol would pass through town. No one was worried. Except Giulia, the dog. She would rush to signal their presence. Seldom would the police knock at someone's door. No one ever came to our door, although someone suspected that Turiddu was at home.

In the meantime the separatist movement had spread across the whole Island and was working to obtain the support of the Americans. They were looking for someone to understand their cause especially thanks to the presence of so many Sicilians across the Atlantic.

But the attitude of the American government proved to be rude and hostile. All this worsened popular discontent. The people of Sicily realized the falseness of all the promises of freedom made to them by the Allies.

On December 9, 1943 the Central Committee for the Independence of Sicily convened in a plenary session. Representatives from all the provinces of the Island came and they decided to make a last attempt to convince the allied government to spare Sicily the disaster of being handed over to the Badoglio government.

While in the high ranks the men with the power were deciding our fate, my brother Turiddu spent his last days of peace and idleness at home.

On the night of December 24, 1943, immediately after midnight, ominous howls vibrated through the air. It was our dog, Giulia. It was signaling the arrival of many officers. Turiddu, as usual, was reading in his room under the dim light of a kerosene lamp. That night the sky was covered with clouds, which were supposed to cover our hearts with peace and serenity like a warm blanket. But the peace was shattered by the dog's howls. In the silence of the night it howling echoed through the air like an ill omen of disaster amongst the town's poor homes.

He shut out the lamp and in a few seconds he gathered his things and was ready to escape. He slowly opened the door leading to the terrace. He crept out with his rifle in his hands. He blew a short whistle. Giulia stopped howling instantly. Silence reigned again. Faraway in the distance the engines of a convoy of motor vehicles could be heard as well as the dull buzzing of voices.

The dog had awakened the whole family. Thinking of what could happen, I felt a lump in a my throat. The only one who was calm was Turiddu. He tried to calm us saying that maybe it was just a normal patrol. But he knew it wasn't true.

The situation remained unchanged for several hours. Only voices, at times whispering, at others excited cries, could be heard in the distance in various parts of town. At about five o'clock in the morning, our father went out and made believe he was going to Mass. He went out to see what was happening. But when he almost reached the church, he was shocked by the sight. The square was full of Carabinbieri, trucks and jeeps. He was dismayed for a few moments. He didn't know whether to go ahead or to return home. But it was already too late.

A carabiniere native of Montelepre recognized him and pointed towards him:

"That's his father! Get him!"

Suddenly four stout soldiers grabbed him. An officer came up to him and slapped him twice:

"Come on! Talk! Where's your son?"

He did not make a sound as some blood started to trickle down his lip and drip onto his shirt. Not a word. Just a big spit in his face was our father's answer. That gesture unleashed the beast-like fury of the officer. He kept punching and kicking our father until he fell to the ground.

"Now take us to your house and we'll have some fun with your son!" he said boldly.

Meanwhile the 800 Carabinieri of the expedition had circled the town. It was impossible to escape from that trap. A group of soldiers dragged father home. Another group, guided by the officer, followed a few steps behind.

They were a few meters away from the door, when my father shouted all of a sudden:

"Maria! Maria! Open the door. The Carabinieri!"

He succeeded in his intent. We all heard him. That call warned us that Turiddu was in danger. He was ready to escape. In a few seconds he gathered the things he needed: the knapsack with the ammunition and supplies, the gun, his jacket and the rifle. He crawled out onto the terrace. He then rushed silently on the rooftops. Like a feline he rushed for about ten meters and then jumped into a garden behind the house from a height of about 4 meters.

He looked around carefully and when he was sure that the coast was clear he tried to reach the mountains. But he could not owing to the presence of the soldiers. He went back and hid behind the wall above the curve leading to the mill.

In the meantime at home we were covering up his escape. To help gain time and to convince the Carabinieri that he was not at home, my mother told me to lay down in his bed and one of Giuseppina's children was put in my bed so that they would not notice that it was still warm.

As we did so, the Carabinieri beat at our door with the butts of their rifles. My mother slowly went and opened the door. She found many rifles aimed at her. But she remained calm. Her maternal instinct had the best over her fear.

She boldly stood in front of those rifles. She opened her arms and she blocked the doorway firmly with her arms.

"You can't come in like that!" she said firmly.

"My daughter Marianna has a weak heart! If you come in with those rifles, you'll scare her to death! Let me wake her up!"

The Carabinieri were dismayed for a few moments. Then, when she started to go up the stairs, a few followed her. The others came in and started to search the ground floor. They found my sister's son in my room on the first floor. He pretended to be fast asleep. On the second floor they found me in Turiddu's bed. As soon as the officer saw me, his boldness seemed to vanish and he asked me the stupidest question on earth:

"Are you a man or a woman?"

"Can't you see what I am?" I replied dryly.

"Get up!" he ordered me.

"Listen, Lieutenant!" I said calmly. "This is my home! If I have to get up, you and your men have to get out of here! You don't think I'll get dressed right here in front of you?"

With an angry face he went out with the others. They went back into road to join the others. They thought that my brother had fallen into their trap, but it was not so. The officer who had beaten my father was absolutely furious and he started to vent his anger with his men.

He started to yell and insult them. He then shouted:

"That son of a bitch has escaped! But we're not leaving here with empty hands! We've lost one, so we'll take away a hundred with us!"

He ordered his men to wake up the people in their homes and to arrest all those with a suspect face, and especially all those who were related to our family.

They started from the house opposite ours. Nino Lombardo, my mother's brother, lived there with his wife and children. They arrested everyone, including Salvatore, our cousin who was born on the same day as my brother Turiddu. That Christmas of 1943 left an unforgettable sign in all the inhabitants of Montelepre. 125 men, women and children were arrested.

Each house, road and alley was scoured. The silence was broken by the cries of pain, curses, insults, and exclamations of surprise and fear:

"What have we done?" "Why are we being arrested?" "Where are they taking us?"

"How many times do we have to pay for being Sicilians?"

These were the questions that no one knew how to answer. Each family lost one of their loved ones.

Turiddu saw everything from his hideout. He saw something that overwhelmed him with horror and anger at the same time. Amongst a group of soldiers walking behind the prisoners there was an old man with his face covered with blood, swollen eyes and a bloody nose and lips. It was our father.

They were dragging him. They pushed him on by hitting him with the butts of their rifles.

Turiddu aimed his gun, but he could not shoot. He risked hitting our father or one of the prisoners. He had to wait a few moments, but he was firm in his intent. He stopped a moment to think. If they had to carry all those people away, they had to load them on trucks. The only place where they could was in the square. That was where he had to go if he wanted to have a chance to free our father.

He ran like hell through the roads. He knew the town well and he avoided all the patrols. From the little road that ran along the tower he looked into the square. It was full of Carabinieri and trucks. But everyone was looking towards via Castrenze Di Bella, the town's main road from where the prisoners were coming.

He came out into open and shouted with the breath he had:
"Cowards!"
"I'm the one you're looking for!"
"Let go my father and those poor people!"
"Catch me if you can!"

Angry blasts of machineguns and rifles followed his challenge. The bullets soared by him without touching him. He ran for cover in the alley. The guns kept shooting as other soldiers arrived. Gunfire was getting more and more intense.

Turiddu shot his gun only three times with deadly precision. One soldier, Aristide Gualtieri, fell to the ground dead. The other two were injured.

The shootout was so intense that Turiddu had to give up the fight and escape. They followed like a beast being hunted down, but they lost his tracks. He had escaped by crossing the bed of the stream than ran through town. He walked in the middle of the water until he reached the "Acqua Alvani" spring and there he found refuge in the "White Cave".

A long time went by before he could come back home. The house was guarded 24 hours a day. The Carabinieri were stalking him. In the town, in the countryside, the patrols were searching everywhere. But my brother knew every ravine, cave and hill around Montelepre. He escaped every ambush and trap they prepared for him with great skill.

Life outdoors, in direct contact with nature, developed in him an instinct for survival like that of wild animals. His extrasensorial perceptions were sharpened.

All those who had been arrested that day were taken to the prisons of Palermo, Termini Imerese and Monreale. There they suffered abuses and torture. Many were whipped, beaten and wet with salt and water to make the wounds burn even more. They even put pieces of paper between their toes and set them on fire. But this was nothing compared to the notorious "BOX".

The poor victim was supine with his hands and feet tied to an empty crate of ammunition on the floor. It was turned so that the handles, located at the extremities, were on the same level as the floor. A carabiniere would sit on his legs and would punch him in the stomach.

While the poor man was still gasping, they would put a gasmask with a long trunk over his face. At the end of the trunk there was a funnel. They would then pour a mixture of salt and water into funnel and the victim was forced to drink it.

In these terrifying conditions the victim would reach the climax of pain. Everything would dim out and he would faint. Then they would show him a list of unsolved crimes. If he confessed to be responsible for them, they would send him back to rot in prison. If he would put up resistance, they would start all over again. They would continue until he confessed anything.

Montelepre: the long line of prisoners.

## Chapter VI

# SOLITUDE

It was since Christmas that Turiddu was living all alone on the Mountain.

His eyes gazed across the horizon until they stopped on his town. Many memories overwhelmed his mind, while he rested in the silent embrace of "Pizzo Saraceno", the hill overlooking Montelepre. By then theirs had become a complete union.

Like a mother, the mountain had welcomed him into its womb and watched over his torment. Cruel destiny had upset his plans and his expectations.

Never had Turiddu wanted or desired to shed blood and with repulsion he cast the evil away from himself. Yet it was a time of catastrophe and aberration, greedy for innocent victims. He was caught and entangled in the tragedy of World War II.

He was not the only one raped of the lightheartedness of youth in those days. Many like him, full of altruism and thirsting for affection, were forced to forget their true nature.

Turiddu was sought-after by all his friends because he would bring joy and peace. No party or dance could start without him.

But now he was alone. As he gazed at the landscape, he flew back into time to those wonderful years of lightheartedness, serenades and songs.

Those images, no longer friendly, suddenly abandoned him in all his desperation. He had let the amours of his past escape from his unhappy destiny. He was alone in that hermitage with his tense senses ready to perceive even the slightest rustle in the surrounding landscape.

In that solitude he could hear every single beat of his heart. There was no peace.

What happened to his dream?

Was it a nightmare? Or just desolate reality?

Suddenly he could hear the voices of his mother, his father, his brother and sisters. They were calling him. . . . It was like a delirium.

From up there he too called them trying to make his way into their hearts.

He shouted with his eyes swelling with tears. He saw from afar. They were there, but no one could hear him. He saw the house that once had been his, too. But he could not go back. Alone!

He called upon the wind, the sun, and the faraway sea. . . . And the mountain remained silent. Everything in and around him was silence, while the day slowly made way for the night.

His crying broke in the echo. Words died in his throat. . . . Alone!

He saw once again before his eyes the threshing floor during the harvest. Many and many times did he joyfully sing his songs while his friends and relatives stood around him or when he spurred on the mule as it ran in circles while the bystanders watched and happily laughed. While the chaff uplifted by the mule's hooves covered him, he, at the center of the floor, would follow the animal in its toil. From his powerful chest a poem would suddenly erupt:

| | |
|---|---|
| Sia ludatu e ringraziato ogni mumentu, | Praise and thanks for every moment, |
| lu Santissimu e Divinissimu Sacramentu! | The most Holy and Divine Sacrament! |
| Oh! Che bedda sta jurnata, viva la Virgini 'MMaculata! | Oh, what a beautiful day, Viva the Immaculate Virgin! |
| E gisa e firria, viva lu beddu nomu Di la Virgini Maria! | Around and around, viva the gracious name of the Virgin Mary! |
| Una pi tia, una pi mia e una pi Santa Rusulia! | One for you, one for me and one For Saint Rosalia ! |
| E si lu ventu veni spissu, viva lu Santissimu Crucifissu! | And if the wind often comes, Then viva the Holy Cross! |
| Semu vinuti fina a cca, pi ringraziari La Santissima Trinità! | We have come all the way, To thank the Holy Trinity! |
| Acchiana e scinni cantannu e ludannu | Up and down, singing and praising all together, |
| Ncumpagnia, viva la Bedda Matri di "Taghiavia!" | Viva the Beautiful Madonna of "Tagliavia"! |
| E vola vola comu n'aceddu, viva la Bedda Matri di lu Rumiteddu! | And flying all about like a bird, viva the Beautiful Madonna of Romitello! |
| E gira e vota comu na picciotta Chianota! | And around and around like a damsel of the Plain! |
| E vola cola comu na farfalla nta li ciuri | And flying all about like a butterfly on the flowers, |

| | |
|---|---|
| E aiuta lu to' Salvaturi! | Please help your Salvatore! |
| Pistamu prestu stu furmentu ringra-ziannu | Quick, let us thresh this wheat, |
| Lu Santissimu Sacramentu! | Praising the Most Holy Sacrament! |
| Si lu suli splenni brillanti, | If the sun shines so high, |
| ringgraziamu tutti li Santi! | Let us thank the all the Saints! |
| Ora ca allistemu, cu tanta alligria | Now that we have finished, |
| Ripitemu tutti ncumpagnia | Let us say altogether, |
| Viva Gesù, Giuseppe e Maria! | Viva Jesus, Joseph and Mary! |

Then, after taking the mule to eat and drink, he would return to sit together with the others.

Now his memories started to fade and Turiddu disappeared under cover of darkness.

He desperately tried to make some light in the place where he was. He gasped during his metamorphosis; he panted and repeated mentally the song.

Just like the last of men he gave no sign of life. A dark cloud was climbing in his sky; handfuls of quicksand would often immerse him once again in his past. During those few moments he was left, his mind went back to the memories of his joyful and lighthearted youth. That time was now gone forever.

Everything for him was over. He saw his beautiful dreams of love and the promising future he would have certainly built for himself thanks to his powerful intelligence crumble before his eyes.

All his hopes had vanished even before they could manifest themselves in all their strength.

How many dreams!

His soul was torn by the immense pain. His life was destroyed. Alone with himself!

He was forced to abandon everything: his home, his beloved family. The only road open before him was that of the mountain, which would have relentlessly driven him towards his cruel destiny.

He had spent already ten days wandering in total solitude. After so many sleepless nights, he laid down tired and hungry between a rock and a bush to rest.

At about one-hundred-fifty meters away from him a small flock of sheep was grazing peacefully in the grass. The young shepherd watching them was the first human being to approach him.

Despite the festivity, the search still continued. A squad of Carabinieri burst suddenly out of the thick patch of olive trees,

Turiddu is alone in the mountains (Publifoto).

reached the boy watching the sheep and started asking him questions.

They asked him whether he had seen Turiddu Giuliano. He looked at them diffidently from the head to the toes and answered curtly:

"I don't know anyone!"

But as soon as the troops moved, he darted away leaving them dumbfounded. He flew as quick as a hare towards Turiddu's hiding place shouting:

"Run! Run! They're looking for you!"

With a feline leap my brother hid behind a fallen tree trunk.

"It's him! It's him!" shouted one of the soldiers.

They started to shoot even though the young shepherd risked being hit. Turiddu peeped out of his hiding place holding his musket, but he couldn't shoot because he was afraid of hitting the boy.

"To the ground! Drop to the ground!" he shouted with all his lungs. The boy obeyed and he could finally fire a shot. A soldier fell to the ground with a wound to his shoulder. All the others dropped to the ground looking for cover and Turiddu took advantage of the situation to escape.

The poor shepherd, just twelve years old, bore the brunt of the consequences. He was beaten brutally and some of his sheep were killed. Some time after, Turiddu bought him some other sheep, even more than the ones he had lost and thanked him with a caress full of gratitude. The boy, beaming with joy, accepted also the clothes and the sweets he had given him.

It was towards the end of January 1944 when we received a letter. Our mother opened it anxiously. She feared that it was bad news from our father who was still imprisoned in Palermo.

When we tried to read it, the letter's contents proved to be obscure and incomprehensible. We didn't know whether it was better to burn it or to send it to Turiddu. In the end we decided on the latter.

We had a vague idea of the area where we could find him. It wasn't difficult for me to find him. To tell the truth, it was actually Turiddu who found me. He had been keeping the mule track coming from town under control and he recognized me.

Turiddu's face was so tired. He had lost several pounds, but he seemed to be fine.

When he saw the letter, he explained to me that it was a coded message from the leaders of the Movement for the Independence of Sicily (from now on I will simply call it the M.I.S.).

The head of the Movement wanted to speak to him. He begged me not to tell anyone of what I had learned.

"I don't want mamma to worry. Tell her that it was just a joke!"

On the day of the meeting Turiddu went to Palermo. He was well aware of the fact that his picture and description had been sent to all police stations. He could not move about without taking the necessary precautions. So he decided to disguise himself.

A relative of ours lived in Palermo together with his family. He too was tall and stoutly-built almost like Turiddu. He was a postman.

Turiddu put on his uniform and borrowed his moped. He reached the address of the appointment and knocked three times as the letter said.

An eye scrutinized him for a few moments through the spy-hole in the door. Finally, the door slowly opened and a middle-aged man peeped out. He was a man of medium height with grizzled hair and moustache.

"Is there any mail for me, young man?" asked the man.

"No, I'm looking for Lady Sicily!" replied Turiddu.

"Here you can find only FREEDOM!" That was the password Turiddu had been waiting for.

"Welcome amongst us, Turiddu Giuliano!" said the man as he showed the most captivating of smiles and opened the door wide.

He was led into a large room covered with wallpaper with a flower pattern. Sunk into an armchair of red velvet sat a man of about fifty years of age, slightly taller than the other man, quite sturdy and wearing eyeglasses.

As soon as he saw him, he jumped to his feet with unexpected rapidity and shook his hand with strength as he looked into his eyes and said:

"Turiddu Giuliano!" "You are little more than a boy! From all I have heard about you I expected to meet someone older than you!"

Turiddu smiled faintly.

"I'm Andrea Finocchiaro Aprile and this is Pietro Franzone, my dear friend and assistant!"

"I've been looking forward to meet you for more than a year now!" exclaimed Turiddu.

"I know! I know! You will never imagine how many things I know about you. But I didn't call you to exchange compliments! There is serious and important news I must tell you!"

With a motion of his hand he invited Turiddu to sit down in the sitting room as he did the same. Then with a paternalistic tone of voice he continued from where he had stopped:

"Dear boy, the situation for Sicily is taking a turn for the worse! The allies want to cast us into hands of Badoglio and his lot! It's only a matter of time! We must prepare ourselves for the worse and fight if necessary! Here in Palermo and in Catania there are many young men ready for anything: all they need is a leader and some training! You have given proof of courage and boldness! You know how to use a gun! We need men like you to train our boys!"

Turiddu was puzzled.

"If I were free to move freely, I'd accept immediately!" he answered. "But I am wanted and coming here to Palermo was a big risk for me! If all these young men could reach me where I am, everything would be much easier!"

"I understand! I know I have asked too much from you! But if you really want to help your land you could set up a group of your own!" proposed the elderly leader of the M.I.S.

"That's possible, although I haven't got the faintest idea of what to do at the moment!"

They shook hands and promised to keep in touch and to inform each other of any news.

At the beginning of February 1944 the worst we had feared took place. The following proclamation was made public in Sicily's major cities:

**"I, Sir Harold R.E.G. Alexander, G.C.E.S.I., D.S.O., K.C.M.G., Governor General of all occupied territories, by virtue of the power conferred to me by the Commander in Chief Sir Henry Maitland Wilson, G.B.S., K.O.B., D.F.O.,**

**DECLARE AS FOLLOWS:**

**THE ALLIED MILITARY GOVERNMENT set up by myself and every and each proclamation and order hitherto issued by myself or on my behalf in that part of Continental Italy, south of the northern borders of the provinces of SALERNO, POTENZA, and BARI, in Sicily and its Islands (save for Pantelleria, Lampedusa and Linosa) HAVE TERMINATED AS OF 0,01 OF THE ELEVENTH DAY OF FEBRUARY 1944.**

**THE ITALIAN GOVERNMENT shall administer the aforementioned territory, save the powers, rights and immunity of the UNITED NATIONS, of the Commander in Chief of the Allied Forces and the Allied Surveillance Commission."**

The Sicilian separatists felt in full the burden of that grave event. Andrea Finocchiaro Aprile spoke on their behalf and expressed publicly their dissent.

In the speech he gave at the Teatro Massimo of Palermo on February 13, 1944 he reaffirmed once again that "the Strait of Messina was to mark a division line not only geographically, but also politically." However, he suggested "the creation of a Confederation of Italian States", of which Sicily could have been a part. But he also affirmed that "of course, the first step was to be the creation of the Sovereign State of Sicily in the fullness of its international rights and obligations."

"We welcomed the Anglo-Saxon troops like brothers, we told our soldiers to lay down their weapons, we covered the liberators with flowers, we expressed them our love and friendship, but, frankly speaking, we would never have expected to be handed over to the Badoglio Government, the worst of our enemies."

"Unfortunately today we have been put before the *fait accompli*. Today, the passage of all powers has already been carried out. Of course, we have no intention to embarrass the Allied Government in any way."

"But it must be clear to all that, should an official representative of the Badoglio Government, a governor, or a high commissioner for Sicily be nominated, he must be appointed by the Sicilian people and he himself must be a Sicilian. Be it Musotto or someone else, he will become our symbol. . . . But, if they intend to send to Sicily a representative of the government who is not Sicilian, a general or an official who has not been appointed by us and therefore does not have our approval, that would mean that we will be forced to fight and we are ready to fight to the bitter end."[1]

---

[1] *The proclamation and the speech are extracts from the book* "Anni Roventi" *by Salvo Di Matteo.*

CHAPTER VII

# THE ESCAPE

As great historical events were taking place in Sicily, Turiddu was in the mountains. In that desolate solitude he often thought of his father, of his relatives and fellow townsmen closed in prison. He was discouraged yet full of anger because he could not do anything.

His hate against the Carabinieri, who in those days were considered to be criminals and tyrants rather than the guarantors of law and order, mounted in Turiddu. He was thinking of all this when a whistle startled him.

It was our messenger who was bringing him food, clothing and a letter.

He opened it immediately hoping that it was from our father. He hands trembled and his eyes were shining for the great emotion. But the handwriting was different. He looked at the signature at the bottom of the page. It was from our cousin Salvatore, the one that was born almost together with Turiddu, the playmate of his childhood, the faithful friend of his youth.

The letter said that he too had been arrested that Christmas day and he was held prisoner in Monreale. He had confessed many crimes he had never committed and said that a whole lifetime would not be enough to serve his term in jail. He ended the letter by begging my brother not to abandon him in jail.

Turiddu could not let his cry for help go unheeded. He loved his cousin very much. They were bosom buddies from their childhood. Even at the cost of his own life, he would try to free he who was suffering because of him. His only fault was that they had the same blood in their veins.

IT WAS HIS DUTY!

The idea of freeing him excited him. The feat wasn't impossible. The more he thought about it the more he was convinced he HAD TO DO IT!

The next day, going along winding roads, he reached Monreale, where he looked for and found the prison. It was located in the lower part of the town, on the edge of the "Conca d'Oro". Three sides of the building were impenetrable, but on the back there was a yard and there were some windows closed with bars overlooking it.

He spent the day thinking of a plan to make our cousin escape. When darkness started to fall, he crept into the garden. He rushed under one of the windows and blew a long and modulated whistle that the prisoner knew all too well. A few seconds went by, but they seemed an eternity for Turiddu. Then he heard his cousin's voice:

"Turiddu! Turiddu! Finally!"

He waved to him to keep quiet. He then showed him a long rope that he tossed through the window. After a few unsuccessful attempts, the prisoner finally grabbed it. At one end an iron bar and two files were tied to the rope. The rope was thrown into the garden below. Turiddu made him understand with his hands that he would come back the next night.

There were eight other people in the cell. They feverishly started to work. They were unusually happy and they started to make noise and sing. But they did it to cover the noise of the file as they cut the bars.

The next day, at sundown, my brother returned to the yard. He whistled again. An arm from the window waved a handkerchief. It was the signal he was waiting for. Everything was ready. Darkness was slowly creeping over the land and with it came the long awaited moment to free them.

Turiddu had got a long ladder. He put it against the wall and he slowly climbed up to the window. He brought along another iron bar and the rope of the day before.

The prisoners tied it to the bars and pulled altogether. But their attempts to bend them were useless even though the bars were already cut at the bottom.

Turiddu told them to use the bars to break the mortar blocking the bars to the wall and went the down the ladder again. He hid in the yard for about an hour as he waited with his gun in his hand. He was ready to kill in case something went wrong and he risked being captured.

Everything went as planned. None of the prison guards noticed anything. When the work was over and the space in the middle of the bars was wide enough, Turiddu put the ladder against the wall again.

After a few minutes, eight of the nine men were free. The ninth preferred not to escape because his release was just a few days away.

The two cousins hugged each other in the silence of the night. Altogether they rushed away from that ominous place and went to hide in the mountains.

When my brother felt that they were out of danger, he invited them to stop and said:

"Picciotti! I came to free my cousin Salvatore, who, as you all know, is like a brother for me. You took advantage of the opportunity, but you're free now! You're free to go wherever you want! I'm responsible for my cousin alone!"

Except for two of them, the others answered:

"You saved us and we'll never leave you!"

Their offer caught him by surprise and he would have preferred to refuse it, but the words of the leader of the M.I.S. returned to mind:

"If you really want to help your land, then create a group of your own!"

He accepted the offer. The six men that stayed with him were our cousin Salvatore, Andrea Abbate, Tommaso di Maggio, Antonino Cucinella, Angelo Vitale and our great-uncle Francesco Giuliano.

A few days later, on February 28, 1944, the Lega Giovanile Separatista (the Young Men's Separatist League) was founded. It was composed mainly of young men full of patriotism who had decided to dedicate their lives to the cause of independence and to support the M.I.S.

After the resounding escape from the prison in Monreale, Turiddu and his men found refuge in the hills of the "Sagana" estate. It lied just a few kilometers away from Montelepre. It was composed mainly by barren hills, rocky walls, natural ravines and caves. At its feet broom bushes, elm trees and other bushes all grew entwined thus forming a thick forest.

Today the "Sagana" estate, in the "Sugarelli" and "Calcerame" contradas, is a holiday locality. There are many small villas and houses full of comforts. In the summer it is full of people. But in those days, the only access road was a trail starting halfway between Borgetto and Giacalone.

The place with all its desolation offered innumerable hiding places in old farmhouses, barns and caves. There were plenty of observation sites, which enabled the sighting of soldiers many kilometers away. On the side overlooking Montelepre, it could be reached only on foot or on horseback by passing along winding trails.

The place was not chosen by chance.

During the first days there was the problem of finding supplies. Turiddu was the only one with a gun and he would spend the whole day hunting for hares, partridges and other game, which was abundant in the area.

But his rifle was not fit for the purpose. If he managed to hit his target, it was thanks to his deadly aim. Afterwards everyone tried to solve the problem with the help of their own families. Relatives and friends would punctually send to Montelepre the food and clothing necessary for the fugitives.

Meanwhile the soldiers continued to comb the area. But my brother was becoming more and more expert in darting their traps, which all failed miserably. In retaliation many farmers from Montelepre were taken from their homes and land and taken to Palermo under arrest. They were all asked once they were arrested:

"Why on that day, at that hour, didn't you rush to inform us that you had seen Giuliano?"

If the poor man did not know anything, he would be brutally beaten. If he confessed, he would then be taken to jail. Although some bore the torture heroically, they were sent anyway to the "Ucciardone", Palermo's prison, awaiting new evidence, testimonies or the confessions of other people arrested.

The torture was brutal. There was not trace of humanity (see Chap. V). When they would finally return home after months and months, they would tell of the horrifying tortures they had to suffer.

The hate and disdain of the town against those who were supposed to be the servants of the State and the government fueled the exasperation of the people to the point that the people hoped that Turiddu, who had become the SYMBOL OF THEIR REBELLION, would avenge the wrongs they suffered.

My brother and his "picciotti" were informed of all the violence, stigmatizing their feelings of guilt, resentment and revenge.

Revenge? But how? Except for Turiddu, they had no weapons. But enough was enough. The time to react had come. He called his companions and said them:

"Picciotti, up to now we've been on a vacation! Our families and our friends have helped us at the risk of their own freedom! The Carabinieri are making them and others who have nothing to do with this story pay at high price their generosity. We are responsible for all this and we must do something! We must find weapons and defend ourselves, our loved ones and our fellow townsmen."

Of course, his words met with enthusiasm. They all went to "Piano dell'Occhio", down to the old semi-destroyed ammunition depot. They started to look through the ruins for weapons and ammunition.

They found a crate almost full of ammunition and hand grenades. They took all they could carry and they went back to their lair. In the days that followed Turiddu and his men set up a shooting range with some cardboard dummies. They practiced every day until they became fierce fighters.

A moment of rest for Turiddu.

Chapter VIII

# THE LAW OF THE JUNGLE

As the days went by the roundups became more and more frequent. The flow of supplies was not as regular as before. Often the Carabinieri came within shooting range. But my brother preferred to avoid them by moving from one hideout to another.

It was during this period that he and his men were forced to ask some food from the shepherds who would take their flocks to pasture in that area. They fed them willingly. In this period of apparent inactivity on the part of my brother and his men, many took advantage of the situation.

Many ruthless criminals would break into homes, stop people and rob them. The authors of these crimes would then accuse my brother of their crimes. In Montelepre too there were some who did the same. One of these was a man named Giacomo N. He would do his wrongdoings blatantly under the eyes of everyone. He would go into town's shops and ask for pasta, bread, wine, cigarettes, oil and other goods saying that he had been sent by Turiddu Giuliano.

The people would hand him everything he asked for in good faith. But as time went by, they waited to be paid in vain. They started to get tired of the situation and they came to complain at our house. We were sure about my brother's honesty, so we paid the creditors and we informed him of what had happened.

Of course, he was unaware of the situation and he got very angry. He could not allow that someone use his name scot-free and ruin his reputation. So one evening he came down from the mountains and he went to see the culprit. He found him as he walked along a dimly lit road. He appeared before him. He took him by the shirt and pushed him against the wall:

"You useless thing! You coward!" my brother said to him.

"I should kill you for what you've done! If you needed anything, all you had to do was ask! I would have helped you! Stop taking advantage of people or I'll kill you!"

Giacomo put his hands in his head meekly. When he looked up

again Turiddu had vanished. A few days later, Turiddu was patrolling outside town in a contrada called "Piano Gallina". He was riding a black horse he had borrowed from a shepherd.

The sun was setting and he was ready to return to the hideout, when he saw an old man crying as he sat on the edge of the road. He spurred his horse towards him and he reached him. He felt pity for that poor skinny man wearing rags. Turiddu was very sensitive to the needs of the poor.

He asked him why he was crying. He found out that a man who was passing himself for him, together with another two men, had threatened the man at gunpoint and they stole his mule and the goat tied to its saddle.

"Giuliano doesn't do such things!" Turiddu reassured him.

"Tell me in which direction they went and you wait for me here!"

The old man looked at him incredulously and with a gesture of resignation he pointed towards the town of Carini. Turiddu spurred his horse in that direction. After a few minutes he sighted the group of men. He preceded them by about a hundred meters and at the first curve along the road he appeared before them pointing his gun at them.

"Drop your weapons!" he ordered.

"Don't try any tricks or I'll kill you like a dog!"

The three men looked at each other trying to understand who was standing in front of them.

"Yet you ought to know me, since you commit your wrongdoings using my name!"

Their faces turned white with fear. They were sure that they were going to be killed. They started to beg him to spare them. But Turiddu put on an angry face to scare them. He noticed that they were so cared that they wet their pants for the fear. He let them go and warned them that if he met them again in that area he would not spare them a second time.

When the old man saw the animals, he went towards him with his arms wide open. He could not stop blessing him and thanking him. He wanted to know his name so that he could thank him in his prayers.

"I'm the one and only Turiddu Giuliano!"

The only man looked at him with his eyes wide open. He went up to him, took his hand and kissed him saying:

"God bless you, son!"

The day after the whole town was talking of the episode. The Carabinieri too found out and they started to comb the area.

Hundreds of soldiers searched for him in the countryside. They arrested all the farmers they met.

From when my brother had pitched camp in Sagana, all those who had been arrested and then released, would reach him in the mountains as soon as they heard of roundups. They would stay there until the alarm had ceased.

Turiddu was no longer alone.

If necessary, together with his group, he could count on many other people. They belonged to all social classes and they had been joined by the common threat. They formed a widespread network of voluntary informers and financiers. Thanks to them, Turiddu could cover the expenses for feeding his men and buying guns and ammunition.

Day after day his fame grew as did his prestige. His name was being invoked by all those who suffered abuses and injustice. People from everywhere were continuously coming and going from our house. They all wanted to meet him.

Some wanted to join him, but very few actually did. My mother and I would look at everyone with diffidence. Who could assure us that there were not any Carabinieri amongst them? On holidays crowds flooded to our house. There were plenty of university students, full of patriotism and sympathy for the cause.

The myth of Turiddu as the defender of the weak and the poor started to grow. By order of Turiddu, our home had become a center of distribution. My mother and I wouldn't let anyone leave empty-handed. We would give clothing, food and sometimes even money to those who really needed it.

People considered Turiddu like a sort of KING SOLOMON. They would come to ask for his judgement on the most varied problems, including private and sentimental affairs. He reconciled whole families divided by old grudges and he saved many weddings. His judgement was unquestionable. His word was law.

The winter was very heavy and rigid. There were great hardships not only for Turiddu and his men but also for the people of Montelepre. The heads of the families went back and forth from jail and couldn't cultivate their fields.

Despite the initial efforts of the Allied government, the food situation had not improved very much: many families were in desperate conditions. Children were barefoot and poorly fed. The men had ragged trousers covered with patches of many different colors. They were desperately looking for a job so that they could earn enough to fill their stomachs. The women would scour the countryside looking for edible herbs. Every now and then some private initiative would temporarily make up for the dearth of raw materials and the negligence of the government.

Soap was made from almond peels, sugar was made from carob, textile fibers from algave and sheep wool was carded. Yet good will alone was not enough neither to solve problems nor to fill stomachs. Although Turiddu distributed three-fourths of the money he collected from friends and sympathizers, the food situation in Montelepre was critical. He tried to do his best but there were too many mouths to be fed.

Our father, before his arrest, had sown 3,000 square meters with fava beans in our land in the "Ecce Homo" contrada. The harvest was abundant and there was a surplus of that legume. My mother informed Turiddu and he was happy about the good news.

He sent one of the town criers with a message wrapped in banknote. As soon as he saw the money and read the message, he took his drum and went through the town crying:

"Listen! Listen!" Ratata. . . Ratata. . . .

"By order of Turiddu Giuliano, whoever wants fava beans can go and pick them in the land of his father in contrada Ecce Homo!"

The invitation was welcomed like a the biblical manna from the sky and many went to take advantage of the offer, including a few soldiers. They went with sacks, saddlebags, baskets and they gathered all they could. Then came the summer.

Many townsmen, taking advantage of the fresh morning air, would go to Palermo taking along with themselves some fresh produce. They hoped to sell them and then buy other products with the money.

Two carabinieri came to learn of what was happening and they would hide along the road leading to Palermo. They would stop those who passed, confiscate their goods and then accuse them of smuggling. They would not inform their superiors. They would keep the confiscated goods for themselves.

But one morning, while they were busy with their profitable pastime, a gunshot in their direction made them freeze with fear.

"Carabinieri!" shouted a powerful voice.

"Drop your guns and return what you've robbed from these poor people!"

The two obeyed and they held up their arms. A man with a rifle came walking towards them with long and confident strides. His townsmen recognized him:

"Turiddu! Turiddu! Make them pay for starving us to death!"

"So you're the ones that steal from my people!"

"Don't kill us! We've got families!" mumbled one of them.

"These people too have families!" replied my brother. With an imperative voice, he ordered them to take off their shoes and to get out of his sight before he changed his mind.

When they reached the police station, barefoot and disarmed, the marshal gathered his men and went out to search for him hoping to catch him. But while they were looking for him in the countryside, Turiddu was at home in our arms.

The two carabinieri were transferred elsewhere because they let themselves be disarmed. The whole town felt relieved.

Towards the end of August, the farmers were preparing the fields for sowing. Many of them who had no land of their own thought of sharecropping the land in "Sagana". This estate was owned by the Opera Nazionale per il Mezzogiorno" (the National Board for the South). The foreman was a native of a nearby town and he wanted to favor his own fellow townsmen by excluding completely the inhabitants of Montelepre.

The Sagana estate was Turiddu's base. When he discovered the man's intentions, he couldn't tolerate that the territory under his control was used with such partiality. He was also afraid that our fellow townsmen would be left without means of sustenance. He decided to intervene.

The day set for the assignment of the land, Turiddu went to the place. He hid his men around the meeting place and he went to negotiate.

Besides the foreman, there was a lawyer and the director of the Opera. He tried to convince them that the farmers in Montelepre had the right to earn a living and work. The assignment of the land had to be fair, without favors. The neediest and most numerous families had to be privileged.

The director and the lawyer agreed with him, while the foreman, who intended to favor his own friends and relatives, insisted doggedly in his intent. All attempts of convincing him were useless. Turiddu placed his hands on his mouth and whistled. His men came out and started to shoot in the air. The foreman and those he wanted to favor ran away. The land was then assigned fairly between the farmers of the two towns.

A few days later, some of the relatives of his men told Turiddu that Giacomo N. started to take advantage of people again by using his name. This time he went to a small milk and cheese shop-owner. He had many children and he barely managed to feed his family.

The sullen individual had asked him fifty thousand Lire telling him that Turiddu Giuliano had sent him and that he wanted them immediately. The poor man promised to pay as soon as possible. But as soon as he went away, he rushed to our house and told everything that happened to our mother. She listened to him patiently and said to him with a smile:

"You know that my son doesn't do these things, especially with poor people! Unfortunately there are rogues that take advantage of the misfortune of others! My son is in Sagana! But they accuse him of all the crimes committed in Sicily. I am surprised that you believe the words of anyone who comes to you even though you live here! Don't worry and above all don't give anything to anyone!"

Of course, we informed Turiddu, who sent a message to Giacomo N.'s victim.

"Tell him when he comes that you've already given me the money!"

After the humiliation suffered, he kept calm for a day. He then thought that the only one who was opposing his profitable activities was Turiddu. He decided to make a deal with the Carabinieri. For half a million Lire he said he would help them capture him.

When Turiddu found out, he got very angry. One night at the beginning of September 1944, he came to town alone. He found him at home and he forced him to follow him up to the mountain. He gathered his men and in front of them he spoke to Giacomo N.:

"You've used my name too many times to cheat people and I warned you not to do so! But you continued anyway! Because of the dearth of this damned period I had forgiven you. But you've done it again and I can't forgive you! You've made a deal with our enemies! With the enemies of our land! With the persecutors of our people to kill me or to capture me! You've betrayed twice: your people and your land! For this, in the name of God, Sicily and your People, I sentence you to death!"

Having said as much, he lined his men up like a firing squad and he had him executed.

The next day some farmers found the body with a message on his back:

"The souls of spies don't go to heaven!"

The local police station in Montelepre was informed. Three carabinieri were sent to the place to check the identity of the victim and to guard the body. They stopped all those who passed from there and asked whether they had seen Giuliano. As expected, no one knew anything, but they started to insult them and hit them with the butts of their rifles.

Turiddu was not very far away on high ground overlooking the site. He watched the scene and quivered with anger. He could not stand the sight of these abuses against his townsmen. He started to come closer and closer.

In that moment Marianna Lombardo, my mother's sister, and her daughter came walking along the road. Her daughter was beautiful.

As soon as the soldiers saw the two women approaching, they rushed to stop them. They asked the usual question. Because they received no answer, they threatened that they would kill them if they did not tell them where their relative was hiding. They threatened them at gunpoint and insulted them. They also told them that they were criminals like all the inhabitants of Montelepre. The women started to cry and they let them go as they laughed.

Turiddu waited until they were gone and then came out in the open.

"Carabinieri!" he shouted.

"Drop your guns and I'll let you go!"

After the first moments of surprise, the three soldiers opened fire, but a burst of machinegun fire lifted a cloud of dust in front of their feet.

They dropped their guns and raised their arms in the air. They started to tremble because they feared for their lives.

"Have you finished bothering helpless people? Did you have fun with the women?"

"Now it's my turn!"

"You were looking for me? Well, here I am!"

Their faces were as pale as death.

"So you've come for him?" asked Turiddu as he pointed his gun towards the body. "If you want to know it, I killed him because he's a traitor!"

"And you'll all finish like him!"

"I could kill you too! If I won't, it's because I know that you have a family too and that you are obeying to orders!"

"Get out of here, before I change my mind!"

The three did not wait for him to repeat it again and they ran back to Montelepre. When they reached the station, they told what happened. The marshal informed the local lieutenancy in Partinico.

Lieutenant Testa had been recently transferred there. He heard the comments on Turiddu around town and he was convinced that capturing him was not at all difficult. That day he happened to be in the office. He had just gotten his wedding license and was elegantly dressed in white.

He received the communication and he thought that it was a good chance to show that capturing my brother was easy, especially since everyone knew where he usually hid. He gathered his men and with a truck he went to Montelepre. At the end of the paved part of the road, they continued on foot to where the shootout with the three soldiers took place. They spread out and shot towards anything that could be a hideout.

Turiddu was not very far and those gunshots attracted his attention. With his binoculars he scoured the surrounding countryside, until he localized the troops at about 500 meters away. He only had his machinegun, while the soldiers had rifles. Although he was outnumbered, he was better equipped. Instead of running away, he stayed to face them.

He recognized Lieutenant Testa at the head of the troops. They had spoken of him as the man who had dared to say in public:

"At the first attempt I'll capture him like meek lamb!"

It was a challenge for Turiddu. And he would never avoid a challenge. It was a personal affair.

He went towards them cautiously. Every now and then he stopped to watch them. It was funny to see them shooting at shadows. At about a hundred meters from them, he climbed onto a rock and shouted:

"I'm here, Lieutenant!"

All the rifles were pointed against him, but before they could shoot he jumped down and hid behind a stone. Their shots missed the target as they whistled through the air. Lieutenant Testa, with two soldiers, charged towards Turiddu. He hoped to take him by surprise while he was still hiding behind the rock. But Turiddu raised his head and shot a blast of machinegun fire. They all fell to the ground wounded. They screamed for the pain. The other carabinieri retreated and were out of shooting range.

Cautiously Turiddu went towards the wounded men and tried to assist them. When he reached Lieutenant Testa, he saw that his wound was serious. He said:

"See what happens for being too bold!"

The wounded man faintly said:

"Let me die, go! I was looking for it!"

Lieutenant Testa died the next day at the Military Hospital of Palermo. In a letter to the press, Turiddu nobly defined him a "victim of his duty". The last few days had been too animated. My brother felt the need to rest in a real bed. He came home to stay as long as possible.

Usually his visits lasted a few hours. We all did our best to make his stay as peaceful as possible. After a bath he ate a large plate of handmade pasta and he had a long sleep. As he rested, my mother and I guarded the house. We would take turns every three hours. He slept for 18 hours.

When he woke up, our mother told him that the night before the mayor of the town had come:

"He came to beg me to give back the weapons you took from the three soldiers! Do it for me, give them back! They risk being put on trial!"

"OK, mother! I'll do it for you! Tomorrow I'll have someone I trust give them to the municipal guard! But make sure that the poor come here to knock at your door! Help them! Don't worry about anything! I'll take care of you!"

"The Lord be with you, son!" said our mother.

They hugged each other for very long. The time had come to leave again. He hugged and kissed us all. He then went out the little door leading to the yard and he went up the hill. Before disappearing from our sight, he waved goodbye.

He had left his horse to a farmer who took care of it as best as possible. He found it already saddled in the early afternoon. In order to reach his men waiting for him in Sagana, he had to go up the usual trail. But he preferred to ride through the plain.

The sun was setting. He was blinded by the last intense rays of sun. He did not notice that there were three carabinieri. He saw them at the last moment, once he had crossed the small stream flowing through the "Valanga" contrada.

It was a marshal and two soldiers from the Borgetto station who were patrolling the countryside.

He leaped off his horse and he dropped to the ground. He shot a blast of machinegun fire to scare them off. They answered fire with their rifles, but they couldn't compete with him. Soon they realized it and rushed for cover behind an old house. Turiddu saw their movements and attacked from their side.

At that point, the soldiers felt that they were in his hands and shouted:

"Why are you shooting at us?"

"I'm shooting at you, because I'm on the hunt for those that hunt me!" said Turiddu.

"But what fault do we have? These are the orders!" continued the soldiers.

"You're under the command of your superiors and I'm under the command of my own survival!" he answered.

"Let us go, we've got family!"

"OK, go, but don't back here ever again!"

The three came out into the open and went towards Borgetto under Turiddu's watchful eyes. He waited until they were far enough and he then returned to his base.

The fame of my brother and his men, who everyone believed to be many, kept spreading like wildfire. They were the heroes of the day and the situation started to worry also the "upper spheres".

The High Commissioner for Sicily, Mr. Salvatore Aldisio, asked the government in Rome to send reinforcements to destroy them. Soon after another 800 soldiers were sent to Montelepre, who started to comb to area. They even came near to the Sagana area. The guards gave the alarm and Turiddu gathered his men, who in that period were only about a dozen.

The binoculars were passed from one to another.

"My God!"

"This time they've sent the whole army after us!" exclaimed one of the boys.

"If I had a hundred men I'd teach them a lesson of strategy they would never forget!", said Turiddu, "but we're too few!" They had to run away.

They went up to the "Rossi" mountain, at 700 meters above sea level. It was a true stronghold.

Turiddu had his men gather boulders to be used in case of an attack and as cover. He then returned to watch the troops' movements. During a wide range operation that lasted till noon, many farmers who were in the area were arrested. In all the chaos our father was arrested for the third time.

A marshal from Palermo named Quardo recognized him and he vented all his anger and disappointment for not having captured Turiddu on him. He started to slap him, punch him and kick him. One of his punches injured him to the point that he felt the consequences until the day he died.

When Turiddu saw that the Carabinieri had gone for the day, he left our cousin at the command of the men and he went down into valley. He went towards the "new houses" in Sagana: they were called new because there had actually been a time when they were new back in the days of King Francis II (called the "Bomb" King). The king would spend his days there resting with his wife, Maria Sofia, or hunting.

At the time of these events the "new houses" were crumbling down.

Once he had come in the vicinity of these constructions, he saw a motor vehicle approaching. He made it just in time to hide behind the "giant's tomb", before it passed a few meters away from him. There were two soldiers and a brigadier.

They had come to pick up some officers. But, since they had gone already, they turned around to make their back to the headquarters.

Turiddu did not expect this change of direction and he came out in the open. He saw them suddenly at just ten meters away from him. He was forced to shoot first and ordered them to surrender. But a bullet ricocheted on a rock and injured the driver in his arm. The vehicle stopped suddenly.

At the sight of the blood, the brigadier raised his arms up to surrender and handed over their weapons. Turiddu went up to the men.

"What are you looking for around here?" he asked.

"We're looking for Giuliano!" they answered altogether.

"Who are we talking to?" they asked.

"I'm the one you're looking for!" answered Turiddu.

"Giuliano? You're Giuliano? Nice to meet you!"

Turiddu smiled and he then saw that one of the men was injured. He threw their weapons away and returned to them. He took his knapsack and pulled out his first aid kit to take care of his wound.

He let the brigadier give him a hand. The wounded man was still under shock and in a moment of discouragement he exclaimed:

"And now that you've bandaged me, you'll kill me!"

"It would be a base action and I'm no coward!" answered Turiddu.

"Tell your superiors that you must not call me 'bandit'. I haven't been banned by the people with whom I have lived. I'm neither a criminal nor the son of criminals! I'm fighting for a cause, for the freedom of my land and people! If I'm up in these mountains, it's the fault of your colleagues who forced me! But you're defenseless. Although you're my enemies, I'll let you go!"

After saying as much, he kindly said goodbye to them and he was about to leave, when the soldiers asked him to leave them a souvenir to remember him. Turiddu was so sorry that he did not have anything with him. He went through his pockets. All he could give them was a lighter.

They thanked him and shook his hand. Then they climbed back onto their vehicle and prepared to leave. But the driver was still shocked and he could not start the vehicle. All his attempts failed.

It may seem funny, but my brother even gave them a hand to start the engine by turning the handle.

When they returned to the headquarters, they told their superiors what had happened. The next day every inch of the Sagana estate was combed. About 1,500 carabinieri, policemen, soldiers and dog units surrounded the area hoping to capture him.

But Turiddu together with his men had moved camp to "Montagna Longa" near Punta Raisi. He had outwitted them once again.

Turiddu with a happy face.

*My Brother, Salvatore Giuliano*

Arrests in Montelepre (Foto Martinez).

The inside of a refuge.

## Chapter IX

# THE E.V.I.S. (VOLUNTARY ARMY FOR SICILIAN INDEPENDENCE) IS BORN

At the beginning of October, after the massive deployment of troops by the government to destroy him, my brother went to Palermo. There he tried to speak to Andrea Finocchiaro Aprile. The meeting was held in a villa near the beach in Mondello. Turiddu told him everything that had recently happened and he asked how were the separatist movement's initiatives proceeding.

The old leader smiled to him. He understood that Turiddu wanted to fight in an official capacity. He invited Turiddu to bear patience and to avoid other shootouts with the Carabinieri. He told him that the Young Men's League of Catania was organizing its first National Congress, which would be held in Taormina. Any future initiative depended on its outcome.

He proposed to him to take part in it:
"You'll see for yourself how things actually are!"
Turiddu accepted.

After a warm embrace they returned respectively to Palermo and Montelepre. Once Turiddu reached the camp he gathered his men and informed them of what was about to happen. He then started to prepare his things. It was not safe for him to travel around, so he got himself a new suit, a fake beard and a pair of dark sunglasses.

He looked like a thirty year old man and no one would have imagined that my brother was hidden behind that disguise. The meeting place was a semi-destroyed hotel.

The proceedings were about to begin; the entrance was carefully guarded, but he had no problems getting in. He sat in the back of the hall and he listened to various men who spoke at the pulpit. They spoke of the future Sicilian Nation and they kept repeating that the movement was different from all political parties.

It gathered amongst its ranks forces of all political colors joined by a sole target: that of restoring Sicily's sovereignty and independence. The young men belonging to the Young Men's League were ready to fight to death for it.

But the news that something very serious had happened in Palermo shattered the calm of the meeting. A terrible event had happened the day before. During a rally to protest against the failed distribution of bread and to obtain a pay raise for the clerks of the tax collector's office, the crowd, composed mainly of women and children were protesting outside the High Commissioner's offices.

The police did not bother about them and let them continue. But someone from a truck full of soldiers shot against the crowd without warning. One of the soldiers launched a bomb. Owing the sudden movement of the vehicle, it fell near the truck itself thus causing the wounding of 9 men amongst the soldiers. The tragic toll of the incident was 30 people dead and 160 injured.

The news shocked the assembly, which was filled with disdain and dismay. It fueled even more the indignation and their protests against the government.

The convention proceedings continued in this climate until the news of further tragic developments arrived from Palermo. The city was on the brink of a revolution!

The High Commissioner, Salvatore Aldisio, who was blatantly hostile towards the separatists and accused them of stirring the crowds and of preparing a revolt against the State, had found a scapegoat. He ordered that the Palermo offices of the M.I.S. be searched and eight people inside the offices were arrested.

Since they had found leaflets of separatist propaganda, he ordered the closing of all separatist offices.

Andrea Finocchiaro Aprile, who had read the news with a broken voice, almost fainted and was forced to sit down. At this point the stranger with the beard stood up and shouted:

"Finocchiaro! Tell us what to do and we will obey till death!"

In all the chaos, shouting, cursing, protests, that voice covered all the others. But patriotic impetus and generosity were not enough to start a war that had to be carefully planned. My brother went back to the mountains to carry out his plans on his own.

As proof of this here is an extract from his diary, published in the weekly magazine *"Epoca"* in 1961:

"ALTHOUGH I WAS IN TERRIBLE CONDITIONS AND I HAD TO FLEE FROM THE CARABINIERI, WHO WERE INTENSIFYING THEIR SEARCH, I WAS ALSO INVOLVED IN POLITICS. SINCE THE AMERICAN INVASION, WITH THE FORMING OF THE SEPARATIST MOVEMENT, I HAD JOINED IT BECAUSE I BELIEVED IT WAS THE ONLY PARTY CAPABLE OF IMPROVING THE CONDITIONS OF THE SICILIAN PEOPLE. FOR THIS REASON I PREPARED PLANS TO

BE PUT INTO ACTION WHEN NECESSARY TO HELP MY BELOVED LAND AND PEOPLE, FOR WHOM I WAS READY DIE, BECAUSE I WAS SURE THAT NEW HEROES AND MARTYRS WOULD BE BORN FROM IT. NO ONE BELIEVED IN THE SINCERITY OF MY PATRIOTISM. EVERYONE THOUGHT I WAS EXPLOITING THE CAUSE TO FORWARD MY OWN PERSONAL INTERESTS TO SAVE MYSELF AND OBTAIN BENEFITS IN THE FUTURE. BUT I WAS CONVINCED THAT THE VICTORY OF THE SEPARATIST MOVEMENT WOULD NOT HAVE CHANGED MY SITUATION AND SO I CONTINUED UNDER THE IMPETUS OF MY IDEA".

In Catania similar steps were taken.

The President of the Young Men's Separatist League, Guglielmo di Carcaci, assigned Prof. Antonino Canepa, a professor of political history at the University of Catania, the task of setting up an underground military organization ready to intervene at the right moment.

He was an expert in guerilla warfare after fighting with the partisans in Tuscany. He had also written a book entitled "SICILY TO SICILIANS", which was considered a cry of rebellion against the misrule of the Italian government and it soon became the "Bible of separatism".

Prof. Canepa's battle name was MARIO TURRI and he assumed the task of saving those young men who the tyrants had sent to their massacre. He was to instill in them the noble ideas of patriotism, the spirit of sacrifice and heroism. With his comrades he set up a training camp on Mount SORO near CESARÒ. There he started to train the young men under his orders with iron military discipline.

In November 1944, the economic and social situation in Sicily was desperate. The chronic poverty of wide strata of the population had worsened even more. Montelepre and the surrounding towns were on the brink of starvation. People were dying of hunger and many asked my brother for help. But his resources were limited and he could not help everyone. Finding food or agricultural products was difficult even for those who had money.

In an estate between Alcamo and Partinico there was a well-organized farm full with all sorts of foodstuffs. It had been signaled by friends in Alcamo. Turiddu sent a message to the owner to ask him to sell his wheat and other cereals. He would have paid them at market price. But he rejected the offer scornfully saying that he could earn ten times as much in the black market.

His answer made my brother angry. He shouted:

"So it's true that those who are full don't care about those who are hungry!"

He was full of disdain. He called his men and said:

"Picciotti, there's someone who needs a lesson! Follow me!"

They moved as one, but he left someone at the camp to guard it. With ten men he went to Partinico, where some friends had been informed of his intentions and lent him a truck. Once they reached the farm, they broke into the farm. There was no need to use their guns. The owner's farm workers helped them load the truck while the owner hid in his room. As his men were about to finish with the job, Turiddu went to find him. He forced him to give all the cash he had and then said:

"I wanted to pay you a fair price for your goods! But you showed me that you don't care about the people starving to death, so from now on I'll take from the rich to give to the poor!"

When the truck was loaded he went back to Montelepre. In contrada "Testa di Corsa" (finish line) he started to distribute the food, after that a municipal clerk had given him a list of all the poor living in town.

He kept the money instead till Christmas Eve. He got some envelopes and he divided it in accordance to the number of family members. During the night he would go around sliding the envelopes under the doors of their homes.

On Christmas day of 1944 the poor of Montelepre found the money with a message saying:

"MAY DIVINE PROVIDENCE HELP YOU! S.G."

But despite my brother's efforts, the cases of extortion committed by people who had nothing to do with him and said to be one of his men continued.

A middle-aged farmer named Orlando Grippi had formed a band of criminals. Together with his lot he stole one evening all the animals of a poor cattle-breeder leaving him in total misery. The victim searched for his animals and he finally found them, the authors of the crime told him that they had received orders from Turiddu Giuliano.

"If you care for your life, don't say anything!"

The poor man came crying to our house. As soon as he saw my mother he dropped at her feet crying and begging her to have pity on him and his family. For days now they had nothing to eat. It was Christmas and at the thought of those hungry children she started to cry.

She tried to comfort the man and she gave him food and money and she told the man that she would inform Turiddu of the incident.

The next day, as we were about to send him a message with a trustworthy messanger, a small landowner from GRISÌ[1] said that Orlando Grippi had come on behalf of Turiddu and demanded 1 million Lire. My mother and I were mortified. We tried to explain to him that my brother had nothing to do with the story and there were many people taking advantage of his being forced to stay in the mountains.

Two days later, on New Year's Eve, Turiddu let his men spend New Year's Day with their families. We asked him whether he was responsible for those shameful incidents and whether Orlando Grippi was really an envoy of his.

The mere doubt offended him. He was very hurt that people still had not learnt to distinguish his actions from those of imposters. Those crimes went against his principles and style. He would never have fallen so low.

He decided to speak to Grippi and tell him to stop. Our mother was worried and told him to be careful:

"Watch out, son! Don't get into trouble!"

"Mother, whoever has done me no harm has nothing to fear! I behave according to conscience! True justice isn't that of courts. It's in the heart of honest people! I don't do anything for no reason at all! If I'm in danger, I'm ready to shoot to save myself! But if there are victims my heart is torn by the pain!"

At midnight he found us sitting around the table already laid. The only who was not there was our father, because he still had not been released after the third time he was arrested. We toasted at midnight with the wine made from our grapevines. Our hearts were full of hope. Then Turiddu put on his white trench coat and he went into the deserted streets of the town.

Silence was broken every now and then by merry voices and the singing of people from inside their homes. Soon Turiddu's search met with success when he found Orlando Grippi at the house of his accomplices. He invited both to come out so they could talk. Once they reached the square, the discussion became more animated:

"Don't ever use my name again in crimes damaging poor and miserable people!" said my brother.

"We don't put our nose in your business, so you don't put yours in ours!" answered the two.

---

[1] *A small village belonging to the town of Monreale and just a few kilometers from Partinico.*

"Since you're using my name for your wrongdoings, it is my business!" replied Turiddu.

"Tomorrow you'll return the livestock you stole!"

"We don't take orders from anyone!" exclaimed Orlando Grippi and motioned to grab his gun in his belt.

Turiddu was expecting that move. Under his right arm he had hidden his machinegun and he had a gun in his pocket. As fast as lightning he pulled out his gun and he rapidly shot twice. Orlando Grippi fell to the ground unconscious, while his accomplice ran away as fast as he could.

There was silence in the surrounding houses. Many lights went out. In the darkness a few windows opened cautiously.

Turiddu made his way for home calmly, walking normally as if nothing had happened. But the shots had scared us and we were worried for him. We saw him coming calmly. He said nothing had happened and that he had shot at a dog. He then went back to sleep in his room.

The next day, at dawn, my mother and I woke up, after having spent the whole night on the terrace on the lookout for Carabinieri together our dog Giulia. We filled his knapsack with supplies and we continued to guard the house. After a hastened hug he left to reach a safer place.

After this episode in which my brother was forced to resort to violence, the livestock was returned to its legitimate owner. A week later, Turiddu was on his way to contrada "Nocella"[1] to see a friend of his who was a small breeder. He asked him to buy two mules for him. He needed them to carry food and weapons.

In order to avoid the Carabinieri he and his men were forced continuously to change their hideout.

That day Brigadier Rossi from the station in Montelepre, together with five other men, were combing that area. They recognized Turiddu by his white trench coat so they prepared an ambush. He hid his men behind some thick bushes along the path and they held their breaths as they waited.

The Brigadiere was excited. It was a once in a lifetime chance! In a few minutes he would have captured the man that everyone considered to be impossible to catch. He would have succeeded in doing what everyone had failed to do. He was daydreaming of solemn commendations and promotions.

When Turiddu, unaware of the luring danger, passed between

---

[1] *A locality between Montelepre and Partinico.*

the bushes, the soldiers jumped on him and blocked him. But as soon as the Brigadier came to disarm him, he gave him a strong kick in his chest and the brigadier fell to the ground. The others were caught by surprise and he managed to escape from their hold. He ran like a wild hare zigzagging across the countryside to dart their bullets whistling near him.

A bullet shot by the brigadier hit his left forearm. He dropped to the ground and answered fire with his machinegun. The brigadier was wounded in his arm. The troops retreated and found cover behind some olive trees, while Turiddu had succeeded to get out of their fire range.

When he saw that he was not being followed he ran off. After having walked around the area, he returned to the place. He scoured the area with his binoculars and once he was sure that there were no dangers he went to meet his friend.

The man watched the whole scene from faraway with great concern for Turiddu. He welcomed him happily, but he noted his bleeding arm and was suddenly worried again:

"They hit you?" he asked.

"Don't worry! It's just a scratch! They came close to catching me, but Our Lady helped me! Get my first aid box in the knapsack and help me take care of the wound!"

"Turiddu, I don't even know how to take care of a cow! Why don't we go to the mill nearby? I know the owner and he knows how to handle these things!"

They went to the mill, where he was medicated and rested. It was almost evening when a 12 year old boy came in. He was tired and hungry. He asked for some food and a job. The boy was so weak and scared that he moved Turiddu with compassion.

More than a job he needed the protection and love of a family. Since it was late, Turiddu kept the boy with him for the evening. The next day, we saw him arrive. He was tired and his clothes were worn and torn. There were holes in his shoes. He gave my mother a message from my brother:

**"Dear Mother,**

**This boy is an orphan. His name is Salvatore, just like me. Please take care of him, just as if he were me. Let him sleep in my bed and my room, try to dress him well, buy him a pair of shoes and feed him. I'm sure of your kindness. A warm hug."**

We were all used to his incredible generosity. Often Turiddu would come home with worn and torn clothing because he had given his to some poor farmer. So my mother did as he asked. The boy lived with us for several months. We gave him all the love and warmth he needed. Then he started to miss his grandmother in Partinico and he left.

In the first three months of 1945 nothing important happened. My brother's generosity was no longer a surprise for us. He kept avoiding the Carabinieri and he dedicated his time to training his men to use their weapons. The searches of the Carabinieri had eased down. Many people were released from prison and came home. My father too was amongst them.

During the week of Easter Turiddu came home. He spent the afternoon and the whole evening with us. Late in the night he left to join his men in contrada "BUONAGRAZIA". Halfway there he heard some suspicious sounds. He was worried, so he dropped to the ground behind a stone and listened in silence.

It was a moonless night. It was pitch black all around. The sound was becoming more and more intense and was coming closer. He could not understand what it was.

He shot a blast of machinegun fire in the air. If they were Carabinieri, they would answer fire and his men would come to help him. He soon understood that they were not Carabinieri but cattle thieves. They had stolen a whole herd of cows and they started to run away after the gunshots.

We too at home heard the shots and we thought that it was a shootout with the police. Our mother prayed on her knees for God to protect my brother and everyone. I ran from one side to the other of the terrace to understand where the shots came from. We spent hours of distress.

At dawn a boy knocked at our door. He said he had met Turiddu and that he had a message for her. We all drew a sigh of relief. She quickly read the message:

**"Mother, don't worry for me. I'm sure you thought that the gunshots you heard were from a shootout with the police. I'll tell you everything when I come home. If someone comes to tell you that their cows were stolen, tell them not to worry, because I have the animals. A kiss."**

Those few lines calmed everyone. Our mother thanked the boy and gave him some money. She then started to thank and praise God and all the Saints for my brother's narrow escape. As soon as we finished reading the message, we heard someone knock at the door. There were two strangers with distraught faces. They had swollen eyes and were very nervous. It looked as if they hadn't slept for days.

My mother opened the door. I was standing next to her.

"We have to speak urgently to your son!" they said.

She feared that they were police in disguise. So she behaved as she normally did in these cases and answered:

"My son was here yesterday. You could have found him if you came earlier! But if you want to leave a message, I'll try send it to him as soon as possible!"

One of the two understood the reason for her secrecy and decided to talk clearly:

"Yesterday evening they stole our cows and calves! We know it wasn't your son, but we're sure that he can help us!"

Reassured by these words, my mother smiled. He went through her pockets and pulled out the message she had just received. The two were left speechless after reading it. Then their joy burst out and they continued thanking us for the good news. They hugged us and kissed our hands. They exclaimed joyfully:

"Now we can go home to Partinico without worrying. The cattle will be returned to us as soon as possible!"

They were about to leave when my uncle, Antonino Lombardo, my mother's brother, came. He had been sent by Turiddu with the task of guiding the owners of the cattle to his hideout.

Their happiness reached its climax. They made their way full of hope towards the "Buonagrazia" contrada, where the cattle was returned to them.

Grateful for everything my brother had done for them, they insisted on giving him a large calf for Easter. He did not want to accept, but he ended up accepting their gift. He thought that it was a good opportunity for feeding the poor.

In no time at all he had organized a feast for Easter day and Easter Monday. He invited all the poor, his friends, relatives and his men's closest family members for a total of two hundred people. For the occasion he asked me to bring him his guitar and accordion. Amongst the guests there were also some of his childhood friends. They too brought along their musical instruments.

The happy and numerous company spent two unforgettable days and nights. We danced, sang and roasted meat on the fire. It was as if we had travelled back in time to the days of lightheartedness. Everything was so peaceful without any soldier being sighted by the many guards surrounding the camp.

The following days were quiet. Turiddu and his men had pitched camp in "Muletta", at 500 meters from Montelepre. He sent a message with a boy to inform us that he was in the area. I wasn't feeling well, so I stayed home, but our mother did not miss the chance of seeing him.

My mother, father, our brother Peppino and our sister Giuseppina went to see him. Turiddu was happy. They withdrew to talk in private of the latest news. Suddenly my mother noticed a well-dressed young man of average height with blond hair, and blue eyes amongst his men.

She exclaimed: "What a shame! Even that handsome boy with you?"

"No, mother! He's just a friend who comes to see me every now and then!"

"So he's armed like the others?" insisted our mother.

"Just to practice! You see, mother, you must understand him. He's looking for adventure. Just think that he enrolled at the age of 17. He was caught by the Germans and he managed to escape. Then he joined the partisans. Now he's a member of the separatist movement. For a few months now he's my contact with the party!"

Turiddu called him and introduced him to my family. That young man was Pasquale Sciortino, the man that one day would become my husband. It was then that my brother noticed my absence and asked worriedly why I was not there.

"Nothing serious!" answered mother.

"She's got a bit of a fever, but she is recovering quickly! Instead, I forgot to tell you that they've installed a meter! Now we need an electrical system! We've installed some hanging wires but we risk getting a shock!"

"If you buy the material, I'll install the system!" said Pasquale Sciortino.

"You're an electrician?" asked Turiddu all surprised.

"No, but I know enough!"

About an hour later, my mother and the others came home. My brother and Pasquale followed them with their eyes until they arrived. At that point Pasquale asked Turiddu a strange question. He asked how was his family composed.

"You've met everyone, except Marianna!"

"Is she married?"

"No, but why do you want to know?" asked Turiddu a bit annoyed.

"Because if she's not married, we'll become brothers-in-law!"

My brother started to laugh:

"You don't even know her!"

"It's true", said Pasquale, "but I know you and I like you, so I suppose that your sister must be the same!"

"What are you saying? I don't even know if she's engaged!"

The next day, around noon, Pasquale Sciortino and Vito Mazzola came to our house. They said they had to make an estimate of the material they needed. Of course, the visit was an excuse to meet me.

I did not know what their real intentions were and I did not pay attention to all their kindness. It was lunchtime so my mother invited the guests to stay. My cousin Giacomo Lombardo came and stayed for lunch as well.

During the frugal meal, the wine finished. I went into the cellar. Pasquale winked to my cousin, who followed me. In the cellar he walked up to me with the air of a conspirator and said to me softly:

"Marianna, do you have a boyfriend?"

"And why do you care?" I answered surprised.

"No! You didn't understand? It's for the young man upstairs. He wants to get engaged with you."

I was shocked and I stuttered:

"No, I'm not engaged with anyone!"

After lunch the three left. Pasquale was informed of the answer. When he saw my brother again, he came back to the subject:

"Turiddu, when I told you that I wanted to become your brother-in-law, I was joking, but now that I've met your sister and that I know that she's not engaged, I'm talking seriously now!"

"You've spoken to her? asked Turiddu.

"No, not yet!"

"So! You've got to get engaged with her, not with me!" answered my brother laughing.

In the meantime the Young Men's Separatist League was in turmoil owing to the negative reactions expressed by all the main Italian newspapers interested in the latest events in Sicily. The heads of the movement did not hand over their weapons. They organized the 2$^{nd}$ National Convention in Palermo on April 14 - 16, 1945. The results of the convention reaffirmed their commitment to fight to death against the Italian State.

The result was a memorandum prepared before the convention and addressed to the delegations of the governments participating in the San Francisco Conference.

Here are some of the most topical extracts:

**"THE NATIONAL COMMITTEE OF THE MOVEMENT FOR THE INDEPENDENCE of SICILY launches its impelling appeal to all the States represented at the San Francisco Conference to invite them to take into consideration the Island's serious situation and to decide on its future.**

Sicily, with its three millennia of history, has always existed as a more or less independent yet sovereign State. Its monarchy, the most ancient of all, lasted eight centuries, during which the Island experienced a long period of prosperity and was at the heart of world's political and cultural life, especially under the reigns of Roger II, the Norman, Frederick II of Swabia and Frederick III of Aragon.

But Sicily always aspired to be independent and fought its greatest battles for it, the most famous of which were the Sicilian Vespers, which were the Middle Ages' most important popular uprising for freedom.

The main target of the revolution of January 12, 1848 was that of freeing the Island from the yoke of the reign of the Bourbons.

In 1860, what great woe was the vile betrayal of our patriots by the Piedmontese government, which annexed Sicily to Italy. This moment marks the beginning of that system of exploitation, oppression and slavery that has lasted for 85 years and against which all Sicilians uselessly protested.

Sicily was treated like a colony and the progress of its civilization was hindered.

The indifferent and widespread hatred of all regions and Italian social classes against Sicily, the complete indifference of all Italian governments towards it, the abusing state of inferiority in which the Island was kept, its systematic exclusion from the benefits granted to other territories, the exasperating fiscal pressure imposed on it, the ongoing draining of all its economic, financial, agricultural and mineral resources, the boycotting of any form of industrial initiative in favor of Northern capitalists and the hundreds of other wrongs have determined the current situation, which can no longer continue.

The union of Sicily with Italy was the cause of our ruin and, should it continue, any form of progress and development in the Island will be doomed to fail as has happened in the past. For said reasons the will of the Sicilian people is to establish an independent State in their land.

This is the will, which is now expressed by the National Committee on behalf of the Sicilian People to all the nations of the world, now solemnly convened. They are exhorted to make their contribution in freeing the Sicilian Nation from its oppression and from the intolerable conditions afflicting it.

We hoped that the government that succeeded the Fascist

government would have given proof of greater understanding for the fervent aspirations of the People of Sicily, but unfortunately this was not the case. On the contrary, the abuses and the vexations have continued. The Island today is living a situation even worse than that experienced under the Fascist regime.

In Sicily, as in the rest of Italy, ruthless parties and men without honor, who care more for their own interests than for those of the public, detain power abusively without having the necessary reputation and support and they continue to defile freedom and democracy, which is based on the government of the people, of the whole people and not only of certain classes or factions represented by those parties and men. They want freedom only for themselves and have dedicated themselves to the most abominable forms of political brigandage.

The spectacle put on by the Bonomi government is literally depressing and is even more so in Sicily, which has been entrusted to ignorant men who worry about themselves and their fortunes.

Today the vast majority of the Sicilian People is in favor of the independence of its land. Yet they obstinately deny this people all those rights which are granted only to small groups of people guided by profiteers and speculators of the worst kind.

The protests made to them in private have met with derision and have gone unheeded. On the contrary, they have worsened the boldness of those responsible for the current disorder, which has exasperated the population. This exasperation is not only the consequence of these days of dire straits but also of the many years of misrule, which have devastated Sicily and continues to oppress now even more than in the past.

Clearly all this cannot continue. The National Committee is firm in its belief that it is its duty to draw the attention of the SAN FRANCISCO CONFERENCE on the situation.

The vilified and oppressed people of Sicily have a limit and an outburst of indignation whose consequences cannot be anticipated is only a matter of time. All this will provide further evidence of Sicily's unquenchable thirst to become a sovereign and independent state, save for the case in which it joins wider forms of confederation with other States amongst which Italy.

No one can dare oppose this sacred aspiration, which is founded on history, law, economy and civilization. Sicily will reach its supreme goal at all costs. Nothing can stop the people of the Vespers. If we need to take up our arms, it will be done with the firm conviction of our ultimate success. Everything is ready.

But if a bloody war capable of upsetting peace in the Mediterranean can be avoided, the Sicilian people would sincerely be glad. It truly believes in an orderly and civilized progress. It wishes to become an element of peace and balance.

The National Committee fervently invites the San Francisco Conference to use its authority to avoid the risk of tragic events. The weak Italian government can lead only to ruin. Only the United Nations, which have fought for the freedom of peoples, whose victorious armies were welcomed fraternally by our Island, can avoid this disaster. This most noble duty of safeguarding the supreme interests of the Sicilian people is entrusted into their hands. We wish that the United Nations will give Sicily its independence as an act of amends and justice, as they have done with Austria and other countries.

**PALERMO, MARCH 31, 1945 (THE 633RD ANNIVERSARY OF THE SICILIAN VESPERS)"**[1].

The vigorous and negative reactions of all the political parties came immediately. There were also acts of intimidation like the police raid in the Palermo offices of the M.I.S. with its total devastation on April 21, 1945.

But all this contributed in creating around the M.I.S. an aura of fascination and romanticism. It was truly the only political force, which proposed something new and different. As a matter of fact, it was the only political force, which awakened a sense of heroism. The idea of breaking the law stimulated the revolutionary in every Sicilian.

The separatists in Palermo were steaming with anger, bitterness, patriotism, but they had no leader and they were exposed to too many dangers.

After another raid on May 1, 1945 in Catania, Stefano La Motta decided to go there. The purpose of his visit was to ask for help from the local Young Men's League, Guglielmo di Caraci. He wanted him to appoint a trustworthy person capable of organizing a group of guerilla fighters like those led by Mario Turri in Western Sicily.

---

[1] *Municipal Library of Palermo.*

The task was assigned to Attilio Castrogiovanni. Without hesitation, they drove together to Palermo in Stefano La Motta's car. They went to see Lucio Tasca, the city's former mayor. He let them use the cellar of his villa. It would be used as a meeting place.

Attilio Castrogiovanni started to work immediately. He summoned all the leaders of the movement to decide what to do, but there was great disagreement on the issue. Andrea Finocchiaro Aprile, Lucio Tasca, Giacomo Vaccaro, Sirio Rossi and Calogero Vizzini were firm in their will to take up arms because they were convinced that it was the only alternative. The others, headed by Nino Varvaro, were against the use of force.

The majority decided to vote in favor of armed combat. But they needed a leader and a training camp in a safe place. Then Finocchiaro Aprile revealed that there was a young separatist who had enrolled in the movement already at the beginning of 1943 and who was just as good as Mario Turri, the head of operations in Eastern Sicily, when it came to courage, loyalty and organizational capacities.

Of course, he was speaking of my brother Turiddu, who was number 138 on the list of the first members of the separatist movement. He was the undisputed leader in his territory, which reached all the way from Bellolampo and Pioppo and included the towns of Montelepre, Giardinello, Torretta, Carini, Cinisi, Capaci, Terrasini, Partinico, Borgetto, Monreale, San Giuseppe Jato, San Cipirello. No one could enter his territory without his approval.

It was the ideal refuge for the separatists. They could use the training camp and count on a man, who was already a legend and was capable of training them to die for the cause. Furthermore, Turiddu had already offered Finocchiaro Aprile his services at the beginning of 1944.

Some disagreed, but Lucio Tasca skillfully managed to overcome their resistance. Attilio Castrogiovanni had no hesitation and he said to the former mayor of Palermo:

"Don Lucio, we must meet this young man!"

They started to look for envoys to organize a meeting with him. Thanks to Vito Mazzola, who had bred some cows for Tasca, and Pietro Franzone, who contacted Pasquale Sciortino, who in turn happened to be a distant relative of his, a meeting was set for May 15, 1945.

That morning Attilio Castrogiovanni and Pasquale Sciortino went by car to Montelepre. They followed the instructions they had received. The car was stopped just outside the town cemetery.

The passengers got off the car and went towards the hill right in front of them called "COZZO VITE". The driver, Salvatore Alimena, started to fiddle with the engine and pretended to repair it so as to avoid arousing the suspicion of the passers-by.

A man walked to meet them. It was Mazzola, who was waiting to take them to Turiddu. The two followed him along a path. They went up the other side of the hill for about a hundred meters. Because of the heat, they reached the top all sweated and tired. From there you could see the whole "Gallina" plain and a number of towns in the background. A man appeared from behind a rock next to a semi-destroyed shack. It was my brother.

As soon as Attilio Castrogiovanni saw him he raised his right hand and greeted him with the salute used by the separatists. He said:

"I can judge a man by looking straight in his eyes. I can see that you're a loyal and sincere man!"

Turiddu exchanged the greeting and he invited the men to sit on the large stones.

Vito Mazzola instead moved away. Castrogiovanni started to discuss the general situation. Turiddu said that he had been waiting for that moment. He was ready to die for the cause. He said he would never have abandoned Sicily and that his men, his camp in Sagana and he were at the complete disposal of the Young Men's League of Palermo.

Castrogiovanni explained that any war operation had to be agreed upon in advance. The person in charge of the E.V.I.S. for Eastern Sicily (Mario Turri) would have come to discuss the plans. He offered him the command of the E.V.I.S. in Western Sicily with the rank of colonel.

My brother accepted with all the enthusiasm of his youthfulness. He promised that as he waited for the orders, the uniforms, and the battle flag, he would have avoided clashes with the Carabinieri. In the meantime he would start the recruitment of new soldiers.

*My Brother, Salvatore Giuliano*

Turiddu in the pose of a strategist.

My Brother, Salvatore Giuliano

Salvatore Giuliano with his dog Giulia.

Chapter X

# THE TWO COLONELS

Until May 19th everything went well. But the next day, as my brother Peppino sat outside on the doorstep of our sister Giuseppina's house, a squad of Carabinieri blocked him and arrested him. His wife, seeing her husband struggle as they took him away, started to scream. I was walking with some friends of mine along the town's main avenue. I recognized her voice and I thought that something happened to my sister's children.

I ran as fast as I could towards the outskirts of town where her house was. My brother Turiddu was at the moment in the "Vallotta" contrada along the road to Carini and he was watching me with his binoculars. He was trying to signal to me with a mirror hoping that my friends or I would see him.

When he saw that I left my friends and ran off, he followed me with his binoculars hoping to understand why I was running. He too saw our brother Peppino as he was being taken away by the police.

I jumped at them like a fury. But they pushed me away and I almost fell to the ground.

Turiddu ran towards town hoping that he could free him. Once he reached the "Vallotta" public wash-tub, he understood that he could not use his arms. It was Sunday and the roads were crowded with people.

As soon as the townsfolk saw him, they understood his intentions. In a few seconds they had all scrambled for cover in the side streets. In the main road there were just Peppino and the Carabinieri, who, once they saw him, rushed along the way using the prisoner as a shield.

It was impossible for Turiddu to free our brother. He followed them from a distance until they reached the station. He then went back retracing his steps. Once he reached the outskirts of town, he blew a modulated whistle. After a few minutes a dozen of his men arrived. They were informed of what had happened and he ordered them to divide into two squads.

Turiddu in a painting by G. B. Di Liberti.

The first squad took position at the "Belvedere" curve along the road to Palermo; the second went to the other end of town to guard the road to Partinico. He was planning an ambush to attack the Carabinieri when they passed from there with their truck. They waited till late in the night but nothing happened.

Clearly the Carabinieri too had been watching them. They waited for him to give up his plan before taking the prisoner to the headquarters in Palermo and they finally managed to do so without any problems. Turiddu could not find peace. Our brother's arrest was worse than a wound burning deep in his flesh. He had to show them that he was not just going stand and watch them do as they pleased. But he had to prove it especially to the leaders of the separatist movement.

On May 23rd he and his men attacked the station in "Piano dell'Occhio". The building was surrounded and battered with their gunfire. The shootout ended when the Royal Carabinieri surrendered. Turiddu avoided humiliating them any further. He knew that they were doing their job. He let them come out with their hands up above their heads and leave without being harmed.

Then his men broke into the station and took all the weapons and ammunitions they could find. Then they ravished the building. When they finished, all that was left were the outer walls.

Meanwhile our brother was being tortured brutally at the headquarters in Palermo. They beat him, they used the "box" on him and he suffered other unspeakable tortures. They accused him of killing Orlando Grippi. He resisted stoically and did not confess anything. Despite all this, after 22 days of torment, they took him to prison with the charge of homicide.

At the beginning of June Turiddu crossed a contrada called the "Piana degli Aranci", the plain of the oranges. He met a poor ragged man and he asked him what happened to him. The man suffocated his tears and said that he had not eaten anything for three days. He asked for some ricotta cheese from shepherds along the way, but they gave him nothing at all.

He told them that even some whey was good so that he could dip his bread in it. But they said they preferred feeding it to their dogs.

Turiddu was moved by his story. He gave the man some money so that he could buy some clothes and food.

The old man took his hand and kissed it. He then said to him:

"You're the father of the poor, blessed the woman that fed you from her breast!"

Turiddu continued along the way and he stopped where the shepherds were. The foreman recognized him as soon as he saw him. He went towards him and welcomed him warmly. He insisted that Turiddu come and eat some ricotta with them.

My brother refused at first, but then decided to accept their invitation. He sat there with them. He took the ricotta and stuck it in his machinegun.

As he watched the gun, he spoke to it saying:

"Do you like it, my friend? Do you want more?"

"Here's another spoonful!"

They looked at him with their eyes full of amazement. They feared that he had gone mad. They asked him meekly what was he doing.

"Your generosity is not for me, but for my machinegun. Just a little while ago you chased away a poor old man and you denied him not only your cheese, but even some whey! You ought to be ashamed! I order you to feed the poor who will ask you for help!"

"It's not our fault!" said one of them. "We were just obeying to the owner's orders!"

Turiddu turned to the foreman:

"Tell the owner to open the doors to the poor who come to this farm!"

He greeted them, climbed back onto his horse and went away.

In the meantime in Eastern Sicily, the men of the E.V.I.S. continued to train themselves under the command of Mario Turri. But in the morning of June 17, 1945, as he was driving to the camp together with five other students, they were stopped by a squad of Carabinieri. It was said that they were waiting for them at the Randazzo-Cesarò crossroads. They were stopped with a gunshot up in the air.

Pippo Amato, who was driving the truck, tried to avoid the roadblock by accelerating. The Carabinieri opened fire. Mario Turri (alias Antonio Canepa) was shot in his left leg. The bullet hit a hand grenade he had in his pocket and it exploded. The passengers were hit by the explosion. Antonio Canepa, Carmelo Rosano, Giuseppe Giudice and Armando Romano died on the spot.

Pippo Amato and Antonio Velis, protected by the truck's cabin, were left unscathed and managed to escape. They ran like hell until they reached the hospital in Randazzo, desperately hoping to help their friends. Here, after certifying their death, the four corpses were closed in just as many coffins and sent to the cemetery in Giarre.

The bodies were left in the mortuary chapel until their burial.

But the custodian saw that Armando Romano was still alive and saved him.

A few days later, the news reached the training camp on Mount Soro. The young troops there were left dismayed by the loss of their colonel and went into hiding in the countryside.

Turiddu too was informed of the incident. But he had no intention of giving up. He was firm in his decision to continue even all on his own. So he founded the M.A.S.C.A. (the Movement for the Annexation of Sicily to the American Confederation).

The movement's goal was to free Sicily and have it annexed to the United States. It would have been the flag's 49$^{th}$ star. (In those days the United States were composed of 48 states). Turiddu called a painter from Montelepre, named Filippo Puntorno, to help him spread his idea. The painter prepared a poster showing a man wearing a uniform (Turiddu) breaking the chain uniting Sicily to Italy as he ties its other end to the United States.

He also ordered to the painter to paint a lion at the head of his bed in his room. One day he would make of this courageous animal the symbol of strength and courage.

In the meantime, the police and the Carabinieri scoured the countryside in Eastern Sicily looking for men of the E.V.I.S. During these operations they found two depots with arms and ammunitions: one near Alcara Li Fusi and the other in the farmstead of Countess Majorca near Francavilla.

The leaders of the Movement summoned a meeting to be held in Lucio Tasca's house on July 25, 1945, to find a way to save the separatist army. During the meeting, the position of commander-in-chief was assigned to Guglielmo di Caraci. His aides were Giuseppe Tasca and Rosario Cacopardo.

Concetto Gallo was appointed commander of the E.V.I.S. in Eastern Sicily with the rank of colonel. He chose "Turri Secondo" as his battle name and with this name he signed his first proclamation:

**"Sicilians! Antonio Canepa (Mario Turri), the first commander of the E.V.I.S. has died by the hand of the Italian forces. Glory to him! All we need is the torch of our ideals. As of today, I hereby assume the command of the E.V.I.S. with the unanimous consensus of our troops. If I too were to die, my successor is ready. Brothers, prepare for the great day! Independence or death!"**

The news that a second Turri was put in charge of Eastern Sicily was ably spread. The politicians in Rome and Palermo were literally terrorized. The time had come to authorize Turiddu to start recruitment in Western Sicily as well.

The leaders of the M.I.S. once again contacted Pietro Franzone, who was in contact with my brother through Pasquale Sciortino. Despite his young age, Pasquale Sciortino had an important position in the movement. He attended many of the meetings held in Palermo.

The meeting was held on August 22, 1945. It was attended by Don Guglielmo, Duke of Carcaci, Concetto Gallo, Stefano La Motta and Pietro Franzone on one side and Turiddu, Pasquale Sciortino, Vito Mazzola and Giacomo Lombardo on the other. Francesco Giuliano and Giuseppe Cucinella were there as well to guard the area.

Guglielmo of Carcaci and my brother spoke for hours in an extremely respectful manner. Turiddu was officially assigned the command of the E.V.I.S. in Western Sicily. He was given a badge with the stripes of colonel, a battle flag with yellow and red stripes with a blue field in the upper corner decorated with a golden Trinacria and some uniforms (khaki-colored trousers, jackets and vests and metal badges showing the three-legged punica).

On that occasion he was promised that once Sicily was independent his position and that of his men would be reconsidered. If everything went for the best, they could have obtained impunity or be rehabilitated. But my brother, who was just 22 and a half years old and quite naive when it came to politics and politicians, did not care very much about those promises.

He was an idealist who was animated by the noble ideal of the salvation of the Sicilian motherland.

They then discussed the financing of the army. Turiddu asked for more information. Concetto Gallo and Guglielmo of Carcaci answered that they had only weapons and ammunition. Turiddu asked whether he could have 10 million Italian Lire to buy food and to pay the troops. They said they could give him only one. The sum was too little for what he had to do.

Stefano la Motta and Pietro Franzone had a brilliant idea, or at least they thought so. They suggested that Turiddu could kidnap wealthy people and ask for ransom. It was the perfect way of getting money. La Motta himself would have given him a list of people.

My brother was disgusted by the idea. Although he was considered a dangerous outlaw by the government, he had never resorted to such means to make money.

Pietro Franzone tried to convince him: he said he would have given him a block of receipts with the mark of the E.V.I.S. so that he could give a receipt to all those who donated money. The E.V.I.S.

would then pay the money back once Sicily was independent. But he added that if they continued to refuse to contribute to the cause he would be forced to kidnap them.

It was difficult to convince Turiddu, but he accepted in the end. Once this problem was solved, the leaders of the M.I.S. left. Only Concetto Gallo stayed to make plans with Turiddu. The two colonels decided to form four small armies to be deployed in strategic positions of the Island.

Carmelo Gallo's brigade was stationed in Niscemi; Turiddu's "Palermo brigade" was to be stationed in Sagana. The other two would be stationed depending on the operations.

The task of recruiting in Montelepre was assigned to Giuseppe Iacona. He had a barbershop in town and had recently come back from Africa. He was helped by Filippo Ferrara. Turiddu offered those who joined a hundred thousand lire a month plus board.

During those days of hunger and poverty, such an amount of money was very tempting. Many young men decided to join both for the ideal and the money. A small army of 80 men, 50% of whom were from Montelepre, was formed.

The third meeting of the M.I.S. leaders was held at the beginning of September. The following material was handed over to Turiddu: 20 uniforms, other badges, 11 machineguns, some grenades, seven automatic rifles, eight guns, three heavy machineguns and ammunition.

But the weapons were much less than those promised. My brother had to get the rest of the arms at exorbitant prices. A military hierarchy was set up with the forming of the army. The ranks were: colonel, captain, lieutenant, sergeant and private. The ranks were indicated with yellow and red stripes near their heart.

There were many meetings between the leaders of the M.I.S. and my brother in that period. the E.V.I.S. started to send more and more detailed instructions. The preparation of the imminent armed revolt, however, were being followed also by the secret services. The government decided to adopt emergency measures and ordered the arrest of the movement's leaders. Sicily's revolt was set for September 27th, but was postponed to October 15, 1945.

A fierce anti-Italian campaign invited Sicilian civil servants to resign if they wanted to save their lives. The most active form of propaganda was the underground separatist radio called *"Sicilia Liberata"* - (Free Sicily). It transmitted the following communiqué:

"ALL SICILIANS HOLDING ANY PUBLIC OFFICE, ALL SICILIAN POLICE OFFICERS AND ALL THOSE ENROLLED IN THE CARA-

BINIERI ARE INVITED TO RESIGN BY OCTOBER 15TH. THOSE WHO DO NOT OBEY TO THIS ORDER SHALL BE CONSIDERED AS TRAITORS OF SICILY AND BE TRIED BEFORE THE SPECIAL TRIBUNAL OF THE E.V.I.S., WHICH SHALL PASS SENTENCE AS THEY DESERVE".

But the armed revolt never took place. On September 15th Attilio Castrogiovanni was arrested and sent to prison in Catania. On October 1st, as they walked home along Via Libertà in Palermo, Andrea Finocchiaro Aprile and Antonino Varvaro were surrounded by at least a dozen cars driving with their headlights off. About twenty policemen came out of the cars and they were arrested.

They were loaded into one of the cars and taken to the port where a Navy corvet was waiting for them. As soon as they were on board, the ship left immediately for the island of Ponza.

On October 2nd the lawyer Francesco Restuccia was arrested in Messina. There were many other arrests and all the offices of the M.I.S. were closed all over Sicily. Private homes were searched, meetings were prohibited, as were the publication, broadcast and sale of the record with the music "SUONI LA TROMBA" (Blow the Horn) from the second act of Vincenzo Bellini's "PURITANI" (the Puritans).

It had been chosen as Sicily's national anthem. The music was the same, but the words were changed:

| | |
|---|---|
| PER LA SICILIA INTREPIDA | FOR BRAVE SICILY |
| NOI PUGNEREM DA FORTI | WE SHALL FIGHT LIKE HEROES |
| PRONTI A SFIDAR LA MORTE | READY TO CHALLENGE DEATH |
| GRIDANDO LIBERTÀ. | SHOUTING LIBERTY. |
| CONTRO I TIRANNI ITALICI | AGAINST THE ITALIAN TYRANTS |
| NEMICI DELLA NOSTRA TERRA | THE ENEMIES OF OUR LAND |
| OGNUN LE ARMI AFFERRA | TAKE UP YOUR ARMS |
| GRIDANDO LIBERTÀ. | SHOUTING LIBERTY. |
| SICILIA! SICILIA! | SICILY! SICILY! |

Palermo and Messina were patrolled by military vehicles in fighting trim and armed with machineguns. All the soldiers of all corps were in their barracks on the alert. Despite the initial disorientation, the arrests of the movement's leaders did not prejudice neither the activities nor the plans of the two E.V.I.S. colonels.

Concetto Gallo intensified preparation and looked for new allies. He reached an agreement with the NISCEMESI BAND (Avila and Rizzo). My brother instead was tired of waiting and at the beginning of December he went to the camp in San Mauro. Together with three of his men he drove there by car. The time had come to coordinate operations with Concetto Gallo. Near the camp they were stopped by the lookouts and led to the commander.

As soon as he saw Turiddu, his face lit up with joy. He ran to meet him and embraced him. He ordered his men to assemble and he presented him to his men as Colonel Giuliano, the commander of the E.V.I.S. of Western Sicily.

After the greetings, they spoke in private to work at their plan of action. They would simultaneously attack the Carabinieri barracks all over Sicily. That was the first step for the conquest of the Island.

Turiddu stayed in San Mauro for about two days. At his return he had the following placards printed and hung in Palermo and all the towns of Western Sicily.

**"PEOPLE! A hundred thousand Lire a month to all those who join the new army formed solely to fight the enemies of freedom, who only have the authority of the government in their hands. Women too can join us in our fight. I promise nothing. No castles in the air: only in case of victory will man's sacred human, social and moral rights be recognized. Beware and be quiet, because there are spies everywhere. If you wish to find the way to join me then look for it amongst friends who are worthy of belonging to me. S. GIULIANO."**

The appeal was welcomed with enthusiasm by many young Sicilians: students, veterans, and jobless people all ran to enroll.

But while the colonels planned the revolt and risked their lives and the lives of many young men, the other separatist leaders were already impudently and carelessly thinking of abandoning them to their own fate.

In order to save the position of the M.I.S., they reestablished contacts with members of the monarchist movement and adopted a political stance in favor of the Savoy family. In Ponza, Finocchiaro Aprile too adopted the new political line without Varvaro knowing anything.

Andrea Finocchiaro Aprile.

The symbol of the M.A.S.C.A. (Movement for the Annexation of Sicily to the American Confederation).

**ANNO II - N. 13**            **15 AGOSTO 1945**

# SICILIA INDIPENDENTE
### ORGANO DEL MOVIMENTO PER L'INDIPENDENZA DELLA SICILIA

## ED ORA, LA PACE

La seconda guerra mondiale è finita.

Dopo cinque anni giusti, in cui i siciliani, aggiogati al carro italiano, ne hanno seguito le sorti, vediamo l'alba della pace.

Non vogliamo stavolta parlare dell'avvenire o ipotecarne le possibilità; non facciamo previsioni sull'immediato futuro o sulle probabilità che si hanno per la Sicilia di una « vittoria sulla pace ».

Contiamo invece di volgere lo sguardo al passato per trarne un monito alla nostra condotta ed un argomento per le nostre affermazioni.

Pensiamo che se la Sicilia fosse stata indipendente negli anni della guerra, essa avrebbe svolto al centro del Mediterraneo il medesimo ufficio avuto dalla Svizzera nel cuore dell'Europa.

Neutrale, essa non avrebbe visto i suoi figli dispersi nei cinque continenti al servizio di ogni causa ed interesse stranieri; avrebbe aumentato il suo benessere economico, come tutti i paesi in eguale posizione ed avrebbe assunto una posizione internazionale di primo ordine, sicura che nessuna delle parti belligeranti l'avrebbe attaccata, per non fornire all'altra parte un'arma terribile, specie nel campo della guerra psicologica.

Purtroppo questo è soltanto un sogno, ed oggi noi siciliani siamo più che abbandonati e peggio che schiavi; la fame e la miseria regnano sulla nostra terra. Le nostre speranze per l'avvenire sono legate di necessità al raggiungimento dell'indipendenza.

**SANDRO DE GIORGI**

**Partigiani Siciliani**, reduci dal Nord continuate a combattere per la libertà. E' un dovere verso la Madre Terra quello di arruolarvi nell' EVIS !

## PROCLAMA DEL COMANDANTE ALLE TRUPPE DELL' E.V.I.S.

### Soldati dell' E.V.I.S.!

Il nostro esercito fu costituito per assicurare al movimento piena libertà di associazione, di riunione, di stampa per il trionfo della nostra idea. Questa funzione, noi la adempiremo fino al suo scopo, con decisione e sacrificio.

Allora, e solo allora, l' E.V.I.S. sarà sciolto.

Ogni notizia contraria è prematura e infondata.

Stringetevi attorno ai capi, pronti a tutto per la libertà della Sicilia, forti della certezza che è di tutti noi: INDIPENDENZA O MORTE !

Dal Comando generale, il 5 agosto 1945

**SECONDO TURRI**

## LA CAPITALE VIAGGIA

I milanesi vogliono che la capitale italiana venga trasferita nella loro città. Un organo molto vicino al presidente Parri si è fatto eco autorevole del desiderio.

I romani cominciano a invidiarci il separatismo, unico mezzo per sottrarsi alla rapacità nordica e si accorgono dopo averci tanto combattuto, della nostra chiaroveggenza.

A noi, questo trasferimento potrebbe apportare più bene che male; servirà a convincere i dubbiosi nel senso che, priva della sua indipendenza, la Sicilia va verso una schiavitù più nera di quella sopportata negli ottantacinque anni di unione all' Italia.

In attesa di trasferire la capitale da Roma a Milano, il governo italiano — ci si passi lo slogan — l'ha trasferita da Milano a Roma; gli uomini del Nord scesi nell' Italia centrale ad impadronirsi delle leve di comando danno la sensazione del dominio esercitato sul paese dal triangolo industriale Milano Torino Genova, immondo Leviathan cui tutto va sacrificato.

**ERNESTO AMORE**

## FIGURE DI EPURATORI

Factotum della commissione di epurazione al ministero della marina italiana è quel V. E. Brusca che i siciliani in genere e catanesi in particolare ricordano come una delle più laide figure di fascista. Antemarcia, profittatore, spione e ladro, vantando attività partigiana si è insediato a quel posto da dove i nostri conterranei che pur detengono ininterrottamente il sottosegretariato alla marina non osano cacciarlo fuori a pedate, come merita.

## TI RICORDIAMO

A due mesi dalla tua morte, ti giunga, o comandante, l'eco del nostro dolente ricordo.

Sotto la tua guida, sfidammo tante volte il pericolo, pronti a far dono delle nostre vite. Infervorati dal tuo esempio e dalla tua parola ti fummo compagni nella buona e nell'avversa fortuna.

Oggi, ancora una volta, ci stringiamo nel tuo nome, sempre più compatti per essere degni di te, del tuo sacrificio, delle nostre aspirazioni. Accogli la promessa che ti facciamo, di lottare come tu ci hai insegnato. Nella nostra opera tu continuerai a vivere.

Il dono di te stesso all'idea è stato immenso, ma non inutile, se è vero che tanti e tanti giovani siciliani si sono arruolati nel nostro esercito dal giorno della tua scomparsa, se tanti altri sono ansiosi di entrare in contatto con noi per seguirci, se il popolo della nostra isola guarda all'indipendenza con maggiore fiducia, sapendosi accanto uomini della tua tempra, decisi all'offerta suprema.

La storia dell'indipendenza, o amatissimo comandante, ha una pagina dolorosa, là dove si dice della tua uccisione, ma noi abbiamo assunto l'impegno di assicurare piena libertà alla Sicilia ed allora il nostro dolore di oggi sarà la tua gloria di domani, solo premio che la vigile coscienza dei tuoi seguaci intende raggiungere.

**LA BANDA TURRI**

Colonel Salvatore Giuliano.

## Chapter XI

# THE WAR FOR INDEPENDENCE

On the afternoon of December 18, 1945, all those who had accepted to enroll were summoned. The meeting point was at the feet of Mount "CALCERAME", south of the cemetery of Montelepre. The men in charge of enrolment, Filippo Ferrara and Giuseppe Iacona, came an hour later, followed shortly after by my brother and Vito Mazzola. Turiddu was introduced to all those who were not from Montelepre by Filippo Ferrara:
"Here's your colonel!"
They went towards him. They had heard so much about him that they were curious to meet him. He spent a few minutes with the men that were expressing all for their sympathy for him. He then invited all those present to come closer because he had something to say:
"Picciotti, many of you know me and know also the purpose of this meeting! We are convened here to prepare a plan of action to be carried out as soon as we receive the orders to enter action."
"From this moment it won't be an easy life for anyone!"
"The Command has ordered us to prepare for the attack!"
"Our idea, as you know, is to separate Sicily from Italy to free it from its subjugation and exploitation! If we succeed, the conditions of our Island will improve! There will be free ports and Sicily will become the emporium of the Mediterranean. Agriculture will be improved with irrigation systems. Our brothers who had made a fortune abroad will come back to Sicily to invest their money! There will be factories and industries and the mines will be reopened and new ones will be exploited. There will be bread and work for everyone! But we cannot and must not hope in the help of others. The struggle for independence for our land must be waged by us! The Americans can't help us, because there would be diplomatic problems with Russia. If they do help us, it won't be officially!"
"The forces of the Italian government are the Carabinieri! We must occupy their barracks, if we want to take power in Sicily!"

*My Brother, Salvatore Giuliano*

> Il giallo e rosso
> son due colori
> che il separatista
> porta nel cuore
> il giallo osar
> il rosso amor
> la terra nostra, Sicilia
>
> pronti, tutti all'assalto
> per liberare la terra nostra,
> il sangue che ci costa
> sarà per la gloria e la civiltà
>
> addio mia bella
> io parto e vo
> vado a combattere
> ma ritornerò
> per ritrovarti
> in una terra libera
> ricca di storia
> e di civiltà

Yellow and red / Are the colors / That the separatist / Carries in his heart. / Yellow stands for boldness, / Red for the love / For our land, Sicily.

We are all ready for the fight / To free our land, / The blood we shed / Is for the glory and culture.

Farewell, my love / I leave to fight, / But I will return / To you / In a free land / Rich in history and culture.

A poem and a song dictated by Turiddu to his sister Marianna.

> O terra mia natia
> madre di nostra gente
> risorgi Patria mia
> sarai indipendente
>
> *ritornello*
> a ferro e fuoco
> noi la facciamo
> se con questo gioco
> non la finiamo
> di Sicilia i figli siamo
> l'indipendenza noi vogliamo
>
> A Montelepre i martiri
> raggio di vera luce
> per la Sicilia pace
> quest'oggi ridestò
>
> *ritornello*
> Avanti avanti Sicilia bella
> di nostra vita sei la stella
> splendi su questa terra
> per la tua libertà
>
> *ritornello* a ferro e a fuoco etc. . . .

My dear homeland, / Mother of my people, / Arise my Land / And you will be free.

*Refrain*

Fire and sword / we shall use / If the end to this game / Is far from sight. / the sons of Sicily / We are, / Independence is what / We seek.

In Montelepre the martyrs / True light for Sicily / Peace has awaken this day.

*Refrain*

Forward, forward, oh Beautiful Sicily, / You are the star of our life / Shed your light on this land / For your freedom.

*Refrain*

Fire and sword. . . .

At the end of the speech a roaring applause broke out. Turiddu motioned them to make silence and added:

"Picciotti! This is no joke! We're risking our lives here. Think well about it before accepting. Many of you are married and have children! If someone has doubts, you can leave freely!"

"Think about it!"

"You have fifteen minutes to think about it, then it will be too late!"

The assembly was over. During the interval there were many comments, then Turiddu called them back:

"Has anyone changed idea?" No one moved.

"Good! Now listen to me!"

"From now on I'm your commander!"

They all applauded.

Turiddu had them bring the flag to him and he waved it. There was another uproar of applause. My brother called the men one by one and had them take oath. They pledged their allegiance to the flag, the symbol of the Sicilian motherland. The ceremony ended with a shout:

"Long live independent Sicily!"

They distributed the uniforms and badges. Turiddu split the men into four squads. The first, the largest, was under his direct command. Giuseppe Passatempo, Antonino Terranova and Giuseppe Cucinella were appointed captains and each was assigned a squad of men.

At the end of the operation the weapons were distributed. Each squad had an instructor that explained how to use them. The sound of the rattle announced mealtime. Everyone rushed towards the center of the field where there were all types of food and plenty of wine. How many of them had finally managed in filling their stomachs?

The next day Turiddu ordered the former tinsmith, Frank Mannino, to prepare some engraved moulds with some sheets of iron, portraying Sicily's break-away from Italy and its union with the USA. At the bottom he was to engrave "LONG LIVE THE E.V.I.S."

The much awaited order finally arrived on Christmas night. On December 26, 1945, towards 11.00 p.m., Turiddu took 10 men from his squad. A Fiat 626 truck painted yellow and red driven by Gaspare Pisciotta (HE WAS NOT OUR COUSIN) was waiting on the outskirts of town in a place called "BELVEDERE".

The men climbed in the back, while Turiddu mounted in the cabin. The truck slowly drove along the road leading to Palermo. Soon after the cemetery, they stopped shortly to get the weapons. The BELLOLAMPO station was located at about 10 kilometers from

Palermo. Turiddu had the truck stop at about a few hundreds of meters away.

Then the men silently got off the truck and surrounded the building. When my brother gave the signal by shaking the rattle, the men opened fire. The shooting lasted a few seconds. He gave the signal to stop.

"Surrender!" someone shouted, but no one answered.

Again the signal and a fierce shower of bullets against the building. Then the signal again and the shooting ceased.

"SURRENDER!" shouted the same voice.

This time the door opened slowly and a white flag tied to a rifle appeared. A few seconds later two soldiers came out with their hands up. Then came out also a brigadier. He told them that there was an injured man.

Turiddu and his men broke in and found him sitting near the window. My brother lifted him up and laid him in the bed, where he medicated his wounds. With the moulds he had prepared, some men started to paint the symbol of the separatists on the walls and they took all the weapons, ammunition and everything that could be useful.

They went back to the truck, where their prisoners were. Turiddu saw that his men were insulting them. He rushed towards them with his eyes full of anger and started to shout:

"Don't you dare do it ever again!"

"A man who lifts up his hands must be considered as dead and the dead must not be offended, not even if they are enemies!"

A few minutes later they stopped a car passing by and they let the prisoners go so that they could take the injured soldier to the hospital. Then they returned to Montelepre. The booty was taken to the camp in Sagana to be added to their arsenal.

On the evening of December 28$^{th}$, another assembly like the previous one was summoned. This operation saw the involvement of Giuseppe Cucinella's squad as well. The target was the station in Grisì.

There were about a dozen soldiers, while Turiddu and his men were about twenty. No one was wounded on either side. The Carabinieri surrendered after the first shots. The station was occupied and the walls were marked with the separatist symbol hailing the E.V.I.S.

The brigadier's wife begged my brother not to touch her possessions. He agreed without much persuading. Then, that station too was treated like all the others.

That day an informer told them that troops and Carabinieri were being sent against the camp in SAN MAURO. Turiddu warned his colleague Concetto Gallo with a letter that was found on him later:

**"About 500 men have been sent against you. I have no news of other movements from elsewhere in Sicily, but I think it's possible. Take all the necessary precautions and eventually counterattack. Let me know if you're attacked, so that we can counterattack with the other forces of the E.V.I.S.**

**In case of success, before proceeding, let us know and wait for orders."**

Turiddu's warning was well-grounded, but it arrived the same day of the attack, before Concetto Gallo could even take the necessary precautions. Approximately 2,000 men, equipped with cannons, mortars, tanks and even two planes, attacked the E.V.I.S. camp.

It was December 29, 1945, when the Italian forces under the command of Gen. Fiumara took position in the "Piano della Fiera" just a few kilometers away from San Mauro. The camp was surrounded. When the shelling started there were only sixty young men there.

Concetto Gallo tried to divert their attention so as to enable his men to escape. He came out into the open with three volunteers, taking the E.V.I.S. flag with him. His position became the main target for the sharpshooters. Their rare shots were always followed by a shower of bullets. They resisted in that position for several hours. One of the volunteers was shot to death and the survivors did not have any other ammunition. The situation was desperate.

Concetto Gallo ordered his two men to surrender and they reluctantly obeyed his orders. He was alone. He took a hand grenade, pulled the fuse with his teeth and stood there. When the soldiers approached him he dropped it to his feet. But the grenade did not explode. As they immobilized him, he exclaimed:

"I've been betrayed once again by Italy" (referring to the grenade made in Italy).

He was handcuffed and taken to prison in Catania. The young separatist troops who had escaped from the San Mauro camp, thanks to the courage and the sacrifice of their colonel, went into hiding in the countryside.

Some of them went to join my brother's men a few days later. The news had awakened the interest of public opinion and had impressed the E.V.I.S. soldiers operating in Western Sicily, but not Turiddu.

On January 3, 1946, Turiddu decided to attack the station in

Pioppo to show that the E.V.I.S. was still alive. He knew that the station was well defended, so he took forty men with him. He ordered that two mules be taken along as well to carry the machineguns, the ammunition and some bombs. They headed towards this small town. Under cover of the night they sneaked up to station and placed a bomb behind the door. They lit the fuse, but the explosion produced very little damage.

Turiddu gave the signal. This time he used a hand siren that emitted a gloomy howl. A powerful blast of machinegun fire was directed towards the station, followed again by the siren.

"Surrender! You're surrounded!"

Many were convinced that the Royal Carabinieri would surrender. But instead they answered fire. It was like hell. Two E.V.I.S. soldiers fell injured.

The siren was sounded once again and they opened fire again. An assault against the station was attempted, but the Carabinieri warded it off with the launch of grenades. They were nailed in their positions. In the meantime news was given that a motor convoy had been sighted. Reinforcements were arriving from Palermo.

Turiddu did not want to risk the life his men for nothing, so he ordered the retreat. They returned to the camp. They positioned some machineguns in case of mass operations in the area. But nothing happened neither that night nor in the following two days, owing to the heavy snowfall that covered the whole landscape.

The patrols sent to the area and the lookouts reported that everything was calm. On the eve of the Epiphany Turiddu sent all the volunteers home on leave. Only a dozen men were left at the camp. Together with this handful of men he attacked the Borgetto station, but this attempt too failed owing to the arrival of reinforcements. It all ended with a few empty cartridges and with the launching of a few bombs.

Many soldiers, carabinieri and police officers arrived in Montelepre in the meantime. They spread throughout the town and started to search the houses. All of the picciotti from Montelepre were warned of the danger and they prepared to return to the camp. Turiddu, who had already been informed by the Commander-in-Chief, Guglielmo of Carcaci, went to meet them and waited for them on the outskirts of town.

In no time at all almost fifty men had gathered. Almost all of them were from Montelepre, because the others from the nearby towns still had not arrived. Turiddu informed them of what was happening:

"Rome has adopted measures to stop our war operations! You've had the opportunity of seeing how many reinforcements have arrived. But more will arrive! Before this happens, we must attack again and this time we must do things in a big way! I have sent someone to call the others!"

"We won't end up like our comrades in Catania!"

"We'll show them how to fight!"

"We can't disappoint the trust and the hope of our people!"

At the end of his brief speech he ordered his men to split in five squads. The largest group made of nine men was under his command. They handed out the weapons and the ammunitions. They gave the men more than one weapon and could produce intense and continuous fire.

On the evening of January 7, 1946, the various squads were positioned along various access points towards town to block the reinforcements. When this operation was over, Turiddu deployed two squads on the "Belvedere" curve in Montelepre. He took his men and went towards the station. They attacked it with bombs and machinegun fire.

25 carabinieri were blocked inside and answered fire as best as they could. Their ammunitions were about to finish. Before surrendering they called for reinforcements from Palermo. The station was conquered without any losses on either side. It was then sacked and stripped of everything in it.

Three hours later the reinforcements arrived. It was a long column of trucks, tanks, armored vehicles, jeeps, mortars and cannons. The squad covering the road leading to town from Palermo asked for the order to attack. But my brother ordered them to pass without problems. He had prepared a "warm" welcome for them.

When the convoy passed the "Belvedere" curve, the squads attacked by launching grenades and Molotov cocktails. The effect was devastating. The convoy was caught by surprise and the vehicles knocked against each other. One of the trucks was burning and almost all the others were damaged. The passengers of those vehicles escaped full of terror. Turiddu did not want to kill them. They were within range and they were an easy target. He ordered a brief cease-fire so that they could save themselves.

In the meantime the Carabinieri and soldiers that reached Montelepre on the Epiphany were spread through town. It was their intention to reach the site of the shootout, but they were blocked by the gunfire coming from the homes. From every roof, window and corner gunfire was directed against them.

The few minutes of cease-fire that Turiddu had granted were over. They opened fire again. The men in the armored vehicles took advantage of the cease-fire. They opened fire on the men of the E.V.I.S. They were hoping to chase off the attackers, but their attempt failed by a shower of hand grenades. Its crew was almost captured.

The intensity of the shootout kept mounting. The battle lasted the whole night. At dawn the other reinforcements arrived. They were soldiers belonging to the "Aosta", "Folgore" and "Julia" divisions and they were supported by other tanks, armored vehicles and cannons. There were about 2,000 government soldiers.

My brother with his squad reached the hill named "Monte d'Oro". The other squads were already positioned on Mount "Saraceno", along the road to Palermo on "Cozzo Vite", on the road to Partinico and in the "Grotta Bianca".

Daylight revealed the flag of the E.V.I.S. waving majestically in the wind above "Monte d'Oro". It could be seen from all towns located around the gulf of Castellammare. The town seemed to be under siege by the E.V.I.S. Suddenly armored vehicles opened fire against the "Belvedere" position, which Turiddu and his men had abandoned an hour earlier. A small house nearby was hit by the cannons and vanished in a cloud of dust.

When they saw the flag on the hilltop, they realized they were shooting against no one. The government forces spread out and started to advance in that direction. Turiddu noticed their maneuver. He was watching them with his binocular. He ordered the men of his squad to reach the masses above the cliff. He then sent a messenger to order the other squads on Mount "Saraceno" to do the same.

The government forces seen from above looked like an immense mass of ants approaching them. The sound of the tanks was becoming louder and louder. The men were quivering.

"Colonel, what are we waiting for to shoot?"

"Keep calm, I'll tell you when!" he answered.

Never-ending moments went by. My brother continued to watch the enemy without worrying. He stayed there until the first shells started to fall around them. With a gesture, one of the men activated the siren and the men opened fire. The squads on Mount "Saraceno" started to roll down boulders. The government forces did not expect the attack from their flank. They were forced to retreat.

They followed them with their gunfire and by launching grenades.

The men on "Monte d'Oro" sighed with relief. They couldn't understand how my brother could always be so calm with the shells and bullets whistling near them.

Although the infantry retreated, the armored vehicles continued to advance. They passed the boulders and went ahead slowly. Two volunteers accepted to try to block them. They went down the hill and when they were near they launched many grenades. The tracks of the tanks and the tyres of an armored vehicle were seriously damaged.

The road was blocked and the infantry soldiers hid behind them. They were euphoric for the success of their raid but other groups were gaining ground hoping to surround them. The attack was followed by powerful explosions of mortar shells.

"Fire! Fire!" ordered Turiddu.

One of the men was overwhelmed by the discouragement and he shouted:

"They're going to kill all of us!"

My brother left the lookout and went towards the man. He looked at him straight in the eyes and shout at him:

"The freedom of my people is more important than a few lives!"

He pushed him away and took control of the machinegun. He started to shoot with such precision that he scared off all those who tried to advance. In order to complete his plan he ordered that other boulders be launched. All the noise and dust forced the government troops to retreat again.

"LONG LIVE THE E.V.I.S.! LONG LIVE THE E.V.I.S.!" shouted the men full of joy for the momentary success.

Meanwhile the artificers pointed against the flag on "Monte d'Oro". They pointed the fire of their 47" mortars on it. A chapel located just a few meters away was hit and disappeared in a cloud of dust. But the flag continued to wave almost like a sort of challenge.

On the outskirts of town there were trucks from all directions. They were transporting troops to surround my brother, but he was not caught by surprise.

He had already sent a messenger to the squad on the road to Palermo with the order to move the machinegun in the opposite direction. He had moved them to avoid surprises from "Piana Gallina" overlooking the road from Carini to Montelepre.

The squad changed position without being intercepted. They managed to place the machinegun just in time because a convoy of trucks full of soldiers was arriving. The head of the squad waited for them to get off in the clearing and ordered to open fire.

Despite their superiority, the troops were nailed where they were. While the battle raged, gunshots could also be heard down in the valley towards Partinico. Soldiers, carabinieri and police feared to be attacked from that side too. They retreated from the positions they had conquered along "Monte d'Oro" with so many difficulties. But it was just a diversion created by my friends and me in case the situation was desperate.

Taking advantage of the momentary calm, Turiddu activated the siren. It was the signal to retreat. All the men converged on "Piano Gallina". Turiddu came running with the flag in one hand and the machinegun in the other. He saw that no one was injured but the ammunition was almost over.

They could not resist for much longer and they decided to retreat towards "LO ZUCCO". The meeting point was the "Princess of Ganci" estate. He ordered his men to leave one at a time. He stayed behind to cover their retreat by keeping the government forces busy. He shot all the bullets he had. When he was sure that his men were safe, he too abandoned the position.

After a day of battle, the police and troops finally reached the top of "Monte d'Oro", but they found no one. Later Turiddu reached his men at the Princess of Ganci estate. He ordered that the gates be closed and he asked to speak with the administrator. He came immediately accompanied by the farmhands and foremen. Turiddu asked that his men be fed, but the administrator hesitated. Turiddu asked him the keys of the pantry. There was plenty of food. He ordered that the food be divided also to all the farmhands and workers there.

At the end of the meal my brother pulled out one of the receipt blocks with the mark of the E.V.I.S. He filled in a receipt and gave it to the administrator for the owner of the estate. He could thus justify the missing food and avoid any accusations of complicity.

In the meantime all the houses in Montelepre from where gunfire came were conquered and about 70 people aged between 15 and 60 were taken away. There were more Carabinieri and police than inhabitants. It was declared a war zone. As of January 13, 1946, the curfew was introduced from 5.00 p.m. to 7 a.m.

The government forces started to carry out war operations against the inhabitants of Montelepre simply because they were Sicilians.

Turiddu was raging with anger. He realized that Montelepre was under siege and was living moments of despair. The population was in a desperate situation. There was very little food and the people could not even satisfy their basic needs.

The soldiers would start shooting for nothing. They were pushing the town on the brink of exasperation. The patience of the town's inhabitants was put to the test and their sympathy and solidarity all went to Turiddu.

During this period of sudden shootouts, a man named Giuseppe Sapienza was killed. He was a poor cattle-breeder who had gone to cut some fresh grass for his animals. To avoid getting the people involved, Turiddu decided to move the area of operations elsewhere.

After his retreat to the estate of the Princess of Ganci he ordered a one-week cease-fire. Then the various squads launched guerilla attacks simultaneously in different places. There were real battles. Some of these battles lasted for days and were waged against forces superior both in number and armament.

But my brother never lost his calm even in the most critical moments. Regardless of the danger, he was always in the front line. Despite the other operations, the hold on Montelepre was not eased. The separatist war became a war against the town. There were torture, and abuses of all kinds every day.

Turiddu decided to hang a notice in the center of the town. He put into force a curfew for the carabinieri. He prohibited them to leave their barracks from 5 p.m. to 5 a.m. in the morning. During those hours the people of Montelepre could come out of their houses. He personally came home a few times or went to walk through town with some of his men.

In the light of the situation High Commissioner Aldisio declared to be ready to resign if he was asked to do so as to avoid a political crisis. But Alcide De Gasperi, the pro tempore Italian Prime Minister, reconfirmed him in his position. Meanwhile, despite the repression, despite the convoys of armored vehicles and the thousands of men deployed, Turiddu's daring had no limits.

On the evening of January 26, 1946 he carried out a sensational operation to prove to his fellow townsmen that he had not abandoned them and that he would avenge them. With about 50 men he attacked the military camp in Montelepre. There were some units of the AOSTA battalion and of the FOLGORE and JULIA divisions.

The attack was so sudden that many tents were burning before the soldiers could respond fire. There was great chaos, a lot of panic but no victims. Another squad had attacked a radio station in the Uditore borough in Palermo at the same time. They were headed by "Fra' Diavolo" (Salvatore Ferreri's battle name).

The target of the attack was to launch a radio message to Sicilians to come and help my brother's army. But the station resisted well and the attackers were forced to retreat. Salvatore Ferreri was one of the few previous offenders amongst Turiddu's men. He had been freed by police inspector Messana to join the E.V.I.S. under the command of my brother.

He was to give him information on how to capture him, but he was so fascinated by him that he too joined his cause. He did not want to betray him so he confessed everything thus gaining his esteem and trust.

On the morning of February 8, 1946, Turiddu took 15 men and went to the houses in "Bellolampo" for a guerilla operation. The men were all wearing the separatist army uniforms and were armed with three light machineguns, over machineguns and hand grenades.

They placed the machineguns on a hilltop over the main road: the position was located above the first curve before the crossroads Torretta – Montelepre – Palermo coming from Montelepre.

They prepared the ambush and waited for the arrival of two jeeps from Piano dell'Occhio to be signaled by the lookouts. Those jeeps were carrying officers who were coming to Montelepre to adopt even more severe measures against the population.

When they were in shooting range, they opened fire with the machinegun. The men in the vehicles were forced to stop. They found refuge behind the vehicles and tried to put up resistance. the noise of the shooting was heard by the Carabinieri in Bellolampo. The commander was informed by the headquarters in Palermo and took all the men he had to the site of the shootout.

The shooting lasted for about an hour. The carabinieri had little ammunition and some had been injured. They would have surrendered, but a convoy of soldiers together with an armored vehicle arrived in the meanwhile.

The first soldiers were caught in the middle of the crossfire of two machineguns as soon as they got off the trucks. Some managed to reach better positions and opened fire. The bullets were flying everywhere. Turiddu and his men made up for their numeric inferiority with their courage and answered.

The fierce fighting lasted for about two hours. The soldiers were nailed where they were. Suddenly five tanks appeared as they came from Palermo. They were followed by other troops and cannons. There were even some troops belonging to the Alpini.

They approached rapidly, took position and opened fire. The situation was too dangerous for my brother. There were even some wounded amongst his men. His position was no longer favorable owing to the arrival of the heavy artillery.

With the support of the cannons, the troops started to advance to surround them. A grenade hit the E.V.I.S. flag tearing it apart. One of Turiddu's men was wounded seriously in his neck; the others started to panic.

My brother moved his men to the hill called Mount "CUCCIO" with his usual calm. He arranged them in a U-shaped formation.

His men obeyed him. He was urging them on especially during the most critical moments. They had barely managed to reach the new positions that they were attacked by many soldiers.

They advanced along the side to the hill. Hidden by the vegetation they tried to catch them by surprise. Turiddu ordered that boulders be rolled down to stop them. The boulders together with the launch of bombs had a devastating effect. Owing to the steepness of the hill a large cloud of dust hid them.

Besides the panic, an unexpected event occurred. One of the mules Turiddu used for the transport of supplies and ammunitions was hit by a cannon shell. As it fell to the ground a cask of red wine rolled off. It started to roll down the hill pouring out its contents.

The soldiers and carabinieri along its trajectory thought that it was blood and retreated full of panic.

Turiddu exploited the momentary advantage to order the retreat. The battle had been fierce and darkness was luring. They returned to base in Sagana by following paths and trails that they knew well.

Day after day the myth of the impossibility of capturing Turiddu grew and his men started to be taken seriously. The government forces were on the defensive and could barely fight off his attacks.

The government was forced to admit that it was fighting against a fierce Sicilian revolt. While the battles raged in the mountains, the police arrested many leading figures of the E.V.I.S. and M.I.S.

Mario Scelba, Minister of the Interior at the time, offered a reward of 800,000 It. Lire for the capture of my brother. Said money would be given to whoever would help to capture him. When Turiddu found out about it, he thought that it was too little. To show his power he offered two million It. lire for the capture of the Minister.

Everyone called my brother now "Colonel Giuliano". He continued unperturbed his unequal struggle against the government forces. Until February 1946 his flag continued to wave over the CALCERAME hill.

But a massive offensive was launched against that position. It was attacked on many sides by a regiment and a thousand carabinieri with modern weapons, armored vehicles and mortars. They were also supported by the troops of the Folgore and Garibaldi divisions with self-propelled artillery.

Death revealed its true face more than once. Many of my brother's men were injured. The situation was critical and Turiddu feared that they would not make it. He did not have enough men to resist. He ordered the ex-tinsmith Frank Mannino to run to Partinico to ask for help. He rushed off without hesitation. He crawled through the ditches as the bombs and mortar shells exploded all around.

A splinter injured him in his ankle. He medicated it as best as he could and continued in his mission. He was exhausted when he reached Partinico. He only found ten men willing to enroll. They all ran to help Turiddu.

In the meantime Turiddu and his men made up for their inferiority with their courage. Challenging death itself, they resisted the whole day. Under cover of the night they retreated and managed to avoid a total defeat.

They found refuge at the base in Sagana. They pitched camp on the sides of mount CANALONE and they stayed there for a few days.

The landscape was made of barren hills covered with stones. The tanks and the other weapons of the government troops could not be used up there. During the brief truce, discontent started to spread amongst Turiddu's men. First they started to argue on general topics, then came complaints and finally accusations.

The leaders of the M.I.S. had promised help but had given nothing. The troops of the E.V.I.S. were tired of risking their lives without adequate support. The weapons and ammunition, which they had promised, had to be stolen instead from the Italian army. They alone had fought against entire armies. If they were alive it was because of their strategic abilities, courage and the courage of the colonel.

Turiddu was very embittered. He knew that he had to face enormous forces, but could count only on promises. (He still did not know that almost all the leaders of the M.I.S. had been arrested). They still did not know that on Januray 9th they had sent Pasquale Sciortino to order the end of hostilities. His operations had already obtained the desired political and propagandistic effect.

But Pasquale Sciortino was arrested that day. He was taken to Palermo in an armored vehicle by Col. Paolantonio. There he suffered abuses and torture. He was forced to confess the names of the other members of the E.V.I.S., who were then arrested.

Turiddu did not receive the orders and continued his guerilla operations. Turiddu invited everyone to bear patience.

He reminded them that they were volunteers and that they had joined for patriotism. If someone wanted to leave he was free to do so. He said they would discuss the matter again the next day so that they all had time to reflect.

The next day he called them and was disappointed to see that there were many who wanted to leave. Amongst them there were some of those that seemed to be animated with fervent patriotism. He had them return the weapons and they left without any rancor. Only twenty men were left.

What are you waiting for to leave? asked Turiddu bitterly.

The eldest of the group answered:

"Colonel! Don't compare us to them! First we were many with little arms and now we are few, but ready for anything!"

Those words calmed Turiddu. The tone of his voice revealed his gratitude:

"Think about it! From now on it will be even more difficult! As for me, I will fight to death!"

"Well said Colonel! After all you only live once!" answered the man.

The day went by peacefully. But the news that the men of the E.V.I.S. were in the mountains of the Sagana estate was sent to the Ministry of the Interior.

The government hoped to dislodge them and sent a airborne unit of Alpini. When they reached the signaled area they started their way up Mount "Canalone". They were used to more difficult terrain and under cover of the night they reached my brother's camp.

The surprise attack would have been fatal for them all. But the moon, up to that moment hidden behind the clouds, suddenly lit the scene. One of the lookouts saw them. He rushed silently to warn Turiddu. When he saw them he realized that they did not have enough time to organize a valid defense with the few men he had.

He ordered to leave one by one and to reach the town of Monreale. Friends would have helped them. They all obeyed halfheartedly. They did not want to leave him alone. But he was firm in his intent.

He let them go until they had a sufficient lead. He then started to make a dummy with some stones. He covered it with his white trench coat. The Alpini were fooled by the presence of the dummy and they directed against it all their fire. But Turiddu crawled through the stones and managed to escape safely.

He reached his men on the outskirts of Monreale, where a safe refuge was found. He discovered that Pasquale Sciortino had been arrested. He received the order to ease his operations. His operations had induced the government to negotiate.

Turiddu and his men stayed in Monreale for a few days and then moved to Mount Gibellinese. They found refuge in a small shepherd's hut. But they stayed only for a day. As they sat around the fire, the lookout gave the alarm. He came running to warn that the house was surrounded by soldiers, carabinieri and police.

The men started to panic. It would have been their last battle. They would have left this life heroically or in the best of cases they would have passed the rest of their days in rest. Turiddu had them swear that they would fight to the end. He placed his men and watched the troops with his binoculars. He saw that on one side the soldiers were still too far away. He wanted to take one last risk. One by one at brief intervals they left safely. The government forces were convinced that they were fighting against thousands of men and did not pay attention to those few men.

They found refuge in the mountains above the gulf of Castellammare, an area full of natural caves and hideouts.

In the meantime the abuses and retaliation against the defenseless inhabitants continued in Montelepre. The town was under the siege of an enormous war machine. All the men had been arrested and sent to prison. They were massed like animals in town square for a whole day without anything to eat or drink. Any act of rebellion was punished with lashes.

Around 5 p.m. news went through town that the prisoners were going to be executed. All the women were shocked with terror. If they were going to kill their sons, husbands and fathers, it was better if they killed them too.

The women of Montelepre became a single body, a single soul. Careless of the machineguns, and rifles pointed against them, they launched themselves against the line of police and soldiers hitting, kicking and biting them.

The alarm was sounded. All the tank cannons and machineguns were pointed against the town. A colonel of the Carabinieri climbed on a truck and shot a blast of machinegun fire in the air.

They all stopped. He threatened that he would raze the whole town to the ground if they did not stop and he assured them that the rumor was false.

The excitement subsided. The women sighed with relief. Only 20 men of all those arrested were sent to Palermo on a truck. Once again the soldiers' behavior, instead of scaring the inhabitants, had fueled even more the feelings of rebellion in their hearts.

*My Brother, Salvatore Giuliano*

One of the many groups sent against Giuliano (Publifoto).

*My Brother, Salvatore Giuliano*

Carabinieri in their positions above Montelepre (Foto Martinez).

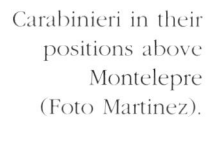

Chapter XII

# CHECKMATE!

After the latest period of fierce fighting, my mother and I found refuge in Palermo. We were guests of the Pizzurro family, which came from Montelepre. My brother had found us this opportunity. He wanted to avoid that we become the targets of retaliation on the part of the police.

Personally I would have preferred to continue collaborating in the fight, but he could not convince my mother to overcome her prejudice. It was not suitable for a girl to stay up in the mountains together with a group of men.

Calogero Vizzini was considered a leader of the M.I.S., but he was also the boss of bosses of the Sicilian Mafia. He was one of the few to be left untouched. He received a message from Turiddu where he was invited to help the separatist leaders that were being held prisoner.

He went to the office of the lawyer Sirio Rossi in Palermo. He too was known to be a leader of the movement. Vizzini thought that it was unfair that the other leaders (Finocchiaro Aprile, Varvaro and Restuccia) were held prisoner on the island of Ponza.

He proposed kidnapping those who had given the order of their arrest: the High Commissioner for Sicily Salvatore Aldisio and Girolamo Li Causi. He had already prepared the plans, but when the moment had come to carry out the operation, he changed idea.

He wanted to send Aldisio an ultimatum. The High Commissioner knew with whom he was dealing with and he understood that he had no other choice. He left immediately for Rome with the intention of pressing for the release of the prisoners in Ponza.

In the meantime, Turiddu decided to launch an attack in the Trapani area to ease the siege of Montelepre. He was hoping to attract the attention of the police. He decided to kidnap Giuseppe Cardella, a rich textile merchant living in Custonaci.

The main purpose of the kidnap was not the money, but that of shifting the attention of the government forces to the Trapani area. If the plan worked, he could have returned to his base in Sagana, which was a more hospitable and familiar area. (I would like to stress that in that period my brother's feats were given great prominence. He received money from voluntary financiers, especially Sicilians living in America. They hoped that independence would allow them to come home and invest their money in their motherland. They believed that Sicily's independence would solve the problem of emigration and underdevelopment).

Since it was a very risky action, Turiddu chose five of the bravest men. They stopped on the edge of the Palermo-Trapani provincial road near the town of Calatafimi. They waited for a car to pass along the road.

They did not wait for long. They saw a truck full of wine casks coming from Alcamo. They put some trunks in the middle of the road to block it.

The driver stopped and got off the truck to remove the obstacle. He was swearing and gesturing with his hands. When he felt the

A convoy of reinforcements sent to Montelepre (Publifoto).

chill of the cold machinegun against his back, he sprung up straight and found himself surrounded by Turiddu's men.

"Friend! I need your truck!"

"If you behave well and don't denounce us, you'll get it back together with a reward!"

"But you're Turiddu Giuliano!" exclaimed the man with wonder.

"I saw your picture in the newspapers! You're fighting for our land and you help the poor! Take my truck! No one will ever know!"

Turiddu thanked him and said:

"You'll have to come with us! You'll watch your load because we need it empty!"

They all climbed on the truck and they took the road leading to Segesta. Near the temple they unloaded the casks and drove to their target. They reached Custonaci in full daylight. They asked where the station was and they were told that it was near Cardella's house. At the other end of town there was another station of the Guardia di Finanza (Italian tax authorities).

The sign of the E.V.I.S. on a station wall (Foto Scafidi).

Turiddu left two men to watch the stations. The fifth man had the task of covering him in case of danger. They went towards the target. Once he arrived there, he knocked vigorously at the door. Giuseppe Cardella looked through the peephole and recognized him immediately. He started to shout and to cry for help. The soldiers of the two stations noticed what was happening.

Turiddu's men started to stop them. They kept them busy very well by launching grenades and machinegun fire. They were nailed in the building. From the shooting Turiddu realized what was going on. There was no time to lose. He broke down the door. He caught the target by the arm and pulled him away like a child dragging his feet.

Once in the street he emitted a modulated whistle. They all ran towards the truck and drove away from Custonaci as fast as they could. The next day the truck was returned to its owner and he received a reward from Turiddu: a large amount of money. Giuseppe Cardella was released a few days later. A ransom of 2 million Lire was paid.

On March 22, 1946, probably after a tip-off, Marshal Calandra found our refuge in Palermo. My mother and I were arrested and taken to Termini Imerese. They arrested some members of the family that had given us shelter: Caterina, Concetta and Vincenzo Pizzurro. I was interrogated without a break. I too was tortured. The soldiers treated me badly. They wanted to know where my brother was.

I did not know, but even if I did I would never have betrayed him for anything in the world. I would have preferred dying. The place where we were held was kept secret for several days.

In the meantime in Rome, after the political pressure exerted by the High Commissioner Salvatore Aldisio, the government sent a delegation to Ponza to meet the leaders of the separatist movement.

The government's envoys told the prisoners more or less the following:

"If you think that you will win independence with your fight, then you can rot in here for the rest of your days! But if autonomy is enough, then you'll be free in no time at all!" Without hesitating, they repudiated their ideals and the expectations of the Sicilian people. Andrea Finocchiaro Aprile answered:

"Who ever spoke of independence? We want administrative autonomy!" They were released. Finocchiaro Aprile, Varvaro and Restuccia were transported to Palermo by plane on March 27, 1946.

A crowd welcomed them and bestowed them great honors with enormous celebrations. On that occasion Finocchiaro Aprile declared to a press agency:

"The goals and objectives of the M.I.S. have been falsified by its enemies. The members of the movement are and intend to remain Italian!"

The government forces, as Turiddu had expected, had moved to the Trapani area after the news of the Cardella kidnap. The hold on Montelepre was eased, although the curfew was maintained.

He was able to return to Sagana. He was informed of the latest news by the people of Montelepre. He was told that Marshal Calandra had found our refuge and arrested us. No one knew where we were being held.

The news of our mother's arrest filled him with anger. He venerated her and had infinite respect for her. The mere idea that someone could hurt her drove him mad. On April 1, 1946, he decided to play the Marshal a nasty trick.

The bus was coming from Palermo and it was directed to Montelepre. In the middle of a curve the driver saw a human body lying in the road covered with blood. He braked all of a sudden to avoid it.

Marshal Calandra was escorting the bus together with some soldiers. He ordered them to move the body out of the way. But they came close enough they saw that it was only a mannequin. There was a message on it:

"April Fool's! Giuliano."

The marshal and the carabinieri were left petrified. They looked at each other with amazement. A wild burst of machinegun fire lifted the dust around their feet. A carabiniere was slightly injured by a bullet that ricocheted. The others rushed for cover behind a short wall.

They hid behind it for several minutes, but nothing happened. It was a trick to scare the Marshal. If my brother wanted, he could have easily killed them. He wanted to show the officer that he knew what happened to us.

Turiddu had informers everywhere. There were even policemen and carabinieri that approved what he was doing. Two days later he found out that we were being kept in Termini Imerese. He sent a message to Palermo to a trustworthy friend. He was a pilot at the "Boccadifalco" airport. He was happy to help him. He climbed into a small plane and flew over Termini Imerese.

Once he identified the prison, he circled around it a few times. Then he flew at low quote and dropped a message from Turiddu wrapped on a stone. It said:

**"My dear, I'm coming to save you. Tell my mother. S.G."**

The message was picked up by a prisoner. Unfortunately she had a big mouth and little brains. She spread the news through the prison and everyone knew about it.

The prison's warden was shocked and he called us into his office. He turned to my mother and said:

"I know that your son's coming to free you! We're ready to welcome him! We've placed machineguns on the towers! Let him know that it won't be easy! But if he manages to get in, I'll personally give him the keys of your cell!"

"How can I let him know?" asked my mother. "You don't even let us write a letter! You won't leave us alone even though you know we're innocent!"

To avoid our rescue, the inquiry on us was accelerated. It was clear that we had committed no crime. After 23 days of prison we were freed. It was April 13, 1946.

After their return from Ponza, the political leaders tried to reorganize the movement. It was officially recognized as a political party. It could now enjoy the rights that it had been denied before.

All the offices that had been closed were now reopened. The red and yellow cockades were free to wave again. Andrea Finocchiaro Aprile's rallies were a success.

In Rome, King Victor Emanuel was satisfied for having supported the separatist cause. Everyone knew of the change of policy in favor of the Monarchy: only Antonino Varvaro and my brother did not know. Actually news that something had changed had leaked, but no one knew how much it.

For many days now Turiddu had no contacts with the movement's leaders. Since they had negotiated with the government thanks to his fight, they had forgotten him. He had the feeling that they had rid themselves of him. He decided to visit the party headquarters in Palermo. It was located in a basement in Via Cavour, opposite the "Birreria Italia".

He found one of the main figures of the M.I.S. They shook hands and embraced each other like brothers.

"What's happening?" asked Turiddu without wasting time.

"Dear Turiddu", he answered, "things didn't go as we hoped!"

"I know it already! You've abandoned me when I most needed you! I had to face the Italian Army alone! I risked my life and the lives of my men innumerable times! We faced the Carabinieri, the army, and the police without receiving guns, ammunition or reinforcements from you as promised! What are you planning to do with this revolution?"

"Calm down! Calm down, Turiddu!" answered the man. "You're absolutely right. But believe me. There have been many unexpected events! For the time being, we need a truce before the elections! Finocchiaro Aprile said that we must be satisfied with administrative autonomy!"

"Administrative autonomy?" repeated Turiddu full of shock.

"You're all crazy! I fought for this? While we were risking our lives, you windbags were sound and safe!"

"Administrative autonomy!"

"Don't you understand that by accepting it, nothing will change? Rome will continue to ignore us just as it has done for the last eighty years. Emigration, underdevelopment and servility will continue!"

Although the interlocutor was scared by his anger, he found the courage to reply:

"No! It's not like that!"

"Your struggle wasn't useless!"

"Thanks to the E.V.I.S. we have obtained autonomy! We've made an agreement. If the statute is approved as it is, it's almost independence!"

Turiddu was very upset. He did not want to give up the fight. But he bent his head in front of the situation.

"OK! Since the damage is already done, I'll grant the truce! But remember! I'm a man of action, not a politician! But I promise you that if nothing changes after the elections I'll continue to fight on my own! I'll rest only once the target for which I fought is reached!"

"Or independence or death!"

Without saying goodbye and with his face red with anger, he left slamming the door. The M.I.S. leader did not have the chance or the courage to tell him that they were supporting the Monarchy.

My brother felt betrayed. He walked along Via Cavour like a robot with his head full of thoughts. Without noticing it, he reached the Cala amongst the houses destroyed by the bombings before the invasion.

He wandered without a destination, when a girl came out of a semi-destroyed home. She was dressed in black. Her head was covered with a veil. Her eyes were dug in and she was so skinny. She was followed by a flock of children. The eldest was not even 10 years old. He held her skirt trying to stop her.

"Mamma! Mamma! Don't leave us! We're hungry!" he shouted as he cried.

"Go home! Mamma's going to work. I'll bring you presents when I come back!"

As he watched the scene, Turiddu forgot his problems. He waited for the woman on the corner and stopped her.

"Excuse me if I'm bothering you! Are they all yours?"

"Yes, they are. I've got six!" she said as she bitterly smiled. "Since my husband has died, it's getting more and more difficult to find what we need!"

Turiddu put his hand in his pocket and pulled out some money. He gave the money to her. The woman hesitated.

"Who are you? Why are you giving me money?" she asked diffidently.

"Don't worry! I just want to help feed your children!" answered Turiddu.

The woman felt reassured by his words and accepted his offer. She asked again:

"Who are you?"

"I can't tell you!"

"Please do! Trust me!"

Due to her insistence, he said:

"I'll tell only if you promise on your husband's soul that you'll keep it a secret!"

The woman swore.

He shook her hand and left her a card. She was so curious that she rushed to read the name. She looked at him full of amazement, but Turiddu had already disappeared.

Full of excitement, she ran to buy food and clothes. Her neighbors were amazed to see her come back full of packages. Her old mother scolded her. She thought she had sold her body to someone.

"I didn't do anything I should be ashamed of!"

"I just met the father of the poor! You think what you want, but I can't tell you more!"

After our release, we returned to Montelepre. The news that my brother had granted a cease-fire had reached also the upper spheres. Almost all the government forces in Montelepre had returned to the barracks. The curfew was still being applied, but not as rigorously as before.

Towards the middle of April I received a letter from the leaders of the movement. It invited me to go to the party offices for a communication that regarded me.

I was left dumbfounded. All I knew of the movement and its members was what my brother had told me. I had never had direct contacts with them. The invitation made me curious. The next day I took the bus to Palermo. There I was welcomed warmly by Antonino Varvaro and Andrea Finocchiaro Aprile.

Despite I had never seen them, they were very kind to me. They also introduced me to Lucio Tasca's children and Varvaro's wife, called mamma Jolanda. She hugged me and kissed me. She then said:

"I'm proud to have met the sister of the legendary Col. Giuliano! I'm sure you will follow his footsteps and help us with the electoral campaign!"

"If my brother agrees, I'm ready and willing to help the cause and the party!" I answered.

I spent an unforgettable day. I was the center of attention. I had always been proud of Turiddu, but that day I was even prouder. I went home feeling satisfied.

The next day I sent Turiddu a message. I told him I needed to talk to him. The next morning a car stopped in front of our door. The driver had been assigned the task to take me to my brother.

I climbed into the car together with my mother and we went to Monreale near a farmstead pompously called "VILLA CAROLINA". The driver stopped the car and rang three times. We looked around suspiciously. It seemed a deserted place. Suddenly ten well-armed men came out from behind the bushes and rocks. They greeted us and took us inside.

Turiddu hugged us. We had not seen each other for two months, but, save for the 23 days of prison, we had always kept in touch with messengers. We were all happy and moved at the same time. Turiddu had prepared a lunch in our honor. During the lunch, he told us everything that had happened to him in the meantime. We were the only ones with whom he could speak freely. We were the only ones who would never betray him or repudiate him.

I would never get tired of listening to him. With other people, he was a man of few words. But with us he could open his heart.

At the end of lunch we spoke in private. I told him of the offer made to me by the party leaders and we asked for his opinion and whether I should take part in the campaign of the M.I.S. He not only agreed but also guaranteed his help. We went home happy and satisfied. I was on cloud nine.

I worked day and night to sew myself a khaki separatist uniform: a khaki skirt and a red and yellow blouse. In Montelepre there was no M.I.S. office. Turiddu had it opened on the ground floor of a house at number 35 of a street called Via Castrenze Di Bella.

I wore my uniform and started to take part in the rallies. I would take with me the E.V.I.S. flag used by my brother during his battles. You could see the bullet holes in it. My brother financed for a month and a half my trips, lunches, car rentals, trucks, planes to launch leaflets.

I traveled through the towns of Western Sicily together with Marianna Alliata, Carmela La Motta, Anna Lanzarotta, Jolanda Varvaro, Lucio Tasca's children and the lawyers Rossi, Micale and Giannola.

The news that I was one of the speakers attracted many people. Large crowds came to hear us and several times the police had to come to control the enthusiasm of the people. They all pressed against the improvised stages hoping to talk to me, to see me, to shake my hand, to ask help from me, to give letters or money to my brother.

The rallies all finished with the following cry:

"For independent Sicily! Hip, hip, hurrah!"

The crowds would repeat it with us.

My brother's popularity was at its acme. If he were a candidate, as Concetto Gallo, Castrogiovanni, La Motta and Cammarata, he would have been the first to be elected, but he could not for obvious reasons.

I could have run in the elections myself with the same outcome, but unfortunately we didn't even think about it. Probably if I did, things would have gone differently.

On May 16, 1946 the SICILIAN STATUTE was approved. It had passed without amendments. The same day the legislative decree was signed by King Humbert II of Savoy. After King Victor Emanuel III abdicated, he had become the new KING of Italy.

The Sicilian people welcomed autonomy with great enthusiasm and celebrated it as the victory of separatism, although it still did not realize its scope and benefits. Autonomy was granted at the height of the electoral campaign for the Constituent Assembly. It was becoming more and more harsh and fiery.

The M.I.S. welcomed the event with great celebrations. They considered autonomy and the approval of the Statute as the greatest result obtained by my brother. The remaining police forces returned to their stations. Everything was normal again.

During the pre-electoral period, my brother too moved to Palermo. He was a guest in the most beautiful villas of the city and beautiful women were competing to have him. They were fascinated by his personality and his muscular body. That was another way of campaigning. He called, wrote or went to visit friends, acquaintances and sympathizers to vote the M.I.S. for the Constituent and the republic in the referendum.

At the same time his men and their families were asking for votes also on his behalf. The electoral campaign ended on May 31, 1946.

The last large rally was held in Palermo in Piazza Politeama. I was amongst the speakers on the stage.

Andrea Finocchiaro Aprile was the first to speak. For the first time in my life I realized what a politician really was. His speech sounded ambiguous to our ears. At first I was surprised, then I felt disappointment, as did Nino Varvaro. In fact, Finocchiaro Aprile had invited in his speech to vote for the Monarchy in the referendum.

He ended his speech saying that King Humbert II of Savoy could rightly call himself the fourth KING of Italy and the first KING of Sicily. Part of the crowd shouted:

"LONG LIVE THE KING!"

But the great majority of people was satisfied with autonomy and was left confused and disappointed. The inconsistency of the leader had dispelled the sympathy for the movement. That was the beginning of the end of the movement.

His speech confirmed the rumors that had been circulating for days and that he himself had denied according to which the leaders of the movement had devised a secret plan. They wanted to offer the crown of Sicily to Humbert II of Savoy if those in favor of the republic won the referendum.

From Sicily he would then conquer the kingdom by force. The KING's "electoral" visit in Sicily on May 28-29, 1946 was further evidence of the plan. Behind the scenes, Varvaro and Finocchiaro argued fiercely after the rally. As Antonino Varvaro climbed to the pulpit to perorate the cause of the republic, I left the stage.

I knew where my brother was and I explained to him the impossibility to reconcile the positions of the separatist leaders. Turiddu was shocked: he realized that the people's right to self-determination was at risk. He picked up the phone to contact trustworthy people to investigate secretly.

In a few hours he was informed of the plot. He found out that the monarchist leaders had reached an agreement with the leaders of the M.I.S. and that they had started to gather arms and ammunitions for the coup.

My brother felt that he had been used and thrown away. He went out into the streets and vanished. I found out the next day that he went to the American headquarters where he met Col. Pollach, who managed to foil the plan.

My brother had checkmated the King!

Rallies in favor of independence (Foto Martinez).

*My Brother, Salvatore Giuliano*

Rallies in favor of independence (Foto Martinez).

Chapter XIII

# THE CEASE-FIRE IS OVER!

The electoral campaign was carried out thoroughly all over the Island. Turiddu left nothing to chance. But during the campaign those who had fought with him and were not known to the police revealed themselves and were discovered.

They exposed themselves to the risk to help Nino Varvaro and Andrea Finocchiaro Aprile. They hoped that with their help once they were elected to the Assembly the other members of the E.V.I.S. in prison would be freed.

In the afternoon of June 1st, Turiddu went to Montelepre. He walked through the town together with Filippo Ferrara and Giuseppe Passatempo. He gave the indications and advice to the electoral roll n° 8.

A police commissioner and a marshal of the Carabinieri met them, but they made believe that they did not see him. They knew they had to respect the cease-fire. The elections of June 2, 1946 went smoothly. In all those town's where Turiddu's popularity was high, the republic obtained the majority of votes.

Although the monarchy had won in Sicily, the republic had won at a national level and Humbert II of Savoy was no longer the King of Italy. Only four representatives of the M.I.S. were elected to the Constituent Assembly. They were Varvaro and Finocchiaro Aprile for Western Sicily and Concetto Gallo and Attilio Castrogiovanni for Eastern Sicily.

The results of the elections were far from being satisfying for the M.I.S. and that led to the dispute between its two different factions: the monarchists on the one hand and the republicans on the other. They had two completely different ways of seeing Sicilian patriotism.

On June 22nd an amnesty decree was approved. It had been proposed by the Minister of Justice, Palmiro Togliatti. The Amnesty and General Pardon decree for petty, political and war crimes had been signed by the pro tempore Head of State, De Nicola. All those who had been arrested for their militancy in the ranks of the E.V.I.S. or the M.I.S. were freed.

When the news was given by radio, my brother and I were home. Thanks to a few of his "picciotti", Turiddu summoned a meeting of all the men on June 25th. The meeting was held at the Sagana camp. The day was beautiful and the temperature was warm. My whole family was together again and it took advantage of the opportunity to go on a picnic.

I preferred going with Turiddu to the meeting, while the others stayed for the picnic in one of our pieces of land in the area.

Turiddu gave a short speech:

**"Picciotti! We have all heard the news we were waiting for. We can go home as free men!"**

**"All those who had a clean record and were involved in the E.V.I.S. operations are free to go home! From this moment there is no longer any reason for the separatist army to exist! We have fought for the independence of our land, but we must be content with Autonomy! If all the men of our party were elected, they would have succeeded in making the Statute work, just like it was approved and we could all be satisfied!"**

They all returned home, save for Salvatore Ferreri and a few others, because they had committed other crimes. Together with them, we went to join the rest of the family. We spent a peaceful day. The men of Montelepre and the nearby towns were free to walk in the streets. They all returned to a calm and normal life and to their previous occupations.

Marshal Calandra was full of anger. He could not bear the idea that those who had given him so many problems were now free again. But those men had committed political crimes and the general pardon had wiped away their crimes. They could no longer be persecuted.

Fifteen days later, when everyone thought that there was no longer any reason to worry, Marshal Calandra and Brigadier Santucci encountered Gaspare Pisciotta, who was in the square with some friends.

Thanks to the help of two girls of the group, Pisciotta managed to escape easily. The soldiers followed him. Once they reached the small bridge on the lower outskirts of town, Gaspare jumped down from a height of about four meters.

He hurt his heels and his lungs when he landed. Panting and limping he managed to get away along the bed of a small stream hidden by the vegetation. The soldiers gave up their pursuit. They went back to the square where they were scolded by a police commissioner. He told them that without this inconvenient they would have captured all of them like mice.

The response revealed the rivalry between the two corps. It was no coincidence, but it had been all premeditated. If Calandra and Santucci would have succeeded the merit would have been attributed to the Carabinieri. As they argued on merits and competence, the "picciotti" watching the scene rushed through town to inform the others. From what the police had said, they heard that other warrants of arrest had been issued against them for petty crimes they had never committed.

The campaign was over and so too the cease-fire. The day after one by one they came to join my brother again. They were complaining that the party had not done anything to safeguard their freedom.

Before nightfall they were all together again in contrada "Cippi". In the morning Turiddu went to Palermo to explain what had happened and to ask for help but he came home empty-handed.

One of the leaders of the movement told him that the E.V.I.S. was a thing of the past. Those who were elected were busy in Rome with the application of the Statute and he could not do anything. The best thing they could do was to look for a good lawyer.

In a few words, they got their seats in the Assembly and they abandoned my brother and his men to their fate.

"Picciotti!" started Turiddu. "We've been used and betrayed! In the light of the situation, the war continues! My M.A.S.C.A. will never surrender! I'll continue to fight for independence even alone! What do you want to do? Do you want to stay and fight or go your own way?"

The men unanimously decided to stay with him. They were about 25 men. All those who were lucky enough not to be recognized, stayed at home and no one bothered them or ever mentioned their names.

As usual the men were split into four squads. Each squad had a captain responsible for the men assigned to him. They were to operate together in case of guerilla operations, but otherwise they were independent.

In the meantime Marshal Calandra was desperately trying to capture them. His mind was full of plans and traps that all failed. He would then retaliate by arresting friends or relatives. They were tortured with the "box" and then accused of invented crimes.

Turiddu's patience had reached its limit. He spread the rumor

*My Brother, Salvatore Giuliano*

Marianna Giuliano in her separatist uniform during three moments of the electoral campaign.

*My Brother, Salvatore Giuliano*

that he would kill Calandra. The Marshal knew that my brother would keep his promise. He always kept his word! As the days went by, tension mounted and fear had caught hold of everyone.

No one was arrested and no one saw him anymore walking through town. The few times he did, he would drive in an armored vehicle. He did not have the courage of going to see his wife and children in Palermo because he feared an ambush along the way. He went only once inside a tank.

The news spread quickly and he had become the fool of the town. He deserved it seeing all the bad he had done to so many innocent people. The Marshal could not bear the situation any longer and he asked for meeting with my brother. He asked Stefano Mannino, the interim mayor of the town, for help. He knew he had been elected thanks to my brother. But the mayor refused.

Once this attempt had failed, he went to my Uncle Antonino Lombardo, my mother's brother. But he too said that he did not know where my brother was hiding. He then realized that the only person in the world that could help him was my mother. He knew that he loved her very much.

One day at the beginning of August 1946, around one o'clock in the afternoon, while everyone was home for the incredible heat, we saw him come into our home. My mother feared that he had come to arrest us again and started to attack him verbally. But he closed the door behind him and motioned to her to calm down. He said he come to talk in peace.

My father was there too. We hesitantly let him sit down. The Marshal was embarrassed and excited. When my mother asked him the reason for his undesired visit, he fell to his knees crying. He hugged my mother's legs. We all looked at each other full of amazement, but we were also glad to see the man that had done so much harm to our family and the town crying.

After a few minutes he started to talk and whimper:

"Donna Maria! My life is in your hands! You must help me! I'm a father! Your son hates me! He let me know that he's going to kill me! Did you hear of the trick he did to me on April 1st? He thinks I'm the one who arrested you, but it's not true! It was Marshal Pinzino in Palermo!"

"Who gave him the address?" I said.

"It was you! To hit my brother indirectly!"

"When I receive orders, I can't disobey!"

"Get up, I'm not the Virgin Mary!" said my mother. "There are many ways to carry out an order! If my son hates you, it's not only because of me and my daughter! The real reason is that you are ruining a lot of people in Montelepre!"

"What can the relatives of those men enrolled in the E.V.I.S. do? The truth is that you couldn't accept the general pardon. So you've accused them for other crimes!"

"It wasn't my idea! I just carried out superior orders! I want to clear the situation with Turiddu!"

"I want to meet him! I'll go wherever he wants, whenever, even disarmed!"

"Very well! I'll tell him you came!" answered my mother dryly as she pointed to the door.

Two days later we received Turiddu's message. He told us he was in contrada "Mazza Martino", about a kilometer away from town. Of course, it was an implicit invitation to reach him. We did so about an hour later.

"Turiddu, my son, do it for me! I'm sure that he has learnt the lesson!"

He adored our mother. He knew how much she worried and suffered for him. After thinking a few seconds, he answered:

"Since he has come to speak to you, I'll give the meeting he wants!"

Some of the men there interrupted the discussion. They said that the Marshal had gone too far and that it was his fault if they were forced to hide. They said he deserved being killed not once, but a hundred times.

Turiddu silenced them:

"Mind your own business! I know what I'm doing!" He then turned to our mother again:

"Tell Uncle Antonino that I will meet him as soon as he receives my message!"

We went home.

My Uncle Antonino informed the Marshal and a week later he was given the necessary instructions. He was to walk along Corso "Di Bella" and wait for a car to come and pick him up. The Marshal was scared to death and did as he was told.

After a while he was invited to climb on board a black car that then drove off towards Palermo. After 500 meters it stopped just outside of town to pick up my Uncle Antonino Lombardo. The Marshal gave him his gun and said it was the only weapon he had on him.

The car drove for four kilometers and reached contrada "Cippi", where my uncle noticed a piece of yellow and red cloth on a rush

Col. Giuliano with Gaspare Pisciotta and Salvatore Passatempo (Foto Scafidi).

along the road. That was the signal. He told the driver to stop the car. The Marshal, my uncle and the driver went up a hill near Mount "Saraceno".

Two men with machineguns came out from behind a shack hidden in the green vegetation. One of them greeted the Marshal and said:

"Wait. The colonel is coming!"

It was about 10.30 in the morning. The temperature was already 30°C. The Marshal was sweating and was looking around worriedly and impatiently.

But Turiddu was there.

He had been there since his arrival. He took advantage of a moment of distraction and came out from behind the shack. As soon as he saw him, he fell down to his knees and he crawled a few meters on the ground in sign of submission. He lifted his eyes up, he saw that many armed men were around him and looking at him with anger. Only their obedience towards my brother stopped them from filling him with lead.

The Marshal's heart was full of terror and he exclaimed:
"You're all here!"
"So it's true what they say in town!"
"Don't kill me! I'm unarmed!"
"Marshal, you won't fool me!" answered Turiddu.
"I know you're unarmed, but I wouldn't trust you even if you were naked!" He smiled to him and gave him a hand to stand up. He kissed our uncle and greeted the driver. After asking for news about us, he took the Marshal arm in arm behind the house.

They sat on the dry grass and their backs against the wall of the shack.

"So Marshal, what have you got to say?"
"You hate me so much because you haven't been informed well!"
"I didn't arrest your mother and sister!"
"It's not just for that!" answered Turiddu. "You're ruining the whole town! Too many innocent people are paying for nothing!"
"We'll see in court, if they're innocent! If they're innocent they'll be acquitted!"
"Lower your voice! This isn't your office, where you can shout at poor people! I'm the boss here!"
"I admire all those who have the guts to come up here in the mountains to fight against me! But I can't stand abuses against meek and defenseless people! I can't let you treat the innocent the way you do! If you come by the hundreds to fight against me I don't care! I

even understand you because you're paid to do so by the government! It's human for me to defend myself because I'm no coward! But what can I say of you who fight against the weak because you're sure of winning?"

The Marshal was silent and he stayed there with this head lowered. He then started to speak softly and changed the subject of the discussion:

"I heard they had proposed you to leave the country? Why didn't you go to America?"

"I'm not the type of man who abandons his friends in a moment of need. I decided to stay for the struggle for independence! If I fail, patience! Anyway I prefer dying than emigrating!"

"You've been fooled by the politicians! They're the true culprits of this mess! They're only scoundrels who wouldn't help you if you were brought in front of a court!"

"We'll see who will have the last say in the end!" answered Turiddu. "My brother Giuseppe is innocent. You had him arrested for the homicide of Orlando Grippi, but I killed him!"

"If it's true then your brother will soon be freed!" replied the Marshall.

"Another thing: tell Brigadier Rossi to let go my relatives. Each time one of my relatives passes through "Bellolampo", he stops them, shuts them in jail and keeps them there until he receives information from Montelepre! Of course, he knows who my relatives are. Or does he think that all those from Montelepre are wanted? No one wants to stop him from doing his duty, but it's not right that he takes advantage of his uniform to abuse people who mind their own business! Tell him that he saved himself once on the "Nocella" bridge, he won't the next time! Tell the same thing to Brigadier Ferrara. It's better if he leaves Montelepre! He's treating the people and especially the women badly! Tell him! Because if he goes on like this, he'll find himself with a bullet straight through his head!"

"I can't promise anything! You know I can't keep all of my men always under control! But I'll tell them what you said and I'll try to satisfy your requests."

"Marshall, let's return to serious business! I know you haven't come only to explain your behavior! I know you want a truce! I'll accept as long as you ease the pressure on the town and stop hunting down my men! As far as I am concerned, I promise that I will shoot only for self-defense and in case of need!"

The Marshall accepted the agreement. They got up, shook hands and the officer made way for home.

An absolutely calm week went by, until one morning Turiddu

was visited by two men. By means of intermediaries they had arrived in Sagana. They were sent by the relatives of Baron Agnello who had been kidnapped.

They brought him a letter with a request: he was invited to treat the hostage well because he was ill. My brother found out that someone was using his name for his dirty business. He took three of his best men and went to search for the hostage.

They looked for him the whole day long without success. At sunset they were tired and hungry. They reached a farmstead inhabited by an old couple who welcomed them warmly.

They were all famished. The poor couple shared all they had with them: a piece of bread, some cheese and a bottle of wine. The woman was sorry she had nothing else to offer. She went to milk the only goat they had to offer them more. She hit it on the back trying to make stand still. Despite her toiling, there was very little milk.

She saw that it was not enough so she went and killed the only rooster of her hen house. She lit the fire in the wood oven and served it to her guests.

Turiddu was moved by so much generosity. The next day he sent the couple two mules full of supplies.

In the meantime many police and carabinieri had come to Montelepre. They were about to launch one of their usual spectacular raids with tanks and dog squads to search for the hostage. The Marshall remembered his agreement and warned me about the raid. He was coming to our house but I met him in the street and said:

"Try to warn your brother! We're moving towards Mount 'Calcerame'! They've informed us that Baron Agnello is being held there. I ran off to find one of the boys used as messengers. I was lucky to find one immediately.

I went home with him and I wrote a message for Turiddu. I gave him our mule. My brother was ready to leave for a new search, when the messenger arrived with the message. He and another three men went immediately to Mount "Calcerame".

Inside the shack they found what they were looking for. Turiddu was surprised and disappointed to see that the man guarding the hostage was one of the men of Antonino Terranova's squad. He was one of his men!

He took the baron and they left quickly. A few minutes later the area was swarmed with police and soldiers. Turiddu and his men watched the scene with their binoculars from the nearby hill. While the Carabinieri and the police tried to beat each other and take all the merit of the operation, they left without being noticed.

The baron's family had been asked 50 million Lire for the ransom. Turiddu let him go without paying anything. The Baron was grateful for what he had done and sent him 20 million Lire. My brother split the money amongst the men that organized the kidnap and he did not keep any money for himself. Encouraged by the outcome of the operation, even Giuseppe Passatempo's squad followed suit and kidnapped the son of Giuseppe Gulì, the owner of a textile factory.

He too was released after his family had asked Turiddu to help them. But these and other incidents greatly disappointed Turiddu. Owing to the cease-fire and to the splitting of his men into squads, he risked losing control of the situation.

He summoned a meeting in Sagana and he said to them:

"For some time now I am not satisfied by your conduct! You stayed with me because we were supposed to organize an army to continue our fight, but you have forgotten or you're pretending to have forgotten our common cause!"

"Someone here has forgotten who gives the orders here! All these initiatives must be discussed first with me. I'm tired of being held responsible for everything that happens in the province of Palermo! From now on whoever disobeys will be punished!"

My brother had a strong sense of responsibility. He was the first to make known those actions and operations that he was actually responsible for. He wanted to avoid that someone could be accused instead of him and that his actions could be confused with those of others.

Of course, when he did not receive money only from volunteer financiers. He was sometimes forced to kidnap someone to finance his operations. But you could recognize his style. Furthermore, he would distribute the money amongst the poor, the needy and families who had relatives in prison. He would always attach a message to the present:

"May Divine Providence always be with you. S.G."

The beneficiaries would come to our house to express their gratitude. During this period he wrote an open letter addressed to the Prime Minister and Foreign Minister Alcide De Gasperi. He explained the reasons behind his actions saying that he did not do it with criminal intentions but he was trying to forward a social revolution:

**"In the name of a great social revolution and of human understanding, awakened by the tears of people afflicted by misery, and having seen that the reforms discussed by the Cabinet are far from being introduced, I claim the right to take from the**

**rich to give to the poor and to those who have nothing and die of the most terrifying of deaths: hunger."**

But as he spoke, wrote and acted guided by his ideals, the newspapers continued to accuse him of new crimes.

The robbery of the Bank of Sicily, the assault against a train on the Palermo-Trapani railway line, the kidnapping of the jeweler Fiorentino, the Lupo homicide, the Orestano kidnap, and many, many more. Light was shed on almost all these crimes in court. As the proceedings of the trials show, the real culprits were found.

At the beginning of September 1946, three young men with a Northern accent came to our house. They told my mother that they had been enrolled by Turiddu and they asked for food. We let them come in the name of Christian charity. My sister and I cooked for them. An hour later, once they had already gone, the police broke into our house and arrested my mother and my sister.

I escaped by rushing out of the door leading to the yard. I was forced to hide and reach my brother in the mountains. I stayed with him for ten days. He then found me a safe refuge in the home of trusted friends.

During the interrogation of my mother and sister, it was clear that the guests were carabinieri in disguise. They accused my family of having enrolled them. This trick cost my mother and my sister six months in jail. I was lucky and managed to get away with it. I was sent a warrant to appear before the court. With the necessary guarantees and the assistance of a lawyer, I went for the interrogation. I was acquitted of all charges.

In the same period, owing to the meeting with my brother, Marshall Calandra was transferred to Delia in the province of Caltanissetta. The episode was considered to be "dishonorable" by his superiors. The news was welcomed with great satisfaction by the townsfolk who could now sigh with relief. Calm had returned and Turiddu came home often.

He missed our family members in jail. He passed hours and hours in his room studying battle plans. He was hoping to reorganize an army to conquer Sicily by force. But he did not have the means to put his plans into actions.

He tried to establish a contact with the American headquarters, but he could not find the right intermediaries. At times he managed to talk on the phone with some senior officers, but their contacts were limited to mutual sympathy.

Help was given by the interim Archbishop of Monreale, since the parish of Montelepre was under his jurisdiction. The prelate succeeded in organizing a meeting with a senior officer of the American army.

I do not remember the exact date. But I am sure that it was in "Villa Renda" (in the vicinity of Pioppo-Giacalone) between September and October 1946. I know that they reached a sort of agreement. The officer promised to provide him with a large load of weapons against the payment of 150 million Lire. The weapons would be consigned in Sfax in Tunisia. From there Turiddu would transport them on board fishing boats from Mazara. He gave the officer a down payment of 10 million Lire, but he never saw the weapons. The officer disappeared with the money.

At the end of the hot summer of 1946, another extraordinary event took place in Montelepre. For the first time in the history of Sicily a cardinal went to visit a small town, especially one like ours, which was considered by the government a den of rebels and the last stronghold of Sicilian separatism.

Two days before, Ernesto Ruffini announced his visit with a telegram. The mayor and the town council were excited and rushed to organize the event.

His Eminence arrived in the afternoon of the next Sunday on board a Lancia "Ardea". The crimson of his habit exalted his person. The town's band welcomed him with a triumphal march. As the notes rung through the air, an uproar of applause broke out.

The event attracted people from the nearby towns. The town's main road was packed with people. When he came out of the car, they took him in triumph to the church. The people celebrated as they followed him in procession. The Cardinal blessed the crowds gathered in prayer. When he climbed to the pulpit, he started to speak and his voice rang clearly through the naves. It reached deep into hearts and filled them with hope.

"I have come to bring you peace!"

"No more pain and tears in Montelepre, but peace and prosperity!"

"The prisons will be opened: your husbands, brothers, and fathers will be free!"

"Happiness will return to your homes!"

He said beautiful words, but everyone asked how were these promises to be kept. The crowd stood around him and begged:

*"N'aiutassi ca li sbirazzi ni cunzumaru li famigghi!"* (Please help us, because the cops have ruined our families!)

"I can help you only if Giuliano and his men surrender! I would like to speak to his father to be informed of his intentions!"

Someone went to look for him to take him to the Cardinal. In the meantime, followed by the crowd, he went to the home of the Galluzzo family, the town's former *Podestà*.

When my father arrived, he welcomed him with his arms wide open. They went to speak in private. The Cardinal repeated the offer to my father. He answered:

"My son will never surrender, nor let the others do so! These young men have fought for their land. They have the right too enjoy the general pardon, because they committed political crimes! So, it's total freedom or they'll stay in the mountains!"

"It's better than spending their life in prison!"

But the Cardinal replied: "If they surrender, I will help them and in a few years they're out of prison!"

"I'm sorry! It's freedom or nothing!" replied my father.

"But what am I to do? I promised the people that everything would finish!"

"You made a mistake, Your Excellency. A life in the mountains is better than rotting in prison!"

"You have no idea of what a prison is! It's easy to say that in a few years they're out! But I know what it means! It's better to die a thousand times than die day after day!"

At the end of their meeting, the Cardinal went to the town hall where he received presents and cheers. He said some more nice words. The whole setting had worked perfectly. He was the hero of the day.

A moment of rest for Giuliano.

Turiddu in the fields.

Chapter XIV

# HURRAY FOR THE BRIDE AND THE GROOM!

Since he had escaped from Calandra and Santucci, Gaspare Pisciotta was feeling worse and worse. The damage to his lung after his jump from the bridge had worsened and had become tuberculosis. The hard life in the mountain was bad for him, especially since he was forced to continuously move from place to place.

He was becoming paler and paler and weaker and weaker by the day. Turiddu could not watch and remain indifferent. He was a friend and a comrade of so many battles. And there he was withering away slowly before his eyes.

He took him to be visited by the best doctors and to be cured with various therapies. But there was little to do about it. The x-rays were all to clear: the tuberculosis gave no signs of regressing.

The chief physician of a hospital in Palermo told my brother that there was only one medicine that could stop the illness: streptomycin. But it was impossible to find it neither in Italy nor in Sicily, not even in the black market.

Turiddu wrote to some friends of his in Brooklyn. After twenty days, he received a substantial amount from the United States. Gaspare's mother, Donna Rosalia, was overwhelmed with joy. She told all the women of her neighborhood:

"God bless him! God must reward him for what he has done for my son!"

Turiddu himself injected the medicine into him. The patient was grateful for all he had done. He knew he owed him his life. The medicine was working. His conditions were improving by the day, despite he could not rest nor have the peace and tranquillity he needed.

As the days went by, he started to recover all his strength and paleness vanished from his face. One day he proposed Turiddu to become blood brothers to show him all his gratitude. The origins of this rite go back to the mist of time. It consisted in making a cut in the left forearm and letting the blood flow out. The two cuts were put one over the other to symbolize the mixing of the blood that become one. In that moment the two "brothers" would swear eternal loyalty and then seal their pact. From that moment they symbolically were blood brothers.

After the elections of June 2, 1946 our cousin Salvatore Lombardo had moved to Tunisia. He was the only person that my brother would trust. He missed him very much, but especially he felt the need of someone he could really trust. So he accepted Gaspare Pisciotta's proposal and became his blood brother.

The news that Turiddu needed the streptomycin to cure his friend had mobilized all those who had relatives in the United States. That miraculous medicine, almost unknown and so rare to find, was soon easy to find. All you had to do was pay and you could find it anywhere. The task of obtaining it was entrusted to the pharmacist Salvatore Baiada. He had worked for so long in Montelepre and he knew everyone and everything about our town. He had moved to Partinico and, upon request of my brother, he gave free medicine to all those who could not pay for it. Every now and then Turiddu would go meet him and pay him for all the medicine.

In the meantime in Rome, pending the approval of Sicilian autonomy on the part of the Constituent Assembly, the immobility of the government gave rise to great concerns on the actual application of the Sicilian Statute approved with the decree of May 15, 1946. This threat was avoided thanks to the new High Commissioner, Salvaggi, who had succeeded Aldisio.

He managed to get through all the red tape and difficulties. During the Cabinet meeting of November 28, 1946 the go-ahead was given for the coming into force of the Statute. It was also decided to announce the election of 90 regional assembly members. The date for the elections was set for April 20, 1947.

The news awoke the aspirations of most Sicilians. The separatist movement too was getting ready for the event despite the internal contrasts (Antonino Varvaro had resigned from the position of secretary of the movement). The leaders of the party organized the 3rd congress to be held in Taormina on January 31, 1947.

A few days before Antonino Varvaro had published an article in a Messina newspaper. He declared to have summoned an interim committee on January 25th. It had deliberated the continuing of the existence of a Sicilian separatist organization by founding the M.I.S.D.R. (Movement for the Independence of the Democratic Republic of Sicily).

This was the first step towards the final split with the other leaders of the movement, who had joined monarchist faction headed by Finocchiaro Aprile. On the eve of the regional elections, the M.I.S. presented itself in two different and contrasting groups, thus helping the other parties running in the election.

At the end of February 1947, my mother and sister Giuseppina were released. The elections were at their acme. The release of my family members coincided with the return to Montelepre of Marshall Calandra.

Col. Paolantonio realized that each time an inquiry had to be carried out in our town they needed his consultancy. So he assigned him the command of the mobile unit. To give proof of his capacity he started the raids again but he could not ignore the agreement he had made before.

So my brother and his men were seen everywhere. They would appear and disappear when you would least expect it. You would never find him where the raids were being carried out. And if they were, they were there to keep the soldiers under control ready to intervene.

During one of these raids, three carabinieri caught a 15-year-old boy who was going to Sagana. He had a kilo and a half of bread and a pot full of boiled fava beans. The soldiers were convinced that he was taking food to some criminal and they started to beat him. The boy was crying and tried to convince them that he was taking the food to his father, a poor farmer working in a field nearby. But they would not believe him and they continued to beat him.

Suddenly a fierce blast of machinegun fire raised the dust near their feet. A few seconds later Turiddu appeared on a nearby rise. The carabinieri recognized him and ran away to town. The boy cheered up. When Turiddu went up to him, the boy vented his anger.

"Three men against a boy!"

He then let him drink from his flask and cleaned his swollen face with a wet handkerchief. He stayed there with him until he recovered from the trauma. He gave him five thousand Lire for his father. The boy hid the money in a sock, thanked him and went away.

Episodes of this kind were normal. More and more often those who suffered these abuses would call the name of my brother.

Meanwhile the date of the elections, set for April 20, 1947, was approaching. The campaign was at its acme and the candidates resorted to all means to win their votes. The monarchists, allied with the faction of the movement headed by Finocchiaro Aprile, asked for my brother's support. Alliata, Leone Marchesano, Cusumano Geloso were trying everything to obtain his help. They met him a number of times.

Although he did not break off contacts with them, he decided to support Nino Varvaro, the leader of the newborn M.I.S.D.R. He was the only one to remain consistent to the original ideology of the party, aiming at Sicily's independence. He was the only one in favor of the survival of the E.V.I.S. as its armed wing and headed by Turiddu. Furthermore, he was the only one with leftist ideas.

As a matter of fact he had excellent relations with the leaders of the P.C.I. (the Italian Communist Party). The only reason of contrast between them was the Communist Party's opposition to any idea against Italian unity. There were no other divergent positions. Turiddu felt to belong to the people, to the poor people. The P.C.I. fought to safeguard the interests of the poor.

Since the failure to conquer Sicily by force, my brother started to share the idea that the only hope for the Island's revival was that of creating autonomous administrative and legislative bodies. With Turiddu's support to the M.I.S.D.R., his campaigning started again.

Once again I wore my red and yellow uniform. I did my best during the campaign, which was almost a replica of the previous elections.

After the general pardon of June 1946 I had gotten engaged with Pasquale Sciortino. This time I went from town to town together with Nunzia Micciché, who would soon have become my mother-in-law, and with Varvaro's wife, Signora Jolanda, whom I would call mamma Jolanda. My rallies were fiery and I would end them all with the following words:

"My Sicilian Brothers! The future of our Island is in your hands! Don't vote for those who make empty promises. Vote only those men who have proven their loyalty to the interests of the Sicilian people and of Sicily. Vote for Nino Varvaro!"

Unfortunately I saw that there was not the same enthusiasm I had met ten months before. The legacy of the M.I.S. was divided amongst all those parties, which had won the support of most of the electorate. There were many that were satisfied simply with autonomy. Pasquale and I decided to get married.

Turiddu had opposed the wedding. He wanted to avoid that, once Pasquale had become his brother-in-law, he would have been involved in the persecution against our family. But Pasquale did not surrender.

He asked for the help of some relatives and influential friends who succeeded in overcoming my brother's perplexity. Pasquale and I set the date of the wedding and we went to the town hall. We went together with my mother, Salvatore Gaglio, my brother-in-law's brother, and Francesco Gaglio (Reversino). The two men were the witnesses.

The mayor filled in the Wedding Certificate and read it to those present. Everything went normally without any surprises or incidents.

The notice was hung on the notice board before the eyes of everyone. In the meantime we applied for the authorization of the diocese of Monreale to hold the wedding ceremony at home. The task was assigned to Fr. Giuseppe Di Bella. He was the E.V.I.S. military chaplain and a firm supporter of independence. He personally went to the bishop.

Monsignor Filippi smiled complacently and gave his approval. The wedding notices were made public, first in the church of San Cipirello (Pasquale's hometown) and then in Montelepre. We set the date of the wedding for April 24, 1947.

We would have had all time to finish the campaign and to see the outcome. My relatives suggested to get married at home so that Turiddu could lead me to the altar. According to the town's custom, the bride was to be led to the altar by a relative.

The nuns of the Santa Rosalia parish, the abbess herself and her assistant, Sister Gioconda, saw to preparing the altar. They wanted to express their gratitude to my brother who had donated large amounts of money and entire wagonloads of wheat for the orphans of the orphanage.

They covered the altar with a beautiful tablecloth embroidered with threads of gold. They decorated it with silver candelabras, candles and flowers. The altar was set up on the first floor. They arranged it in my parent's bedroom after taking away the bed.

My mother went to visit and invite all our closest relatives in the morning of the ceremony's day. Towards seven o'clock in the evening the guests wearing their best suits started to arrive. There were many men around our house. On the terrace and the roofs of the nearby houses several machineguns had been arranged. At each corner and window, along all the roads leading to house, armed men were positioned.

It was a mere formality. About a hundred Carabinieri were stationed at the time in Montelepre, but they had to watch out for my brother's curfew. That evening no one of them dared to go out in the streets or to bother us.

After half an hour all our relatives were waiting in a room on the ground floor. Someone started to get impatient:

"What are we waiting for? When will the ceremony start?"

At about 8.30, one of the lookouts came in and announced:

"The Colonel's coming!"

Some of the guests found out that I was getting married at the last minute. Turiddu came in together with the squad leaders and his most trusted men: Frank Mannino, Gaspare Pisciotta, Salvatore and Giuseppe Passatempo, Nunzio Badalamenti, Rosario Candela and Salvatore Ferreri.

At his arrival they turned to look at him and the crowd opened to make way. The guests started to whisper. Turiddu shook hands, smiled to all the relatives and hugged our parents. He then went upstairs into his room on the second floor.

Everything was ready for him to wash up and get dressed. He wore a light gray suit in pure lambswool, a silk shirt, a dark red tie and shiny black shoes. As he was getting dressed in his room, I was doing the same in mine. Three friends of mine were helping me to put on the wedding dress and to do my hair.

My future husband too was very elegant. He was wearing a dark gray suit, a white shirt and a light gray tie. He was waiting in the room on the ground floor. He was together with my mother, my sister and some relatives. Turiddu finished getting dressed quickly and came downstairs to see the bridegroom. He shook his hand and hugged him:

"This is my present for you!" As he said these words, he took off a ring he had with a large diamond.

Pasquale was moved and excited. As he did so, he said:

"I'm especially grateful for your gift! It means a lot to me!"

As Pasquale showed it to all the relatives who gazed at the jewel admiringly, one of the bridesmaids came to announce that I was ready.

It was 9.30.

On the first floor Fr. Di Bella was lighting the candles and putting on the paraments. Turiddu came upstairs to my room.

He looked at me intensely for a few seconds: he was deeply moved. For a moment I thought that he was shy owing to the presence of the bridesmaids. But his face lit up with joy and said:

"You're incredibly beautiful!"

He took me by the arm and together we went down the stairs. We were welcomed by a warm applause. All the guests were moved, because Turiddu had had the joy of seeing me get married although he was an outlaw.

We slowly went towards the altar, where Pasquale took his place near the altar. Turiddu went to the other side of the room. He took his accordion and started to play Schubert's "Ave Maria".

He played those notes with great skill. The atmosphere seemed so heavenly. My friends were in ecstasy. They sighed, as they desired him intensely with their eyes. Turiddu was handsome, strong, and marvelous. But dressed as he was, his sex appeal was multiplied a hundredfold. He was even more manly and fascinating.

The ceremony continued in this magic atmosphere. During his homily, Fr. Di Bella gave the usual advice, he explained our mutual duties and cited the relevant articles of the Civil Code. At the end of the ceremony, all the guests came to kiss the couple according to customs. Turiddu too kissed us and greeted respectfully the priest, who took him by the arm and said:

"Of course, you know the results of the elections. You must have realized by now that the party has lost the race! Why don't you leave everything and everyone and go away?"

"I'll think about it. . . . I'll think about it, father!"

As soon as the priest finished taking off his paraments, we went down to the ground floor and refreshments were served. One of our relatives went around the room with a tray full of pastries and invited the guests to help themselves. Another guest was serving wine and liqueurs.

In those days there were no music bands or stereo equipment. All we had was a gramophone and old records. But Turiddu had hired two musicians for the occasion. One played the mandolin, the other the guitar. My brother joined in with the accordion.

After toasting with our relatives, Turiddu and I opened the dances with a waltz. He moved on the floor with great confidence, grace and speed. The other couples started to dance together with us. Turiddu was the tallest. With his solid build he towered above all the guests.

At the end of the dance, he started to play again. After playing some songs with the others, he stopped the music and whispered something into the ears of the musicians. He started to play and sing a song he had written for me. His beautiful voice rang sweetly and passionately:

| | |
|---|---|
| Sei bella, | You are beauteous, |
| Sei splendida, | You are splendid |
| di bianco vestita, | All dressed in white, |
| la fronte coperta | With your face covered |
| da un poetico velo, | By a poetic veil, |

| | |
|---|---|
| in mezzo ai profumi | In the midst of the scents |
| e agli omaggi di festa, | And the joys of the feast, |
| il suo cuore | His heart |
| s'infiammò per te. | Was set on fire by you. |
| | |
| Ma ancora la vedo più bella | But I see you even more beautiful |
| la gioia sui veli rialza | Joy below your veil lifts |
| il tuo piccolo piede | Your small foot |
| simpatico e snello, | So nice and slim, |
| allora il tuo cuore | Your heart |
| ti parla d'amore. | Speaks to you of love. |
| O vaga fanciulla, | Oh vague Maiden, |
| o angelo divino, | Oh divine Angel, |
| nel cielo fu scritto | In the heavens it is written |
| in un libro divino, | in the Divine Book, |
| che un giorno sposa | that one day |
| dovevi essere tu. | You were to wed. |

My mother was moved. The tears were running down her sweet face. That tall and unlucky man was the light of her eyes. She seldom could spend an hour of joy with him. He shared that great love with the same intensity and, when he had the chance, he would overwhelm her with kindness. At the end of the song, she went up to him silently. Turiddu hugged her and had her sit next to him. They sat their for a minutes without saying a word.

Turiddu saw that she was looking to the other side of the room. In a corner there was a man who seemed to be a shady type of individual.

"Mamma, why are you looking at him? Don't you know him?"

"Oh! No! I know that he's Giuseppe Passatempo! But his face looks so. . . !"

"A shady type, isn't he?" answered Turiddu.

"I always have to keep him under control, because he's always risking to get into trouble! Don't you see how mean his face is? His heart is as black as night! We call him the HANGMAN!"

"So, why don't you send him away?" asked my mother.

"Because I've got very few men! In battle he fights like ten men. He's as courageous as a lion, aggressive as a tiger and as dangerous as a snake!"

The party lasted till five in the morning. At dawn Turiddu put on his usual clothes and said goodbye to those who were still there. He gathered his men and went to Sagana.

Partinico: a slogan for Nino Varvaro (Foto Martinez).

Giuliano's mother too is active in the political struggle.

1947! Marianna Giuliano wears the separatist uniform again.

CHAPTER XV

# MY BROTHER
# AND PORTELLA DELLE GINESTRE

The desolate day I am about to talk about was the main cause that obscured and dimmed the fame, the ideals, the generosity and love that my brother felt for the Sicilian people. For decades it has been exploited politically. No one had any interest at all to shed light on what actually happened. It was easy to attribute all the responsibility to my brother.

To make the whole episode clearer, I will leave out some of the dates to summarize the main cause. As stated previously, owing to the split within the M.I.S. during the third party convention in Taormina on January 31, 1947, Antonino Varvaro had set up another party called the M.I.S.D.R. (the Movement for the Independence of the Democratic Republic of Sicily).

When Turiddu learnt of the news, he tried to mediate between the two groups to avoid the split in the movement. He tried to convince them that they had to put aside their personal interests and rivalries and think only of the interests of the Sicilian people. But his efforts brought to nothing.

While Varvaro and his supporters seemed ready to reconsider their stance, Finocchiaro Aprile and the others of the monarchist faction left his appeal go unheeded. It was obvious that Turiddu would have chosen to help Varvaro during the electoral campaign. He knew him for many years now. He had been his lawyer during the trial for the killing of the carabiniere in Quarto Molino and he also shared his ideas.

In February 1947 Varvaro sent a message to my brother. He invited him to meet some leaders of the Italian Communist Party with whom he and other members of the M.I.S.D.R. had established contacts. It was a necessary step because many Sicilian communists shared the opinion that Sicily had to break away from the rest of Italy. The leading figure of the party was Girolamo Li Causi.

To overcome his doubts and perplexities, Varvaro had organized a meeting. He would thus have the opportunity of personally dis-

*My Brother, Salvatore Giuliano*

Marianna Giuliano and Pasquale Sciortino on the day of their wedding.

cussing the details for a possible agreement. The meeting was to be held in villa Surisi, an edifice located on the outskirts of Borgetto and owned by a nephew of Varvaro. The participants were Varvaro and Girolamo Li Causi on the one hand and Turiddu and two friends on the other.

On that occasion they spoke clearly of the role of the Communist Party in Western Sicily. At the time it had joined with other forces of the left to form the "People's Bloc". The agreement reached regarded the election of Varvaro. Many communists in the towns of Alcamo, Piana degli Albanesi, Altofonte, San Giuseppe Jato, San Cipirello, Termini Imerese, Bagheria and others would have voted for the M.I.S.D.R. and Varvaro. That was the agreement reached with Li Causi.

Turiddu, on his part, would have done the same in the area he controlled. Furthermore, he had guaranteed my involvement in the campaign and promised he would cover its expenses. After the first meeting there were two other meetings with Li Causi to define the details of the agreement: one was held in a place called "Lo Zucco", the other in Palermo.

Faithful as always to his commitments, Turiddu kept his promise. He paid many millions for the renting of trucks, cars, amplifiers, posters, leaflets, luncheons and banquets. Many of Varvaro's votes were the fruit of the efforts of my brother, his men and myself: he obtained 2612 votes in Partinico, 1521 in Montelepre, 443 in Giardinello, 508 in Borgetto, etc.

The results of the elections of April 20, 1947 were made public on April 23. They were disappointing for Turiddu and not only for him. I too shared his feelings. The towns that according to the agreement with Li Causi were supposed to give their full support to the M.I.S.D.R. thus making the most of the parallel electoral roll were much less than their worst expectations.

Nino Varvaro and the M.I.S.D.R. in the two constituencies where it had run, i.e. Catania and Palermo had obtained 19,542 votes tantamount to 1% of the total. Despite our support he had not been elected.

It was a moral and material defeat. Li Causi had betrayed us and Varvaro must have known from the outset. Turiddu had summoned him to Sagana immediately after my wedding. But his fatalistic and submissive behavior confirmed his suspects.

He clearly expressed his resignation and intentions to dissolve the party. He was thinking of joining a party of the left, as he actually did a few months later when he became a member of the Italian Communist Party.

My brother's doubts and perplexities on the agreement were now a reality. The two politicians had taken advantage of his idealism and his love for Sicily for their own interests. Their conduct could not be left unpunished!

We had lost our money and credibility. Li Causi had to give us an explanation. As for Varvaro, my brother had limited himself to chasing him away, but Li Causi had to explain why he did it. Turiddu wrote to him some letters, which were given to him by Gaetano Pantuso, one of his closest assistants, but he did not answer.

Li Causi's behavior exasperated my brother. On April 28th he sent him the last letter with the same messenger. He told him he would meet him at Portella delle Ginestre, where he would hold a rally on May 1st every year.

More than an appointment, it was a challenge. Turiddu wanted to capture him and make him confess what he had done. The crowd would then have judged him and decided his fate. He informed his men of his plans and told them when he handed the letter to Gaetano Pantuso that the time had come for him to get into politics and to run for a seat.

The man greeted him with the separatist salute, jumped onto the red motorcycle he had borrowed from a man named Remo Corrao and left for Palermo. Salvatore Ferreri, alias Fra' Diavolo, the informer sent by the police, who for a long time now had not carried out the tasks assigned to him by inspector MESSANA, secretly left the camp.

The news was too big. He had to TELL THE INSPECTOR. He went to Monreale, he picked up the first phone he could find and told him the news. Then he went to see the inspector in person to discuss what he was supposed to do.

But the inspector too did not keep the news for himself: he informed the local Mafia boss Calogero Vizzini and Carabinieri Colonel Giacinto Paolantonio. The inspector knew that Don Calò hated Turiddu, because he had denied his authority and because Turiddu had not allowed him and his men to commit their crimes in his area.

On his part Don Calogero realized that this could be the chance to make peace with Li Causi. In the past he had tried to stop him and even to kill him. But now that Li Causi was a leader of the Communist Party, doing him a favor meant obtaining his complete support.

Gaetano Pantuso gave the letter to Li Causi, but that very evening Col. Paolantonio warned him that if he went to Portella he would risk getting killed.

In the meantime Turiddu had summoned a meeting of all his men on April 30th. At the time he had a total of 40 men, 25 of whom were up on the mountain. Antonino Terranova and his whole squad were absent: Francesco Pisciotta, Francesco Abate Palma, Rosario Candela, Frank Mannino, Francesco Motisi, Giuseppe Sciortino and Angelo Taormina. Salvatore Passatempo and Antonino Cucinella were on a mission in the Trapani area.

Terranova's squad was for two days now near San Cipirello. They had been assigned the task of buying two mules and to get the supplies and ammunition ordered in that area. Besides these men, there were at least another one hundred. They had fought with him during the struggle for independence. The police did not know their names and so he did not call them for any reason and did not even mention their names.

At the meeting held in the afternoon of April 30th on the hill called Mount "Finocchiara" only 14 men including my brother were present: Salvatore Ferreri, Giuseppe Passatempo, Nunzio Badalamenti, Giuseppe Cucinella, Pietro Licari, Giuseppe Di Lorenzo, Salvatore Pecoraro, Giuseppe Pianelli, Fedele Pianelli, Castrenze Madonia, Tommaso Di Maggio, Giovanni Genovese, and Giuseppe Genovese.

Turiddu started with a brief speech:

"Picciotti! Tomorrow is May 1st and I need you for an operation in Portella! Some of you already know what it's all about! It won't be difficult. We just have to scare some people!"

As usual they all accepted, save for Tommaso Di Maggio and Giovanni Genovese. They were the eldest of the group and they did not want to go on that walk. Gaspare Pisciotta too was absent. He was still ill: he had been temporarily "discharged" with a million and two hundred thousand Lire.

While the meeting was being held in the mountain, my husband had felt ill during our honeymoon. He twisted with pain and his face turned blue. I feared for his life. I was so desperate. I sent for my mother who had gone to the bakery. Pasquale was feeling worse and worse. I went on to the balcony and started to cry for help. Many neighbors ran. Someone went to call Dr. Salsedo, the town's doctor.

The passers-by noted that something was happening at our house. My mother had been called and she rushed back home as fast as she could. When she came, she found the doctor there: he diagnosed an attack of appendicitis and had administered some sedatives.

Turiddu in the meantime was explaining his plan to his men. He traced the map of Portella delle Ginestre on a sheet of paper: it was in a large valley quite difficult to reach. The river Jato ran along one side of it. In that area more than a river it looked like a stream. To the south there are two hills with exotic sounding names: Pelavet (or Spiked) and Kumeta (or Comet). Probably their names came from the local dialect spoken in Piana degli Albanesi, located in the valley. It was founded around 1450. Its inhabitants are the direct descendents of a colony of Greek Albanians.

Turiddu decided to split his men into two squads: the 11 men there would go with him, while Antonino Terranova's squad would have positioned itself on the other side in case of an emergency. They were to leave for Portella at about 10 o'clock in the evening and to send immediately for the other squad that was to position itself at the feet of Mount Kumeta.

In Palermo another meeting was being held at almost the time. Inspector MESSANA, the Mafia boss CALOGERO VIZZINI and some members of the CHRISTIAN DEMOCRATS had prepared another plan, which had two targets. That year the PEOPLE'S BLOC had obtained the relative majority and the Christian Democrats could not take it. Although the alliance between Li Causi and Turiddu had failed, my brother's popularity was at its peak. If he were to run for an election, he was a great threat for those petty politicians, SERVANTS OF ROME, who could no longer continue to sell Sicily and the Sicilian people. He could have influenced political choices. Soon the Italian government would have been forced to grant Sicily independence. His popularity had to be destroyed and at the same time a political crisis was needed to avoid that the left reach power.

Calogero Vizzini would have taken care of the operations. It was not difficult to find men ready to do the job, but he needed also logistics. One of his men had been infiltrated amongst my brother's men: Giuseppe Passatempo!

In Sagana the weapons and ammunition were taken at the hour set. Turiddu gave orders to take only Breda caliber 6.5 automatic guns with three charges and some 1891 model rifles, but Giuseppe Passatempo, as suggested by Salvatore Ferreri, wanted also a Breda caliber 6.5 machinegun. He was loading it on the mule with the other weapons, but Turiddu noticed it:

"What do you need it for? To make noise! Along the road you risk making undesired encounters!" he answered. "You head is harder than a stone! Discussing with you is useless! Anyway, you're not loading it on the mule. If you want it, carry it yourself!"

Giuseppe Passatempo made an angry face and answered rudely:

"OK, I'll take it! I prefer saying .... who knows? Better than saying.... if I had known!"

Turiddu's squad reached Portella at seven o'clock in the morning. The whole valley was deserted. They climbed for a hundred meters up the "Spiked " hill, they lit the fire and prepared some coffee. A few minutes had gone by when one of the lookouts saw four armed men. They were dressed like hunters and they were approaching their camp. The lookout blew a short whistle. Two other men were alerted by the signal. They caught the intruders on the flank and disarmed them. They asked for their documents to check that they were not police officers in disguise. Their names were Salvatore Fusco, Gaetano Cuccia, Giorgio Sirchia and Antonio Riolo. They said they were hunters who had taken advantage of the holiday to go hunting for hares. They were led near the camp, tied and seated near a boulder. They were left there under the surveillance of Pietro Licari.

It was about nine o'clock when the first people arrived. They came on foot, by bicycle, on motorcycles, by horse and in decorated wagons.

Like every year for many years now the workers from Piana degli Albanesi, San Giuseppe Jato and San Cipirello would meet at Portella delle Ginestre to celebrate on May $1^{st}$. It was a political and trade union event. During the feast lamb meat would be roasted, there was plenty of drinking and singing as well as political rallies. That May 1, 1947 was a special occasion thanks to the excellent results of the PEOPLE'S BLOC in the whole of Sicily. At about ten o'clock more than three thousand people had already gathered. You could hear the singing and laughing. The celebrations had begun: about a dozen fires were burning and the people were crowding around them as the women prepared the food.

In the meantime a truck had arrived from San Giuseppe Jato and about a hundred meters away from Portella it was making a U-turn. Once it finished, six men got off that truck and advanced disorderly. They went to sit amongst the rocks at about ten meters away from fires.

From the ridge Turiddu looked over the valley with his binoculars. He was waiting for the arrival of the other squad and the speaker. But Girolamo Li Causi NEVER came! He had sent a young communist and trade union activist, Francesco Renda, to speak officially on his behalf. But even he did not go to Portella. A "fortunate" breakdown of his motorcycle with sidecar had left him blocked in the small town of Altofonte. At least that was what he said.

Of course, these things were discovered when it was all over. My brother was unaware of it all. Around 10.15 all hope in the arrival of the other squad was lost. It was then discovered that they were blocked just below San Cipirello in contrada "Balletto" because of the presence of many carabinieri.

While Turiddu looked towards the Kumeta hill with his binoculars hoping to see the other squad, a small group of people broke away from the crowd. They climbed unto a slab of rock called the BARBATO PODIUM. On May 1st of every year Nicola Barbato would climb onto that slab of stone to speak to the workers.

Giacomo Schirò, the secretary of the local office of the Socialist party in San Giuseppe Jato too had waited in vain for his official speaker. The feast without an official speech would have lost its traditional meaning. So he decided to take his place. The crowd was getting restless. Some started to walk up to the podium.

Turiddu could not see him in his face. He was positioned behind the speaker. He was convinced that he was Girolamo Li Causi. So he shouted:

"You're finally here!"

He then turned to his men:

"Picciotti! Ready to shoot when I give the signal!"

A few seconds went by, then the speaker started his speech:

"Friends, companions, every year, with or without Fascism, we have met here for Labor Day. . . ."

"Fire!" ordered Turiddu.

The rifles and machineguns were pointed up into air and they started to spit fire. Eleven men emptied their cartridges, but no one in the crowd moved. The shooting lasted a few minutes, but the crowd continued to laugh and clap their hands. It noticed nothing: they probably thought that the gunfire was fireworks.

The orator continued to speak:

"This year with the victory of the People's Bloc, we can open our hearts to hope... Our children can learn to read and write and there will be water and electricity in the countryside. . . ."

The arms remained in silence for about a minute. The men loaded new cartridges. Turiddu gave new orders:

"Picciotti! Shoot at about twenty meters above their heads! They'll hear the bullets whistle and start to panic. We'll go and get Li Causi! Watch out! Amongst the crowd there are some relatives of my brother-in-law, Pasquale Sciortino!"

After the new blast of gunfire, they all looked up to the hill. The speaker too turned around. Turiddu was looking at him with his

binoculars and saw him in his face. He immediately ordered:
"Cease fire!"

But Giuseppe Passatempo rushed towards the machinegun that had not been used yet and shouted:

"What! We're leaving without even scaring them a bit?"

He started to shoot together with Salvatore Ferreri. At the same moment that the machinegun opened fire, the men who had got off the truck pulled out their Beretta machineguns and opened fire on the crowd. Their first bullets hit the horses, which fell to the ground and left the poor people without cover. The other bullets went to hit the poor victims, especially the people standing around the podium. There was chaos everywhere: shouts of pain, the animals were running wildly, everyone was searching for cover behind the rocks.

Turiddu saw the dust rise around the podium. He could not understand what was going on. How was it possible? He started to shout desperately:

"You scoundrels! What are you doing?"

Jumping from rock to rock, like a furious lion, he leaped on Salvatore Ferreri and Giuseppe Passatempo. He started kicking them as he shouted:

"You scoundrels! What are you doing?"

The men had a tough time trying to keep them away from him. When they finally managed to calm him down, he ordered to let go the four hunters. Unfortunately they were the witnesses of what had happened. He gave them back their rifles and documents. When the hunters were far away, he ordered his men to return to the base in Sagana, hoping with all his heart that no one was hurt. But the sad truth was that 11 people had been killed and 27 were injured more or less seriously. The premeditation of vile and ruthless people had transformed Turiddu's revenge against Li Causi into a tragedy. Here are the names of the victims:

Giovanni Megna, Vito Allotta, Vincenza La Fata, Giovanni Grifò, Lorenzo Di Maggio, Francesco Vicari, Costanza Intravaia, Giorgio Cusenza, Margherita Clescari, Serafino Lascari, Filippo Di Salvo. They were all from Piana degli Albanesi.

Alberto Borruso, a boy who had gone to Portella with his bicycle, declared to have seen 6 men of the Mafia clan of San Giuseppe Jato come out from behind the rocks. He was sure that he had seen them and that they were responsible for the massacre. He then saw them escape along the road leading to their town. He realized that they were trying to find an alibi. He mounted on his bicycle and started to run as fast as he could. After a few minutes he was passed by a truck running on the road. When the boy reached town, the men that he had seen at Portella delle Ginestre were standing in front of their homes so that everyone could see them. Alberto Borruso's testimony was useless against those men protected by the Mafia and the "reason of State".

Two hours after the massacre the place was swarmed by police and carabinieri. Major Agrisanti surveyed the area and realized that there had been other gunmen besides the group on the hillside. He found six other positions on the same level and on the same trajectory of the shots that hit the victims. Around the positions he found 81 cartridges from Beretta caliber 9 machineguns. A few hours later, the same operation was carried out by Capt. Carmelo Ragusa and Commissioner Frascolla. They counted 800 cartridges from various types of firearms, but in their report no mention was made of the 81 Beretta caliber 9 cartridges or of the six positions where they were found.

The ballistics and postmortem exams revealed that both the victims and the injured were hit with a horizontal trajectory with Beretta caliber 9 guns. These weapons were used exclusively by the Italian armed forces. If the shots had come from the mountain, the trajectory was to be oblique and the caliber ought to have been 6.5.

But why did they shoot on the defenseless crowd?

Who could be interested in sacrificing men, women and even children to ruin the myth of the defender of the weak and of the people that my brother had won over long and terrible years?

Why this bloody reaction? To stop the farmers' movement, which was starting to organize itself to claim its rights in the new republic that was forming?

The Mafia at the time did not have the political intelligence to plan such an episode that shocked the whole country. After that incident the parties of the left were expelled from the Italian government to the advantage of the Christian Democrats who were to govern the country for 50 years. Only a top-level politician could have devised such a diabolic plan. Up to this very day the Italian government has kept the utmost secrecy on the episode. It is a STATE SECRET until the year 2016.

These questions risk to be left without an answer forever. But those who wish to analyze the facts that I have told as they were told to me personally by my brother and together with the other facts discovered afterwards in the minutes and the statements of the trial of Viterbo can draw the obvious conclusions.

The next day when the newspapers with the headlines of the

massacre arrived in Sagana, Turiddu was overwhelmed with anger. He jumped on Salvatore Ferreri and slapped him twice. Then he caught Giuseppe Passatempo. He gave him a punch in the jaw and tossed him to the ground.

"Look here idiot!" he said as he pressed the newspaper into his eyes.

"It's not my fault! I just shot a bit lower, but not against the crowd!" he answered.

Turiddu had no intention of listening to his excuses, although they were plausible. He continued to beat Passatempo, who supported everything for the guilt.

"Look here assassin! Men, women, children!"

Every word was followed by a kick or a punch that Giuseppe Passatempo tried to ward off with his right arm as he sat on the ground.

"It was you! As you were shooting I could see the dust rise from off the ground!"

"It's not true! I didn't shoot at them!"

Turiddu tore the page with the article and stuffed it into his mouth. He pulled out his gun and was about to kill him. For a few seconds he stared into his eyes with hatred. Then he slowly lowered the gun and said with great despise:

"You're not even worth this bullet!"

He looked at his men who were silently watching the scene. Anything he did, no one would have moved a finger. The unexpected massacre had shocked all the men. Their eyes were full of dismay. They looked at each other to understand who else had disobeyed Turiddu's orders.

He ordered two of them to strip off Giuseppe Passatempo's shirt and he gave the same order to another two to do the same with Salvatore Ferreri: the order was executed without hesitation, without resistance and without any comment. They were tied to two olive trees and they each received thirty lashes. The silence of the mountain was broken by the cracking of the whip and their moaning. Despite they continued to say that they were innocent, he kept them tied there for two days. He then sent them away saying that we were not worthy of staying with him. When Turiddu thought of the incident, he cried in silence the death of those innocent victims.

In the meantime thanks to the medical assistance of Dr. Salsedo my husband started to recover. He spent the whole period in bed. I did not leave his bedside even for a second.

On that tragic May 1$^{st}$ we heard on the radio what had happened at Portella delle Ginestre. My husband was worried for his relatives.

He was born in San Cipirello and his family too would go to that festival. He calmed down only when he was sure that none of his relatives had been hurt.

**At the trial of Viterbo, Giovanni Genovese stated that my husband had given my brother a letter a few days before Portella. I can swear before GOD that it is absolutely false. My husband never left home for at least eight days. How could he? He was so sick that I feared that I would soon be left a widow. According to Genovese, that letter allegedly gave the order to shoot at Portella. Maybe he was hoping to give the case a political motive? He knew the true motive and the person who was the cause of that tragic expedition. But the trial had taken that turn. Soon the court strategy was centered on his statement. This false story was believed.**

When my husband was arrested in the United States and then repatriated, he discovered that he had become the scapegoat. He was furious with my brother's men especially with those who had been his comrades. But he realized that they had been tortured to make those statements. It was his firm intention to inform the judge, but that very night he was taken from his cell and handed over to the executioner "Don Pasquale", alias Carabinieri Brigadier Nicola Sganga. He was tied hands and feet to an overturned crate of ammunition. First he was punched twice in his stomach. As he panted and writhed for the pain, they put the gas mask on his face. They had attached a tube to it that looked like a trunk. Everything was so fuzzy. He felt nauseated. All he could hear was Don Pasquale inviting him to sign the confession. With great scorn he said no with a movement of his head. Then another two punches in his stomach. Once again the mask and more salty water. The procedure was repeated three times, but my husband resisted. "Don Pasquale" lost his patience. While one of his assistants continued to pour the salty water into the tube, he started to cut the victim's chest with razor blades. He stopped only when he moved no longer. He feared that he was dead. They untied him and let him fall to the ground. But my husband had only fainted. He started to throw up the salty water he had been forced to drink. After about half an hour he recovered and Don Pasquale ordered him to sign the confession. Despite he was exhausted, he refused.

He was tied in the same position again and the wounds on his chest were covered with salt. This time the pain was too great and unbearable that my husband was forced to sign to make him stop. Until the day he died he had 32 scars on his chest.

The only relevant letter that was received at the beginning of May was from Monsignor Filippi, the Archbishop of Monreale. The prelate made my brother concrete and peculiar proposals. Since the separatist movement had lost its effectiveness, he invited my brother to leave Sicily. To assure him that the proposal was not a trap, he offered to him a guarantee: the Archbishop had an eight-year-old grandnephew called Carletto, who he dearly loved. He was the son of a nephew of his, an Air Force colonel called Alessandro Garacci. Turiddu was to leave the country and take the child with him as a hostage. He would keep the boy with him until he crossed the border. Furthermore, to prove the sincerity of his proposal, Monsignor Filippi would set no condition for the release of the boy. He could leave him in any foreign country, as long as it was not in some abandoned place. Thanks to the local police, the hostage would be sent home. If Turiddu agreed, Monsignor Filippi also guaranteed that a plane was ready for him at the Boccadifalco airport of Palermo.

My mother gave the letter personally to Turiddu. She insisted that he accept the offer. But he answered:

"My story started here and here it will end!"

When my mother and I were interrogated we said that we did not know anything of the letter and that the only letter we knew of was that with the offer to leave the country. (Of course, we made no mention of who had sent it).

In the meantime the investigations on the Portella massacre were requested insistently by all political parties. The shock it had caused in public opinion demanded the identification of the criminals responsible for it and their severe punishment. No one could imagine that the plot had been devised to blame my brother of that horrendous crime. Giuliano had dedicated his whole life to help farmers and small landowners, the poorest members of society. How could he deny the principles for which he had always fought?

The police was groping in the dark. The uniqueness of the crime led in completely different directions. Probably they were put on the right track by Girolamo Li Causi himself who feared Turiddu's retaliations. He declared:

**"The names of those who may have organized the massacre are: the Terrana, the Zito, the Bosco, and the Riolo-Matranga families; they are the Mafia bosses, the excisemen, the representatives of the monarchist, liberal-political apathetic party of San Giuseppe Jato."**

All these people, approximately 70 people, were arrested. About fifty were released after about ten days. Only the police inspector Ettore Messana, who knew all the truth, had sent a report to the Minister of the Interior, Mario Scelba:

**"Reliable informers (Salvatore Ferreri) had immediately warned that the author of the crime was Salvatore Giuliano and his gang. However, for the time being, it cannot be excluded that the crime was inspired and supported in particular by other external political activists in close and unspeakable relations with the outlaw Giuliano, although hitherto no evidence has been found".**

But no one took seriously the inspector's report and dozens of other people were arrested, especially because during the parliamentary debates Li Causi continued to launch accusations against the landowners and the Mafia gangsters of San Giuseppe Jato.

The news that the shooting had been caused exclusively by Salvatore Giuliano and his men was made public on July 14, 1947. On the next day, July 15, 1947, after having reflected for two and half months, the Minister of the Interior Mario Scelba dismissed inspector Ettore Messana.

All this was the result of the "confession" extorted from Francesco Gaglio (alias Reversino, the witness of my wedding in the town hall) with the usual barbarous methods. He had brutally massacred him. A few years later, during an interrogatory on April 15, 1951, he declared:

**"The carabinieri stretched me on a table, covered my face with a gas mask that they filled with salty water, they burnt my body with lit cigarettes, and they crushed my testicles. One of them now is completely dry.**

**When I was taken back to jail, I wasn't visited by any doctor. When I told the judge what had happened, he told me that I was saying rubbish."**

All those who had been accused by Li Causi for being the authors of the massacre were set free. On September 12, 1947 their release was ordered for lack of evidence. Turiddu and his men were the scapegoats to be sacrificed for "reason of State".

The consequences of Francesco Gaglio's "confession" were devastating. A raid was launched in Montelepre: about twenty boys between 16 and 18 years of age were arrested. But the terrible tortures of the vilest individual that has ever worn a uniform of the Carabinieri, Brigadier Nicola Sganga, notoriously known as "Don Pasquale", did the rest. Not only did they accuse themselves but they also made the names of other boys of their age and said that they were involved in the Portella massacre.

Years later, during interviews with the protagonists of this sad episode, it was confirmed that Francesco Gaglio himself, whose statements and accusations led to the identification and arrest of the people allegedly responsible for the massacre, died without knowing where he was held prisoner. This is the only explanation for his continuous contradictions, his confessions to the Carabinieri that he then denied before the judge. This is the only way to justify and comprehend the absurd reconfirmation of the statements he had denied.

He was scared of being sent back to the police station and tortured again. Some even reached the point of accusing their own brothers. All this was unnatural. A similar behavior can be explained only with torture. Of course, the opposite happens. It is more likely that a brother sacrifices himself by confessing that he is responsible for a crime to save his own brother.

Those young men were all innocent, they confessed what they had been told to confess. The whole trial on the Portella massacre was organized around imaginary offenders. The only true thing that the judges believed was the partially involuntary nature of the crime, i.e. they had no intention to kill, which however they did not take fully into consideration when they passed sentence. If all the 719 shots blown that day on the crowd had been directed all against it, the death toll could not have been of just 11, but at least of 500. If they wanted a massacre all they had to do was to point their guns lower. Each shot blown with a horizontal trajectory could have passed through two or three people. But as described above this was the result of the 81 shots blown by the gangsters from San Giuseppe Jato with their Beretta caliber 9 guns.

Those condemned for the massacre were the other victims of that tragedy. They spent decades in prison dying day by day paying for a crime they had not committed.

Turiddu wrote to Giuseppe Montalbano, a member of the Italian Parliament, to declare his innocence and deny the terrible accusations. He sent the letter to the editorial offices of a local communist newspaper *"La Voce di Sicilia"* (Sicily's Voice). Here are some of the most interesting extracts from that letter:

**"Dear Director, if as they have told me, we are not enemies, please publish this letter in your newspaper:**

**As regards the latest news reported in the newspapers, I am dumbfounded by the delirium that has led prominent "gentlemen" to mention my name with their shameless mouths. It is all too obvious that the support for their defense, the only way**

they have to hide their crimes is to blame me for them. Do they believe that a bandit, an outlaw searched by the police, has no right to have his own moral dignity?

Maybe is it because I am not entitled to the freedom of press especially when I speak of the police and these honorable "gentlemen" and because I do not have their same culture and education, so I have no right to defend myself from their slander and accusations against me?

They are free to accuse me of whatever they please. They are free to use me as a scapegoat so that they can sleep peacefully at night because no one is interested in shedding light on these crimes that they accuse me of, since a criminal like me cannot absolutely be defended.

If my question meets with the comprehension of some reasonable individual, I would like to ask: why then Giuliano, the defender of the poor and the enemy of the rich, has turned against the working class?

All the evidence collected by those butchers known as Carabinieri is the result of torture. If you want proof go and ask those poor innocent people who have been forced to confess the names of those responsible for this war? The flagellation of Italy? Of course, they will answer that they did it. It is blatant that it was all the torture that made them say and sign everything they wanted. If they were told to confess other crimes, they would have done it.

**Dear Montalbano, I am sorry that you, a mature man, fail to understand all this. GIULIANO."**

Someone may be led to think that I have spoken of Li Causi to cover up my brother's responsibilities with regard to the events at Portella delle Ginestre. But there is evidence of the contacts between my brother and Li Causi. Furthermore, the Anti-Mafia Committee, whose vice-president was the Communist senator, received two letters which confirmed these contacts.

But, taking advantage of his position within the Committee, he ably succeeded in covering up the evidence.

Luckily the texts of the two letters were published by the newspaper *"Telestar"* on April 12, 1966. Without this evidence, probably the exploitation of the massacre for purely political reasons risks lasting forever.

These men have no intention of revealing the TRUTH.

My brother used to say:

"History will judge me."

Yet impartial evidence of his statements and deeds needs to be found so that the final judgement can truly be fair and definitive. These are the two letters he wrote:

"I, Vincenzo Petrotta, was a Communist activist for many years. For seven years I was the political secretary of the party in Piana degli Albanesi and local inspector. Therefore, I can freely and sincerely speak. Mr. Li Causi states that he is the champion of the fight against the Mafia. He finds many men like Dolci to speculate in favor of his party. The Vice-President of said Committee has forgotten that the communists have used both the Mafiosi and those against the Mafia to reach their targets, because all they care of is the advancement of their party. Do not pretend to be a saint, Mr. Li Causi! When we started to organize the Italian Communist Party in Sicily, we worked with the son of the famous Mafia boss Ciccio Cuccia, Dr. Giuseppe Cuccia. I do not want to question the honesty of this intelligent professional, but his being Ciccio Cuccia's son opened many doors for us wherever we went. We had protection everywhere. Mr. Li Causi was aware of all this. Mr. Li Causi, the Vice-President of said Committee, has eaten many times with the Cuccia family in their home.

In those days everything helped.

This is how things are. The Communist doctrine taught that also Stalin robbed banks, so the Communists of those days could ask for the help of anyone, including the Mafia. This most honorable Committee was unaware of this small detail. Danilo Dolci himself thought that it was useless to investigate into the relations between Communists and the Mafia. Dear Mr. President, I hope that this testimony were taken into consideration in the light of the high and noble purposes for which this Committee was established and for the benefit and the peace of Sicily and the whole country". Signed, Vincenzo Petrotta.

This letter was followed by another from C. Carignito:

"Danilo Dolci asked for information about me from a lady living opposite my house, where he could find me. The lady told him that I was about to come home. Danilo Dolci came again to see me and we met in the street. He asked me strange questions trying to obtain information against Minister Mattarella. But I frankly could not give him the information he wanted because it was false. They asked for documents that could damage Minister Mattarella, documents that I have never seen and whose existence even ignored. They wanted me to declare that I was in contact with Giuliano. But as far as I know there have never been contacts with him.

What I do know is that I was hunting in contrada ZUCCO in Montelepre in 1947. In the middle of the countryside, near a well, I met Giuliano and other people who were talking of politics. I remember that I went up to the group and Giuliano on that occasion introduced me to Mr. Li Causi.

I felt the impelling duty to inform you, because I have suffered very much and I feel that I must tell the truth as truth must always triumph over friend and foe".

Partinico, January 13, 1966. Signed C. Carignito, via Stazione n° 47.

Chapter XVI

# THE ORDEAL OF A FAMILY

An American journalist arrived at the Boccadifalco airport in Palermo on May 7, 1947. His name was Michael Stern. During the war he was a captain in the U.S. army and now he was the Italian correspondent of the American weekly *"True Magazine"*.

He had received the order from his director to interview Giuliano. His fame had crossed the ocean and had reached the United States. He was well prepared for any eventuality. He had all the authorizations and letters of presentation he could need. As soon as he arrived in town, he went to see Inspector Messana to see my brother's file.

He was authorized by all the competent authorities not only to read it but also to copy everything he could need. After this first phase, he asked how he could reach Montelepre. In those days there were police blocks everywhere. The police was still looking for the authors of the massacre at Portella. He got his pass and the next day he left Palermo on board a jeep together with Wilson Morris and a Spanish woman. He and his friend were wearing US army uniforms, the former with the rank of captain and the other that of sergeant.

Once they reached Montelepre, they started to drive through the roads of the small town. They wanted to understand the conditions of the town's population. The townsfolk looked at them with curiosity. Those two men with the American uniform and the woman were smiling at everyone and they soon won everyone's sympathy.

When they started to ask questions on my brother. Sympathy soon changed into diffidence. They could have been policemen under disguise who were looking to damage Turiddu. The people suddenly became deaf, mute and blind. The only answers to their questions were mumbling and evasive replies. Insisting was definitely a bad idea. They would turn around and leave them.

The journalist did not surrender. He went into a bar and offered everyone a drink. He hoped that with the help of some liqueur,

*My Brother, Salvatore Giuliano*

Giuseppe Passatempo.

Some burning truths of the past came to the surface, but were ably hidden.

someone would start to talk. It was all useless. But perseverance had its fruits in the end.

Someone came to our house to tell my father. The news made him curious and he went out to meet the strangers. If they were not spies, they could have been real American officers. My father had spent about one third of his life in the United States and knew how to speak English. It was no coincidence that he was known in town as Turiddu Giuliano, the American.

My father spoke in English to the strangers: he asked who they were and what they were looking for. They explained to him why they had come. My father felt reassured by their answers and invited them to our house to speak freely. They drove there on their jeep. The journalist spoke with my mother and me for a long time. We all understood that an interview could have helped Turiddu so we sent him a message to inform him.

Turiddu accepted only once he had been reassured from Palermo that the strangers were not spies. My father himself took them to the meeting place. When they finally stood one in front of the other, Michael Stern spoke first:

"I'm glad to shake the hand of the famous outlaw that has aroused the curiosity of the United States!"

"Outlaw?"

"You too believe what the government says about me? What a shame! The partisans too were considered outlaws and now they are heroes of the Nation!"

The journalist was soon fascinated by his words. He realized that his image had been faked by media and that Turiddu was no common criminal. He had ideals and he loved his land. He could not help not calling him a revolutionary fighting for the freedom of his land.

Michael Stern and his entourage were Turiddu's guests for a week. They lived the same life, they ate the same food, and they slept in the same hideouts that changed from day to day. He also visited the scene of the many battles during the fight for independence. Those battles had contributed greatly to the granting of Sicilian Autonomy and the Statute.

The presence of the American reporter had reawakened Turiddu's hope of seeing his dream come true: the dream of making Sicily the $49^{th}$ State. Michael Stern instead was looking for a scoop and the money he would earn. He took a picture with Turiddu, as did Wilson and the Spanish woman. With all the information they gathered and the pictures they put together a file. The interview was published in *"True Magazine"* and then also by other newspapers.

Even a book was written. It was entitled "No Innocence Abroad". When he left, he promised Turiddu to keep in touch and he kept his promise. A few days later my brother sent him a letter in Rome. This letter included another two letters: one was for the President of the United States, Truman at the time, and the other for the American Command.

Here are the most interesting passages:

**"Dear President Truman, if I am not bothering you and if you are well-disposed, please accept the humble appeal of a young man who is very far from America, yet well-known. I ask for your help to make my dream come true.**

**After the war we have lost, we are in a desperate situation and we risk becoming the victims of the foreigners. In 87 years of National Unity, or more precisely, in 87 years of slavery under Italy, we have been plundered and treated like a mere colony. For this reason we wish to become part of the United States.**

**In 1945 the walls of most Sicilian cities including Palermo were covered with posters showing a man (me) cutting the chain tying Sicily to Italy, while another man in America tied the other end to the United States. This symbol stands for my hope that Sicily become a part of the United States: I have always been in favor annexation to the United States, but owing to the Fascist regime I could not express my feelings. Once I was at large, hoping to enjoy the political freedom brought to Italy by the Americans, I thought that this was the only way to see my greatest aspiration become a reality.**

**I immediately joined the politicians of the Sicilian Independence Movement to give my contribution from the very outset to annex my land to the United States after the breakaway from Italy. Unfortunately my movement, which I called the M.A.S.C.A., was destined to fail for obvious reasons. But I did not surrender and I have no intention of surrendering, because for the love of Sicily and of the United States, I would even die for this cause.**

**What we need most desperately is your great and powerful moral support. Dear Mr. President, please remember that hundreds of thousands of men wait to be freed. My best regards. Your most humble servant. Giuliano."**

"To the American and British Command.

Dear Sirs,
A few days ago I sent a young man to inform you of my real position. When he returned he informed me of something, but it was nothing concrete.

If you do not believe that I am an outlaw as the Italian government calls me and if you believe that I am worthy of fighting, please send someone to contact me, to make an agreement and to gather information here in Sicily so that I can personally show you what is happening . I would like to inform that many parties would have wanted to help me, but I hope you will understand me.

My pure and sincere feeling has never wavered from that ideal that I will follow to death. But I also believe that any effort to resist is useless. The Italian government has decided to put an end to all this. I am not scared, but it grieves me.

I cannot fight against a tank or a plane with a machinegun. Please send someone. I am sure I can be very useful to you. This is my address: Via Castrenze Di Bella n° 189, Montelepre.

If someone will come, please do not come in uniform, but in disguise for greater security. Mr. Stern can guide you here. Giuliano."

Stern sent these letters and he promised to forward my cause with the competent authorities, but Turiddu obtained just his sincere friendship and fame at an international level. Nothing more. As the days went by, this burst of hope subsided until it completely vanished.

Towards the end of May, my husband was still recovering from his appendicitis. We were thinking of renting a house in the town of Terrasini to spend the summer by the sea. So my husband went there and he came back once he had found what he was looking for. There were three large and comfortable rooms, a kitchen and bathroom and it was very close to the beach.

In the afternoon of May 27th, my husband rented a car. It was driven by a friend of his. He had been told to come to Montelepre to take me there. But my mother feared the prejudice of the people and did not let me go alone. She decided to come as well so that I would not have to travel with a stranger.

We took all the clothes we needed for the summer and plenty of food. We climbed into the car and drove along the road to Carini. After a few kilometers we were stopped by a roadblock. Contrada

"Piano Gallina" had been invaded by hundreds of Carabinieri searching the area owing to a kidnap by some strangers in Partinico. Other cars were stopped, too. As we waited for our turn it got dark. The driver was asked to show his documents. His name was Giuseppe Cracchiolo. The Brigadier pointed the flashlight to his face.

"Who are these women?" asked the officer.

"My fiancée and her mother!" he promptly answered.

"Where are you taking them?" asked the soldier.

"To my house in Terrasini!" answered the driver.

His story could have been credible, if Marshall Lo Bianco who knew us well was not there. He noticed the ironic smile on Cracchiolo's face as he answered.

He reacted suddenly. I turned to the driver bitterly:

"Where did we get engaged? Here in the car?"

The brigadier pointed the flashlight towards me and then towards my mother.

"What's your name, ma'am?"

"Maria Lombardo!" she answered.

Then came my turn.

"And you?"

"Marianna Giuliano Sciortino! We're going to Terrasini to spend the summer there!" I replied.

Then Marshal Lo Bianco stepped in.

"Let's cut the whole comedy!"

He told us to get out of the car and to climb into the truck. They took us to the San Vito station in Palermo. The driver was closed in a cell, while we spent three days and three nights in a room. We were left on some chairs, without any food or water. The car was searched. They found 500,000 Lire in cash, my jewels and the pictures of my wedding.

After the third day in those conditions, I started to feel ill. As the minutes went by I was feeling worse and worse: I felt nausea. I was about to faint. I asked insistently for a doctor. After two hours they finally decided to call him. He was captain of the Carabinieri Medical Corps. He examined me and asked:

"Are you married?"

"I got married a month and six days ago!" I answered.

The doctor looked at my breast: he understood immediately. He called the soldiers that were guarding us.

"How long haven't you fed them?"

Their silence was more eloquent than any explanation.

"Watch out! The lady is pregnant!"

The Captain himself took care of us. He ordered them to transfer her us to prison.

In the meantime Turiddu had found out that we had been arrested and he got very angry. He went to "Bellolampo", a locality overlooking Palermo. There he climbed to the top of telephone pole and he connected his radiotelephone to it. He called the Carabinieri Col. Paolantonio. He said straightforward:

"I'm Salvatore Giuliano".

"I'm calling to warn you! If you don't release my mother and sister in three days time, I'll do things that I would never have wanted to do! The first thing I'll do is to blow you up with the whole station!"

"Are you really Giuliano?" asked the Colonel dumbfounded. "Where are you calling from?"

"I thought you were smarter!" answered Turiddu. "Don't ask me stupid questions!"

"So! Did you understand what I said?"

"Three days time! I understood! They'll be out in three days time. There is no charge against them!"

"I know it! What I can't understand is why you keep on taking advantage of those who can't defend themselves! If you want me, come and fight in the mountains! I'll give you fight!"

Turiddu interrupted abruptly the conversation just as he had started it. But his words and threats were all too clear. Col. Paolantonio and Marshal Lo Bianco came to interrogate us the next day. They asked us who did the money belong to and whether Turiddu had made an agreement with Marshall Calandra. They wanted to know if my brother had paid him.

We immediately understood what they wanted. My mother and I looked at each other in agreement. We said that we did not know where the money came from and that we did not know if Turiddu had paid Calandra.

Eight days later, before the deadline of my brother's ultimatum, they let us go. The Colonel preferred to avoid the risk. As soon as we got home, Turiddu came to see us. He told us about the phone call and then exclaimed:

"After all he's a good man!"

My husband too came back. I told him I was pregnant. He was overwhelmed with joy. Since he rented the house, he said that we might as well go to Terrasini. I answered that I would be happy to go, but I needed some rest.

During the first ten days of June 1947, Turiddu went to Palermo with three of his men. He wanted to capture Girolamo Li Causi. He went to his home and said that he had a letter for him. He was convinced that this time he would catch him, but he went encounter to another setback.

Girolamo Li Causi had left for Rome a few hours before. Turiddu had always been calm and reflective, but he would get furious at the thought that that man was involved and that he was morally responsible for what happened in Portella delle Ginestre. He just could not stay calm. He was always so phlegmatic and when he talked he would almost stutter. But he wanted him at all costs directly or indirectly. This new failure led him to decide a demonstrative raid against the Communist party offices headed by Li Causi.

The date for the beginning of the raids was set for June 22, 1947. Turiddu invited his men not involve innocent people. Their attack was to damage without destroying and to scare but not to kill.

Turiddu would have attacked simultaneously the offices of Carini, San Giuseppe Jato and Borgetto. It went according to his plans: three different squads went into action simultaneously at 9 o'clock in the evening. They launched Molotov bombs and shot blasts of machinegun fire against its walls. The explosions and the fire of the machineguns created a lot of chaos, without any bloodshed.

The same happened at the offices in Cinisi and Monreale. But an unexpected problem occurred once again and ruined Turiddu's plans and strategy: Giuseppe Passatempo had learnt of my brother's plans from his brother Salvatore and decided to intervene.

He was angry with Turiddu because he had unfairly accused of the massacre at Portella delle Ginestre. He had humiliated him and sent him away. He wanted to avenge himself in the way he preferred the most. That same day Giuseppe Passatempo came alone to Partinico.

The office to be attacked was in Corso dei Mille. He had sneaked up to it in the dim light. Although he saw that there were about a dozen people who were talking in front of the building he jumped out of his hiding place and opened fire on the group of people. To complete his terrible action, he launched a grenade inside the building: Giuseppe Casarrubia and Vincenzo Lo Iacono died on the spot, another four people were injured.

Once again that bloodthirsty beast had worsened my brother's situation. But this time he who had armed his hand did not limit himself to continue the destruction of my brother's myth started at Portella delle Ginestre. He also gave him leaflets signed by Salvatore Giuliano, inviting the people to join his absurd anti-Communist crusade.

Giuseppe Passatempo had spread them where he had committed his crime. This time as well his desire for revenge against Li Causi had rebelled against Turiddu. He learnt the news on June 24$^{th}$ and he immediately ceased all hostilities. That was not the only bad news he had to hear that day. A spy inside the police station had confirmed his suspects. Inspector Messana had been warned before the expedition to Portella by Salvatore Ferreri. But he was not the only spy amongst his men. The Pianelli brothers, who belonged to Ferreri's squad, were the informers of Col. Paolantonio. Turiddu finally had a clear picture and did not waste time to inform Messana and Paolantonio that he had discovered everything.

Two days later, exactly in the morning of June 26$^{th}$, Capt. Giallombardo, the commander of the Carabinieri station in Alcamo, received a letter. It was given to him by a boy. It was from an anonymous informer. That letter informed him that that evening some men of Giuliano's gang, amongst whom Salvatore Ferreri, alias Fra' Diavolo, would be in Alcamo.

The Captain kept the secret until evening. Around nine o'clock he called his men and told them get ready because an important operation had to be carried out. They all followed him to the town's outskirts in a position where they could watch from above the road from Calatafimi.

He divided his men into two groups to set up two roadblocks. He positioned one group behind the town's first houses so as to create two obstacles at about twenty meters away from each other. The wait was long and exhausting. It was past midnight and they started to think that the informer had made a mistake or that Fra' Diavolo had sensed something and would not have fallen into their trap. But their perseverance was rewarded.

Around three thirty in the night five men appeared. They were unaware of what awaited them and they were proceeding calmly. The soldiers of the first block stayed where they were and let them pass. They found themselves caught between two fires and without cover.

At that very moment Captain Giallombardo shouted in the silence of the night:

"Ferreri! Stop! Surrender! You're surrounded!"

The five men were no novices. They had fought dozens of battles. He rushed here and there looking for cover. They preferred dying that spending the rest of their days in prison. They put up fierce resistance. They shot up to the last bullet and launched all the grenades they had. After a short yet intense shootout in a disadvantageous position they were are all killed.

Four of them died on the spot: Giuseppe and Fedele Pianello, Antonio Coraci, and Vito Ferreri, Fra' Diavolo's father. The man who was supposed to be the operation's main target was still alive. He had been wounded, but it was not serious. He had thrown away his machinegun to surrender.

He looked at Captain Giallombardo with his eyes full of anger. He ordered his men to put him into the car and took him to the station, where he was then interrogated.

Salvatore Ferreri refused to speak and continued to look at him with despise. Finally he exploded:

"I'm Inspector Messana's informer! I want to speak to him! You can't arrest me!"

Having said this, he pulled his documents out of his pocket. According to the documents, his name was Salvo Rossi: the name of Messana's driver. He then showed him the pass given to him by Messana. Ferreri continued to shout. He wanted to be taken to Palermo. He said he could not be arrested without the inspector's approval.

Captain Giallombardo was dismayed. He called Palermo to have his story confirmed. Probably it was that phone call to sentence Ferreri to death. He could no longer be used as an informer. What happened after in that station can easily be deduced. According to Captain Giallombardo's statement, Salvatore Ferreri had assaulted and disarmed him. He would certainly have been killed, had it not been for the fact that the gun was blocked by the safety catch. Luckily he had another gun in his pocket and killed the outlaw.

After this incident, which, depending on the points of view, could have led to his promotion or demotion, he was simply transferred instead to a small town in Calabria. But a month later Inspector Messana too was transferred elsewhere. He was replaced by Inspector Coglitore. The latter did not even finish one month of service that he asked to be transferred too. He was replaced by Inspector Spanò.

While all these replacements were being decided in Palermo, the trial against my brother Giuseppe was being prepared in Cosenza. The date was set for July 12, 1947. My parents and my sister-in-law left by train to reach that city. The trial was held. He was accused of having killed Orlando Grippi.

Thanks to Turiddu's confession to Marshall Calandra during their meeting, my brother Giuseppe was acquitted. But he was not freed. The Surveillance Committee convened a month later and decided to send him to the island of Ustica for five years.

Towards the end of July an Italian American arrived in Montelepre. He was an old friend of Turiddu and he wanted to meet him immediately. He looked for envoys. He went up to the mountain many times. He finally came to speak with my mother.

The first evening my brother came to sleep at home, we sent for him. Turiddu was both anxious to see him and curious to know why he was looking for him with such insistence. When his friend crossed the threshold of our door, Turiddu went up to him smiling: they hugged each other fraternally. Then the guest was seated between my parents. He started to speak. He explained the details of a plan to have Turiddu expatriate to the United States. Everything was ready. At his arrival in that great country he would have found all the support needed, documents, a new identity, a job and protection. He could have started a new life.

My brother let him speak without interrupting. When he finished he answered:

"I've said it many times already, but I'll repeat it again!"

"My story started here and here it will finish!"

But the guest replied: "But if the people doesn't care anymore about the Independence movement, what use is there to continue?"

"If politicians don't care about Sicily and the Sicilian people, I can't do the same! My people, my comrades. . . . I can't behave like a coward and abandon them to their fate!"

"But why do you want to refuse an excellent opportunity like this? This people who you care so much about isn't politically mature: they're selfish, apathetic, they are always ready to betray and to support whoever makes them a promise or does them favor! Listen to me! No one deserves your sacrifice! Forget about everyone and everything!"

"For once in your life think about yourself!"

"Am I speaking Arab or you just won't understand?"

"I'm not leaving!"

"Since you want to take someone to America, why don't you take my brother-in-law and my sister, before they get into trouble again?"

"Tomorrow we'll go see them and we'll see what they think about it!"

The guest was disappointed. He left in silence.

In the meantime my husband and I did not go to stay in Terrasini and we were staying in Villa Trabia in Bagheria. The place was beautiful. The house was enormous. There were 120 rooms in the villa. It was in the middle of a large park covered with flowers of all colors. Age-old trees of all kinds surrounded the house. Behind it the crystal clear water of the sea with its emerald green reflections was an irresistible temptation.

Besides my husband and I, two friends of mine were there as well. I took them along to keep me company when my husband was away. And there were also the servants of the owner of the house. When Turiddu and his friend arrived, we went to meet them altogether. My friends welcomed them warmly and looked at him as if he were the apple of the original sin. They were attracted to him in an almost morbid manner. But Turiddu was too busy with his thoughts and he knew that he could not have a lasting bond with a girl. He just smiled at them and shook their hand. He then left my friends and came to hug my husband and me. He greeted everyone kindly including the workers and the servants.

We went into the great hall on ground floor. As we waited for lunch, Turiddu wanted to visit the villa with his friend. Wherever they looked there was marvelous furniture, precious and antique paintings, tapestries, vases, sculptures, and frescoes. The art and richness transpired even from the simplest objects.

In a large room on the first floor they found four pianos of different shapes and brands. We were all surprised when Turiddu sat down to play a German piano there. His fingers moved with confidence over the keys. With his innate skill he played a tune that was very popular at the time: "Bambina Innamorata" (Girl in Love). My friends were in ecstasy as they watched him play. I was dumbfounded. When the song was over, I asked him:

"When did you learn to play the piano?"

He looked at me and answered with a smile:

"Do want to know the truth?"

I nodded yes.

"It's the first time! I thought that if you know how to play the accordion, then you can even play the piano!"

Turiddu continued to play and sing together with my friends and me until lunchtime. Deep down in his heart he was still the same romantic boy he had always been. After the simple lunch, my husband, Turiddu, his friend and I went to speak in private and we discussed whether we were to leave the country.

First of all, I pointed out that I was not in the right conditions because I was pregnant and things were getting more difficult by the day. I could not travel in my conditions especially if were to leave in secret. I would have been an obstacle for my husband. We decided unanimously that it was better for him to leave alone. It was much easier for him to escape the controls and to prepare everything for my arrival. I would have come after the birth of the baby.

The date for his departure was set for August 20, 1947. That day inexorably arrived. I had a sort of premonition. The thought that I would lose him obsessed my mind. I was upset. I hugged him as I cried. It seemed, as if it were the last time I would see him. A few hours later he left for Genoa, where he left for New York on board the "Saturnia".

We had been forced to leave each other only 3 months and 26 days after our wedding. Once he reached destination, Pasquale took the name of Anthony Venza. He went to work for a radio station and there he had a radio show of his own in Spanish. He then joined the United States Air Force with the name of Frank Catalano.

After my husband's departure, I returned to Montelepre. After about a week I was visited by a man named Miceli. He worked for a lawyer who was a friend of our family. Unfortunately I was to discover later on that he not only was a friend of my family, but also of Marshall Lo Bianco.

Miceli had come to warn me about a possible arrest warrant for me. On behalf of the lawyer he had come to tell me to go to Palermo, in Via Siracusa, so that I could live there with his wife and daughter-in-law.

The idea was not particularly appealing. I still had not recovered completely from my previous visit. I was worried so I let him convince me. I spent a few days there. I felt that the atmosphere was tense. Instead of being a guest, I felt like a prisoner and as the days went by my suspects grew and grew. Miceli daughter-in-law started to ask me questions on the money found in the car when I was arrested.

"You say that the money isn't yours. But the Marshall says it is!"
"If you say that the money is ours, they'll give it back!"
"Otherwise they'll keep it! Why lose half a million Lire?"
"I can't lose money that isn't mine!" I answered.
"Ma'am, you haven't understood anything? If you say it's yours and then you give it to the rightful owner, you will have no problems at all!"

Their plan was finally clear. They had organized everything for the money. In order to get out of that situation, I exclaimed:

"I'll do as you want, but leave me alone!"

She took me to the Calatafimi station. I signed a statement, but they did not give me the money. We returned to the place where I was staying. Miceli said that there was no longer any threat that I would be arrested. I could now go out freely.

I decided to stay another week in Palermo. He had things to do. But three days later, as I was going down via Materassai, I was surrounded by the Carabinieri. They arrested me and took me to the "Benedettini" prison, where they told me the reason of my arrest. This time they accused of an alleged attempt of kidnapping a famous surgeon, Prof. Orestano.

I shouted, protested and swore but it was all useless. They closed me in a wet and dark cell. For three days and three nights I was not allowed to see anyone for no reason at all. I was in my sixth month. My thirst and hunger were worsened by my conditions. I was finally interrogated by the investigating magistrate and by Judge Urso. I did not hesitate to ask for a confrontation with Prof. Orestano. He knew me and I knew him. I was curious to see how I could have done what they accused me of with my belly!

According to the accusation, my friend Caterina Pizzurro and I had gone to the clinic, asked for the doctor to lead him into a trap organized by our accomplices. Owing to the hunger and the lack of water, I was very ill. It was so obvious that one of the magistrates tried to console me by saying:

"Ma'am, we've got families and we understand your conditions!"

"Stay calm, stay calm! There is nothing to worry about! There is no need for the confrontation. The professor and his wife have declared that you are not involved. Resist! Do it for the child in your womb! Now we'll let you go home!"

But his words were false. His assurances were groundless. I was considered a guerilla fighter and my brother's advisor. By hitting me, they wanted to hit him. What better chance was there to keep me off the scenes for a while than this alleged kidnap?

The next day, instead of releasing me, they sent me to the jail in Termini Imerese. Turiddu knew the conditions in jail and was very worried. He wrote to the newspapers and to the magistrates. He declared my innocence and at the same time threatened terrible retaliations if something happened to me. Fearing his retaliation, they moved me to the prison in Caltanissetta and then to Catania. After 44 days of suffering and imprisonment, they granted me freedom on parole on October 26, 1947.

In December of that year, in the light of the persecutions against me, I tried to leave the country secretly. But unfortunately it failed.

## Chapter XVII

# ILLUSIONS AND DISAPPOINTMENTS

1948 seemed to start in the best of ways. After the latest events that had animated our lives there was a calm period. It seemed almost like a sort of truce. Turiddu had suspended his activities. The police continued to search for him and he would just avoid any encounter or clash with them. He limited his range of action to the area around Montelepre. He was much closer than they could imagine. He was often at home together with us.

Despite the tragedy we were forced to live, having him around the house every now and then was our only comfort and moment of rest. If his informers would tell him to stay away from town, he would spend a few hours of the day on the surrounding hills. He would stop at the feet of "Picco Saraceno" or he would hide amongst the boulders of Mount "Calcerame".

If the situation were calm instead, he would rest under an olive tree in "Montedoro" or under a large carob tree at the feet of "Cozzo Vite" at just 500 meters away from our house. From there he could follow the life of our family. He would watch our movements in the garden of our house with his powerful Navy binoculars.

First he would just watch us. Once he had ascertained that the coast was clear, he could contact us directly. He always had a little with mirror for the purpose. He would reflect the sunrays on a window of our house or he would move the mirror with a particular rhythm and flash it on one of us.

This was just the first step. He would use it to attract our attention. After we would notice the signal, he would use other vague movements and then other more precise ones. Turiddu had invented a code of his own, which he taught us. By moving the mirror in a particular way he would transmit his message.

He would tell us if he needed something or he wanted one of us to reach him. If we would send him the signal that the coast was clear, Turiddu would come down the hill and join us at home. The system worked perfectly as did our surveillance system when he was at home.

*My Brother, Salvatore Giuliano*

Salvatore Ferreri, alias Fra' Diavolo.

His dog Giulia, which he had personally trained, was a real phenomenon. It was capable of signaling a police patrol within a range of 500 meters. If they were less than three it would just whimper, wag its tail and bark every now and then. If they were more than three, he would start to bark and howl intensely.

If we were all sleeping at night, although it happened seldom, we all had nothing to worry with that dog. The Carabinieri and the police would patrol the town two by two. They would check the streets and alleys and see who was walking in the streets. Surprise raids in homes were seldom.

Of course, there were officers who knew or imagined that Turiddu was at home, but there were never unexpected surprises. It was not worth breaking the truce. Towards mid-January Turiddu tried to contact the leaders of various political parties. Everyone knew of our activism during the previous elections in favor of the separatist movement.

Now that the M.I.S. was declining, and that Antonino Varvaro had dissolved the M.I.S.D.R. and had joined the Communists, the votes that my brother and I could guarantee were very appealing. Now that the parliamentary elections were approaching, the various leaders had remembered us again.

The reporter Michael Stern between Salvatore Giuliano Senior and Salvatore Giuliano Junior.

Turiddu had very little to choose: the American government, from which he had hoped to receive help to see his dream come true, did not take him seriously. But deep down in his heart he had not forgotten his idea of an independent Sicily. He was forced to take seriously into consideration the offer made to him by the Christian Democrats.

If he was to be consistent with his ideals, he was to support the parties of the left, but those parties were now asking for his head after "Portella delle Ginestre". He was forced to put aside his ideals and do the wisest thing. Many Christian Democrat leaders and monarchists assured him that if he supported their campaign his decisive contribution to the granting of Autonomy and the Sicilian Statute would have been recognized publicly. They would even propose a general pardon for him and his men.

He was tempted by these promises. He was tired of wandering from one place to another. So he decided to meet these politicians. He realized that things would have changed much for him with the general pardon, but many of his men could have finally returned to their homes.

His generosity and altruism always had the upper hand. The idea had rekindled hope in everyone's hearts once again. Turiddu met them various times. The most famous of these meetings were held in contrada "Parrini" in Partinico and in Castellammare del Golfo.

The date of the elections was set for April 18, 1948. We all started to campaign for votes. A new truce was reached with the police. This time I could not travel from town to town as I did the first two times. My pregnancy was now approaching the end. I simply sent messages to people I knew.

At midnight between Thursday and Friday February 5, 1948 I gave light to a baby. My friends and relatives were waiting anxiously for the big event. The next day the news spread across town and reached Turiddu too.

In the evening of February 8th, the first day of Carnival, it was a custom to play music in every home. In our home too the gramophone was playing without rest and amplified the sound of our records.

Carnival in Montelepre was far from being like that in Viareggio or Rio, but all the same people would have fun. Groups of young people wearing costumes would go around town: they would enter the homes where music was being played to dance a bit. They would continue to go from house to house all night long.

That year Minister Scelba had issued an order by which it was forbidden to go around with masks. But with the taboos and prejudice of the time the only hope for people and especially women to go out freely thanks to the mask without risking their reputation was lost. Many picciotti too could not come to town to have fun, so they asked Turiddu to help them. No one wanted to miss all the fun and celebrating.

His answer to the order was a proclamation that he hung on the police station door during the night. It was both a challenge and threat:

**"Whoever dares to hinder our traditional Carnival celebrations ought to go and confess himself and say his prayers"**.

As was to be expected, no one heeded the Minister's order. Around 10 o'clock in the evening a large group of people all wearing costumes came in and started to dance. One person of this large group distinguished himself from all the others. We noted him both for his height and the beauty of his costume. He was wearing a 15$^{th}$ century aristocratic costume. I was sitting in a corner with the baby in my arms. That individual with his costume had attracted my curiosity from the moment he came in. He looked so familiar.

I looked at him, but was he looking at me?

But I could not find any detail that could help me reveal his identity. Suddenly he came towards me, took the baby delicately and started to dance with it in his arms. My face lit up with joy. He could only be my brother.

There was no need to speak. From the look on my face he understood. He nodded to me and climbed the stairs to go into his rooms. I whispered the news into my mother's ears. In his room he took off his mask and hugged me. He told that some of the men in the group were his "picciotti" with their girlfriends or fiancées. They would have spent the Carnival in town ready to intervene in case the soldiers bothered the people dressed up in their costumes.

A few minutes later they left and started to walk through town: they went into houses and danced. They even fooled around with a patrol of carabinieri and invited them to come and dance with them.

The townsfolk knew who the king was and laughed at the sight. Maybe even the carabinieri imagined who he was, but they knew that it was better to make believe of nothing and join in the game.

The campaign for the parliamentary elections started off in an extremely fiery manner. Both Turiddu and I had believed in the promises of the Christian Democrats and we decided to support their campaign. All the men, their families, their relatives and friends did their best. It was easy to expect the final outcome in our area where the results were very satisfying.

The Christian Democrats won the elections hands down and the Monarchist party did well too. What happened now in favor of the Christian Democrats was the replica of what had happened in favor of the M.I.S.

Only Bernardo Mattarella hugged my father in public during a rally in Montelepre. In that area alone he won 1,800 votes. The Christian Democrats and the other lay parties had obtained the absolute majority in the whole country.

After the elections Turiddu hoped that the Christian Democrat leaders would have kept their promise. He hoped in that general pardon that would have enabled his men to be free again. Only then would he have taken seriously into consideration one of the many proposals of emigration and put an end to the game.

But once again those politicians who thanks to our help had won their seats in Parliament turned their backs on us. My brother could not believe what had happened. He deluded himself that others were just as loyal and sincere as he was. This aspect of his character caused him many illusions and disappointments. He learnt only not to trust the "cops".

In those days, while the election results were still being commented and the truce was still in force, the raids were rare. Turiddu was informed in advance of the few patrols that carried out. There were informers both amongst the police and the Carabinieri. There was also a fierce rivalry between the two law enforcement forces that favored my brother.

But on May 1, 1948, something did not work. An unfortunate incident occurred: a carabiniere was killed. There is a letter from Turiddu written to the mother of the victim telling how the story went:

**"Dear Mrs. Esposito,**

**At the culminating moment of your immense pain, I feel the need to express my sympathy for your great suffering. Please do not consider this as an insult. This is the sincere act of solidarity of a young man, who, although he is defined as an outlaw, has a heart, which is even larger than other people, a heart that beats and suffers for similar tragedies, which unfortunately and painfully occur.**

**During the five years hitherto in the mountains, I have never felt so greatly the loss of a man and especially a carabiniere, as in the case of your son. Since your son came to Montelepre, I had been informed he had behaved well, no complaints were ever signaled to me and what hurts me most is that he did not deserve to end his days so prematurely and in such a violent**

way. For these reasons I have felt the need to write to you and to explain how your only son, your only support after so many family tragedies, lost his life. I hope that my modest words of comfort can ease your pain and console you in this tragic moment.

I was sure that there would be movements of police forces in the mountains so at dawn on Saturday morning we had set up a network of lookouts to avoid unpleasant surprises. As a matter of fact there was a patrol and from the top of the mountain I followed the movements of the Carabinieri, amongst who was your son. I followed them along their way with my binocular as I moved farther and farther away from them.

Everything went well until about 3 o'clock in the afternoon. I lost sight of them for a moment and I thought that they had returned to the station owing to the late hour of the day and not having seen them anymore. So we had calmed down and we were sitting and playing cards, when all of a sudden one of my men stands up with his hands up in the air. He managed to shout my name to warn me. Having heard that desperate cry of alarm, I collected all the courage of my desperation. I found myself just five meters away from the carabinieri. They had managed to come so close under the cover of a large boulder that limited our view. Seeing my man with all those rifles pointed against him, I was forced to shoot against them to scare them and make them drop to the ground so that my men and I could escape.

We left all our arms, ammunitions and coats there and rushed off without worrying if someone had been injured or killed. The fact that I ran off without continuing to shoot is proof that I had no intention of killing anyone. Owing to the danger of the moment, I was forced to react to save myself.

This is a brief description of how things went. I hope you will understand that your son's death is not my fault, but the fault of a cruel fate that put us both in such a desperate situation during which I forced to defend myself.

Please accept my most sincere solidarity and this token of 50,000 Lire as a sign of my sympathy and pain for the loss of your beloved son. GIULIANO."

Fifteen days later this tragic episode, an officer came to the door of our house. As always the sight of a uniform was a shock for us. We lived with the constant fear of being arrested with just any excuse.

I went to open the door.

"Are you Giuliano's sister?"

I nodded affirmatively.

"I'm a friend of your brother! They have sent me here to tell him that this story must come to an end!"

I was bothered by the tone of his voice. I asked him:

"Who are you?"

He answered immediately:

"I'm Commissioner Celestino Zappone from the police station in Partinico!"

"So you seem to have forgotten that my brother is no friend of yours! I don't trust you cops!"

The commissioner insisted.

"I have a message for him from some very important people! Turiddu must decide whether he wants to emigrate or surrender! If he doesn't the government will send the army again and, if it does, this part of Sicily will be covered with blood!"

We had received many similar threats over the years. We had received hundreds of this kind. Turiddu would never have surrendered because of these threats.

Soon the commissioner realized that he was wasting his breath. He turned to my mother to ask her to organize a meeting with my brother and said to her:

"You don't trust me, do you? You think that I'll hide a gun on me to kill your son by surprise? I'm ready to go up into the mountains wearing only my underwear so that they can all see that I'm clean! You must realize that he has to leave Sicily and Italy! He must go! I must convince him to leave! I received the task from my superiors! Your son has three choices: emigrating, surrendering with the promise of a lighter sentence or dying in battle!"

"This situation has gone too far!"

Commissioner Celestino Zappone was not diplomatic at all. My mother and I tried to avoid his requests by repeating to him:

"Turiddu is no little puppet that we can keep here in our pockets and pull him out whenever someone asks to meet him!"

Finally he understood that we had no intention of cooperating with him. So he decided to resort to threats:

"You hope that I never meet him!" he said bitterly. "If I meet him face to face, it'll be either me or him! You can be sure that it won't be me!"

Before he left my mother replied:

"I hope you never meet. I'll pray to the Lord to help the both of you!"

"This gun here will help me!" answered the commissioner, as he laid his hand on the machinegun hanging from his shoulder.

As my mother closed the door behind him, she added:

"Let that gun help you and God will take care of my son!"

In an ambush in the center of Partinico Commissioner Zappone was killed together with two carabinieri three days later. The rumor spread that my brother had accepted his challenge, but he had nothing to do with it. That ambush was organized by the relative of a criminal that the Commissioner had killed some time before during a raid.

A few days later, on June 12, 1948, a shepherd boy came to knock on our door. He insistently asked to see my mother. I told him that if he had something to say he could speak with me, but he kept on insisting. I called my mother. When he saw her he pulled a message out of his pocket.

To be sincere, it was so dirty and wrinkled up that you could barely call it a message. The shepherd waited for her to open it. He then smiled revealing his yellow teeth. My mother recognized Turiddu's handwriting. She gave me the message and I read it anxiously:

**"Dear mother, I'll be waiting for you and Marianna in contrada "Calcerame". Bring something to cook so we can eat together".**

My mother and I looked at each other. There was no need to speak. We were both filled with joy for his invitation. We looked at the clock. It was about 10 o'clock in the morning. Turiddu had no need of an answer. He knew that if we received his message we would have done everything possible to reach him. During those years spent in the mountains we had gone to see him at least a hundred times. If he did not see us come, he would soon find out the reason by contacting his many informers.

We went straight to work. I baked a cake covered with cream. My mother went to buy some fish and vegetables. We took two bottles of our best wine and the bread we had baked in our wood oven. Around noon we were ready. We put the food into two bags so that no one could notice. Before leaving, we check if the coast was clear. It had been a relatively calm period, but you could never be too cautious. I climbed onto the terrace of our house. From there I had a view of the whole town.

I looked towards the center of town, where the police station was: everything was calm. I did not see any suspicious movements, not even outside town along the road to Palermo. The road was deserted. There were no carabinieri or police in sight. We then made our way towards the trail leading up to the mountain. Almost halfway up it was a mere path amongst rocks and boulders. Not even the tanks had managed to climb there.

We would take all these precautions each time we were to go see Turiddu. It was not easy to follow us. Anyway, there was no risk that anyone could follow our traces up to my brother's hideout. When he would wait for visits, even us, he would choose strategic points of the mountain. From there he could watch the area for kilometers and kilometers all by himself.

Whoever tried to surprise him, even without being noticed by the people being followed, could reach him without being seen. He would have surely noticed anyone and have all the time necessary to get around him and catch the pursuer by surprise.

If there was a large number of enemies instead, he would have escaped to a more favorable position already chosen in advance. In the worst of cases the only inconvenience was that my mother and I would have walked the whole way without seeing him.

But let's get back to our story.

My mother and I had walked for more than an hour. We went along paths and trails we knew well. We reached the meeting point without any problems. Turiddu was there waiting for us and as we arrived he came running to mother and he hugged her closely to his heart. Then, as usual, he kissed her on both cheeks. He hugged and kissed me too and then he hugged our mother again.

She was short and in his arms she looked like a small child. All that affect had moved her: she was looking at him with her sweet eyes veiled by tears, she caressed his hair and touched the firm muscles of his arms as if she wanted to see if he was as strong as always.

I stood there watching them a few meters away. I was moved by so much tenderness. When their embrace eased, my mother said:

"Watch out son! Beware of those who are with you! Don't trust even the air you breathe!"

He answered with a smile:

"Mother, don't worry! I know where I am going and what I am doing!"

He changed the subject and pointed out that he had already lit the fire on the grass under the olive tree. Around the fire he had made a circle of stones to avoid that the fire spread. He had then placed a grill to cook the fish. As we waited for it to cook, Turiddu started to slowly eat the fresh bread we had brought from home.

When the fish was ready, we started to eat that long and joyful lunch. Turiddu ate heartily and he drank a few glasses of wine. This happened seldom. Then for dessert he cut a large piece of cake. He had a sweet tooth and then he poured himself a nice cup strong black coffee.

Every now and then he would stand up on the large rock he was sitting on and scour the surrounding area with his powerful binoculars. Then he would come back and sit with us. At the end of the lunch conversation moved to the various proposals to emigrate:

"They want me to emigrate to Brazil! Go! They tell me! So that this story can finally come to an end! Especially those from the police! They promise me ships and planes! They want me to abandon everyone and everything! But I'm no traitor! I can't abandon these men to their fate! If I did, they would all get arrested or killed in no time at all! I must resist! Those in Rome have realized that neither those with me nor myself are criminals! They must understand that we were caught in this situation and that it's not our fault. But the situation escaped our control: the war, need, hunger and the especially the betrayal of the politicians! They must grant us a pardon!"

Listening to him as he said all this our hearts were filled with hope. A peaceful solution was desirable and possible. Towards sunset we went home. Turiddu's words had given us new strength.

Salvatore Giuliano amongst the vineyards in Contrada "Cippi".

Chapter XVIII

# DESTRUCTION ALL AROUND TURIDDU

It was the end of June. Nothing new had happened, but one morning I was awakened by a loud noise from the house opposite ours. My baby too was awakened and he started to cry. I rushed onto the balcony to understand what was happening.

I saw a team of workers bustling around some strange machines. I asked what they were doing. They told me that two men from Palermo, called Davì and Cusimano, were opening a pasta factory. I begged the workers to make less noise because it bothered the baby. But they continued the whole day long. That evening Turiddu came home to visit us. I told him of all the noise they had made and of the workers' rude behavior. He went to speak to the two partners to complain with them. He invited them to try to make as less noise as possible.

The two partners of the new firm came the next day to excuse themselves for what had happened. They were very kind and cordial. As we spoke, a relaxed and friendly climate was created.

At the end of our conversation they proposed my mother to join their company. The share for joining the company was a million and half Lire. My mother accepted and paid the amount. Of course, we informed Turiddu of the news. He was happy about our mother's initiative. He had always dreamed of going into commerce. In order to help this new enterprise, he wrote the owner of a mill in Partinico. His name was Cassarà. He asked him to offer a discount on his prices if my mother decided the buy flour and bran from him.

But in the first decade of July, Cassarà was killed in Palermo. He was killed by a jeweler named Fiorentino, because Cassarà had tried to rob him. When the inquirers went through his pockets to find out his identity, they found Turiddu's message. Davì, one of the company's partners was arrested immediately.

They interrogated him with the usual "democratic" methods and they made him declare that he had been forced by the threats of brother to become my mother's partner. The police had been looking for an excuse for some time now. They immediately issued an arrest warrant for my mother and they arrested her for aggravated extortion. It was July 15, 1948.

We are dumbfounded. But the worst was yet to come. We had no idea that the arrest was just the beginning of a long series. It was all part of a cynical and diabolic plan to isolate my brother. In those very days the Parliament had debated the "Giuliano" case. Its envoys together with those of the police and Carabinieri had failed to convince him to emigrate or to surrender. Their only choice was to put an end to the story. They launched a massive offensive against him to force him to surrender or to eliminate him physically once and for all.

The interim Minister of the Interior, the Christian Democrat Mario Scelba, issued the arrest warrant even for the cat of the Giuliano family and all the able-bodied of the town of Montelepre.

Our town suffered another invasion by the Italian State. Soldiers, carabinieri and the police: they all came by the thousands. They were equipped with tanks, cannons, armored vehicles and self-propelled mortars. It seemed as if we had returned to two and half years ago during the struggle for Sicilian independence.

Massive raids of three thousand men were launched. The town was under siege. My sister Giuseppina and her husband were arrested on October 10, 1948. I cannot remember the excuse they found. All I remember is that they were interned in the island of Ustica. On October 15th my father was arrested again and he too was sent to Ustica.

To arrest me they had no need to invent anything. They suspended my freedom on parole, which I had been granted once the case of attempted kidnap of Prof. Orestano was cleared. I was arrested and taken to jail in Termini Imerese. They left the child with me because he was only eight months old, otherwise he would have suffered the same fate of my sister's children. They were captured and sent to three different institutes.

Half of Montelepre's population had been taken away. There were more internees in Ustica than inhabitants. The jails in Palermo and the other towns of the area were full of people from Montelepre. Each family was deprived of two or three members. Their economic conditions, which were already desperate, worsened even more leaving them just the means for survival.

My brother's reaction was easy to imagine during the persecution of our family and the whole town of Montelepre. He wrote letters to or called newspapers, magistrates, politicians and he stigmatized the abuses committed.

This letter was sent to the Minister of the Interior during that period:

**"Dear Scelba,**

**You are a villain, a shameless man, you are the worst of men. You have found the right way. Do you think that you will find here those miserable Mafiosi of 1926? There are men here. Do you think that by arresting women you will get us? Leave the doors open! Poor beast! You're an ugly beast. All I can say to you is that I will not surrender to a miserable man like you, capable of fighting only against women. I am a man and I behave like a man. With my men I will show what it means to be a man. We are not afraid of your threats. You dog, remember that the responsibility for all the blood that will be shed will fall on you. I am defending my mother and the honor of Sicily. Honor: a word you have no idea of what it means.**

**PS: Prefect Vicari and Spanò, you beasts, what I said to your friend Scelba, goes for you too. Send this to that cuckold, who is more than cuckold than you.**

**GIULIANO"**

He waited a few days for a reply, but the arrests, persecutions and abuses not only did not stop but they continued more than before. In the light of the failure of his diplomatic efforts to stop the retaliation against our family and our fellow townsmen he went into action.

On October 17, 1948, he attacked a police vehicle full of soldiers with some of his men. During the shootout an officer, a petty officer and three agents were seriously injured. In the days that followed he attacked many stations, prepared ambushes, and used every type of guerilla strategy against those forces superior both in number and armament.

Antonino Terranova's squad started to kidnap rich people. With the money they bought ammunition, food, and supplies for them and for the abandoned families. Our house was empty. It was occupied and transformed into the largest police station in Montelepre. They stole all we had. They drank our wine, used our oil, wheat and all our supplies for the winter. Most of our furniture was used as firewood.

Despite the massive deployment of men and army vehicles, the government forces failed to capture my brother. They used all means against him. First they started with the ordinary systems and then passed to extraordinary measures. They organized the most diabolic traps and strategies. But he always escaped.

During the fight for independence many believed that he was aided by expert officers who told him what to do. But the hypothesis was now to be ruled out. Now that he was alone with his men, he was putting on a fierce fight with his men. It was my only meager consolation in my cell.

This is a letter he wrote in that period to the Police Inspector's Office.

**"Spanò and Scelba, you miserables!**

**I am writing to you to inform you that it was I, Giuliano, to do it. So put your hearts at rest. Don't do as usual! Don't blame innocents! The only to do all this is I and no one else. And you still haven't seen anything yet. You bastards! You should be ashamed to take advantage of poor women. I could do the same to your women and there are many targets I could hit. Not like you! The only target you have is my mother. But it's a shame for me to behave like you. Are you planning to arrest all families? All relatives? You're a mass of beasts! Do you really think that you can reach your target by doing this? I cannot understand what kind of stupid idiots you are! Where are your brains? Do, as you like!**

**But remember and don't forget. I told you once and I'll tell you again. The Italian government with all its strength never has and never will scare me! GIULIANO"**

The roundups continued. Many poor farmers were caught during that ruthless manhunt.

At the end of November Turiddu was tired and exasperated by the state of things. He tried a last desperate diplomatic effort. He sent a letter to the Christian Democrat Members of Parliament elected in Sicily.

**Here is an extract:**

**"The current situation requires an explanation. You need it more than we do. The police forces of our leader and friend, the Christian Democrat Scelba, has invaded our territory and perpetrated all types of abuse and violence.**

**Our women and relatives are the favorite targets of this terrible fight.**

**What blame do they have?**

**You do not know it, the police does not know it nor do the women know it. We ask you nothing. We do not even ask you**

to stop this war against us, the victims of these damned post-war years, although we would have the right to do so. But at least leave our women and children alone.

Members of Parliament, these women which are being maltreated in your prisons voted for you during the elections because they had hope in your sense of justice and above all in your promises. In our area we voted only for you. We have kept our promises, now you keep yours.

GIULIANO"

On October 2, 1948 he sent this other letter to the editor of L'Unità, an Italian newspaper of the left:

"Mr. Scelba is lying. He wants to rid himself of the responsibilities of he and his Christian Democrat colleagues. They had promised to grant a general pardon, not only for me and my men, but also for the many people who fought for the honor of the Sicilian motherland. But he does not even know the meaning of the word "honor". All this depended on the victory of the Christian Democrats. They won but Mr. Scelba has forgotten.

Evidence of this was that the Christian Democrats obtained the absolute majority of the votes. If it were not for the great sincerity that nature has given me, I could show you a letter given to me by a close friend of Mr. Scelba on the eve of the elections. This letter contained the aforementioned promises. I tore the letter to pieces to eliminate the evidence.

Scelba, this is what I say to you: "You feel to be safe in your iron tower. With cynicism and wickedness you are waging a war against me. If I agreed to accept the agreement, it was not because I felt to be in the wrong, but to avoid new suffering for everyone.

Do you think that I'm afraid of your emergency measures? I have always told you that I fear no man. Remember that I am afraid of no law, because I can act freely and forcefully. So do as you please. But listen: if God gives me the chance of having you in my hands, I will tear your skin off like a pig. I will make you pay for every minute of my mother's suffering".

On the morning of November 24, 1948, after a tip-off to the Carabinieri, a squad of carabinieri caught Giuseppe Passatempo in his hideout. He was hiding for some time now in his house on the outskirts of the town of Giardinello, where he returned at night to sleep.

The soldiers surrounded his home in silence. They took position and waited patiently for him to come back from the mountain. As soon as the carabinieri saw him, they told him to freeze. His instinct of self-preservation, which had been greatly developed during all those years of hiding, led him to react immediately by shooting a blast of machinegun fire towards them. The men were injured, while the others reacted promptly.

Their bullets hit him many times. Although he was wounded, he crawled to a small cave from where he shot with great fierceness fueled by his desperation. He hit another three carabinieri and continued to shoot until he finished all the ammunition. During the shooting he had been hit again. He had a last bullet in his gun. Since he was no longer answering fire, the soldiers unleashed a German shepherd against him.

Giuseppe Passatempo felt his life, as it escaped from his body as the dog's barking was closer and closer. Probably to put an end to his agony, probably to deprive his enemies of the satisfaction of catching him alive, he pointed his again to his head and shot himself.

The terrible "hangman", the accomplice of the Mafiosi of San Giuseppe Jato that committed the massacre at Portella delle Ginestre, the killer of the Communists in Partinico, the assassin of dozens of men, most of whom belonged to the government forces and had the misfortune of fighting against him, died just as violently as he had lived. When the soldiers reached him. They were surprised to see that besides the hole through his head his body was full of wounds.

The whole territory around Montelepre was scoured daily. Turiddu and his men were forced to be always on the move. They had little time to sleep and very little to eat. Some of them did not want to continue that life anymore and they told my brother their idea of emigrating. He let them decide freely.

On December 8, 1948, a fishing boat set sail for Tunis with the following men on board:

Antonio Terranova, Francesco Motisi, Antonino Cucinella, Frank Mannino and Andrea Palma Abate. Mannino, Candela and Palma Abate joined the foreign legion, while the others were in the hands of the French police about a year later.

Turiddu was alone with very few men. The members of Parliament he had written to did not answer. Of course, they could not expose themselves. It was then that he decided to put an end to the situation like the "Orazi and Curiazi" did.

He challenged Minister Scelba and the whole Italian government in the newspapers:

**"Ten against one, that is ten of them against me alone. They must face me one at a time. If I win I will take over the government, if I lose I shall surrender to them, as long as they release all the members of my family."**

As he waited for their answer he put into force a cease-fire. He left Montelepre and the surrounding territory and he went down to Castellammare del Golfo. One day, as he walked along the shore, he was watching the eternal movement of the waves when an idea flashed in his mind. He could use that force for the benefit of humanity. He started to plan the construction of a machine capable of transmitting the movement of the backwash. After a few weeks and many failed attempts, he managed to build a rudimentary device. He had used the parts of an old car and the beams of an old fallen-in house. It was placed above the waves, which transmitted the movement to a gear. By means of a pinion, it too cogged, the movement was transmitted to a pulley. He called it "perpetual motion".

He said that once it was started it would never stop. Unfortunately all traces of this device were lost.

The answer that Turiddu was waiting for was given in the newspapers. As he expected, the members of the government did not accept the challenge. It would have been interesting to see the duel between my brother and Minister Scelba. He still had not realized that those who reach the top have no intention of coming down again. The situation was difficult. He was trying to solve it in the way he knew best. He would never surrender.

"They'll never catch me alive!" he would often say.

Although he had understood that the Ministers had not taken his proposal seriously into consideration he tried again. He sent some of his men to hang the following notice in Montelepre and in many parts of the city of Palermo:

**"Since the press fails to satisfy my requests, here is this notice outlining my program. If my thoughts are not misconstrued, I hope that no more blood is shed. I will write again to explain my insistence on the challenge I launched in the newspaper in which I gave my ultimatum.**

**I have heard that it has been considered as INCREDIBLE because the members of the government cannot accept a challenge from A SO-CALLED OUTLAW.**

**I would like to know whether important men like Scelba or De Gasperi, who for twenty years gave no sign of their exis-**

tence and then appeared suddenly in a tragic moment for our country with the support of an invading army, have given their fatal blow in a moment in which Italy can be considered dead.

They are responsible for the most terrible and bloody fratricidal war that the world will ever see. As for me I won my fame honorably, by facing the most dangerous risks of life. Looking at my adventurous life, can it be denied that I am no common criminal?

What outlaw ever in the world launched himself in hand-to-hand combat risking his own life to save innocent lives?

If I were an outlaw as they say I could continue to fight from my hideout without ever being caught. This is the reason why my challenge cannot be considered as something extraordinary, because, despite its preponderant forces, the Italian government has failed in reaching its targets and must now take me seriously.

So, since they have no intention of putting an end to the situation with my challenge, I propose that the people express its opinion on a general pardon with a referendum.

Has the government forgotten that they were considered outlaws before me and did they not call Mussolini a tyrant because he considered them criminals and arrested their families? When they resort today to those same means used by that tyrannous government, do they believe that theirs is a government assuring peace and justice?

The newspapers accuse me of carrying out a fratricidal fight. So I ask whether all my considerations were useless?

I have proven time after time that I am no bloodthirsty criminal searching for the blood of the innocent. If I have killed it has been for self-defense. When it was possible, I was the first to help the wounded by medicating them and setting them free.

PEOPLE! Who is more bloodthirsty?

The government that is hunting me down like a fierce animal or he who kills only to defend himself and suffers to see the bloodshed trying to avoid it in every possible way?

As you can see, as regards both the challenge and the referendum, the government says that it is a member of the Atlantic Treaty for security to bring peace and tranquillity to this tormented people. If it is truly so, why does it not solve first this internal crisis and bring peace amongst these exasperated souls who continue to fight each other?

PEOPLE! Try to persuade them, because they are ready to shed innocent blood to quench their thirst for blood.

Remember that in this land we have all made mistakes. Understand our desperate situation. Think of the sacrifices you have borne to grow your children and the risk of seeing all this lost because of this unfair fight in which they risk to die a cruel death. Their death will cast you into eternal mourning!

And you Carabinieri! For a meager sum you renounce the sacred rights of a mother. Stop to think for a moment. I do not fight for money, but for the love of my mother and my land, God's greatest gifts to us. You who are the long arm of the law must recognize that you are defending injustice.

REBEL! Because you are the strength of those buffoons and tyrants. Without you they are no one. Proof of this is their refusal of my challenge. Think of your mothers who anxiously await your return with their arms wide open ready to press you against their hearts.

Remember that you are dealing with a man of honor and that continuing as you are doing, your only hope is that of not being killed with my own hands.

I will give my last ultimatum on March 30th (1949) if nothing happens in the meantime.

DEFEND YOURSELVES! Because, with great woe, I will have to resume my fight. I hope that you and the people will understand me. My best regards to the people!

GIULIANO"

A few days of waiting went by even after the deadline of the ultimatum. But nothing happened. On the contrary, there was a further intensification of the retaliations and arrests. In the eyes of Turiddu, this behavior of the soldiers was a provocation. His reply came on April 6, 1949, when he and his men attacked an army truck with 12 carabinieri on board. They were returning from an operation in the countryside around Torretta. Ten of them were wounded during the shooting.

This attack was followed by other more fierce clashes. The roundups with the deployment of thousands of men and dog units were carried out almost daily. But my brother had become an expert in guerilla warfare. He managed to coordinate each attack perfectly. He always got by safely and he continued to live free as bird in the mountains around Montelepre.

In the meantime another change was made at the head of the

police station: Spanò was replaced by inspector Ciro Verdiani. Up to that moment he had worked in Sicily. He knew the mentality and the expectations of the Sicilian people perfectly.

His methods gave rise to lively arguments between the carabinieri and the police. He counted heavily on the help of informers, he established contacts with the local Mafia bosses in Monreale, Borgetto and Partinico. Thanks to these "men of honor" he managed to meet my brother a number of times. First he tried to convince him to surrender or to expatriate, then, during these meetings, something that had happened to all those before him: the new inspector was fascinated by Turiddu. He not only forgot his innate cautiousness and the uniform he was wearing, but he ended up offering him his help and friendship.

Towards the end of May 1949 a young captain of the Carabinieri came to inspect what had been the house of our family and was now the largest station in Montelepre. They all sprung to attention before him. They bowed in front of him and were very respectful. They followed him into the various rooms.

He spoke very little. He just looked at the devastation of the building. The officers were embarrassed. They tried to find plausible excuses to explain what had happened. Suddenly he caught everyone by surprise. The captain turned on his heels and went towards the door. They all sprung to attention again and they saluted him.

As soon as he was about 10 meters away, he loaded the machinegun, suddenly turned around and opened fire against the walls of the house. Everyone was caught by surprise and scared. They asked themselves why the officer was behaving like that. The answer was immediate. The captain tossed away his jacket and hat and revealed his true identity. That man was Turiddu in disguise.

It was too late when the carabinieri realized that they had been fooled. They tried to react but they did not even have the time to react, because my brother shot a second blast that wounded two of them. There was total chaos and everyone rushed for cover.

Turiddu had gone to see for himself what they had done to our house. When the soldiers tried to close ranks, he had already disappeared.

In that period more than 3,000 people in Montelepre had been taken to jail or interned. The more the government forces raged against the population, the more Turiddu reacted with anger. Inspector Ciro Verdiani tried at first to contrast Turiddu's initiatives as best as he could, but the Ministry was dissatisfied. It wanted to put an end to the whole story as soon as possible.

Colonel Ugo Luca was sent to Palermo to help him. First he put back into force the curfew and then inflicted new suffering onto the remaining inhabitants, that is to say women, the elderly and children.

For my brother that measure was the last straw and he decided to make him pay for it dearly. He organized an attack on the station in "Bellolampo" but that was only a diversion. The real target was that of attracting the main body of the army out of town.

As he planned, about a half an hour after the attack, a whole convoy of armored vehicles full of soldiers and police headed for there. They started to scour the whole area looking for Turiddu and his men. Of course, they found no one. The two commanders ordered the retreat to Palermo. As they wandered uselessly around in the mountains, my brother placed two mines along the road to Palermo.

The mines were for Luca and Verdiani, but their vehicle passed without being damaged. Unfortunately one of the vehicles following them pressed the mine with the rear wheel and exploded. Many soldiers were killed and others were wounded. All this happened on August 19, 1949.

This attack by Turiddu led to the fierce reaction of the Ministry of the Interior.

Five days later the Police General Inspector's Office was suppressed. The C.F.R.B. (Bandit Repression Forces Corps) was set up instead with the same powers and competencies. Col. Ugo Luca, aided by Capt. Antonino Perenze, took over the command of this new corps. He had fought in the Far East in the military secret services. He was an expert in guerilla warfare.

Inspector Ciro Verdiani did not take the change in command very well. He refused to hand over any document he had and he kept secret the network of informers he had set up and used up to then. So the C.F.R.B. had to start from scratch. Meanwhile Verdiani had found the right envoys to organize the meeting with Turiddu.

At first, as he himself confessed later, he wanted to find a way of catching him, but then, as stated above, he changed his mind. During one of the many meetings with him, the inspector made him a strange offer: Turiddu was to shoot a movie telling the story of his life. Verdiani himself would have given him the movie camera. The movie was to end with the death of the protagonist. Of course, it was supposed to be only a stage illusion.

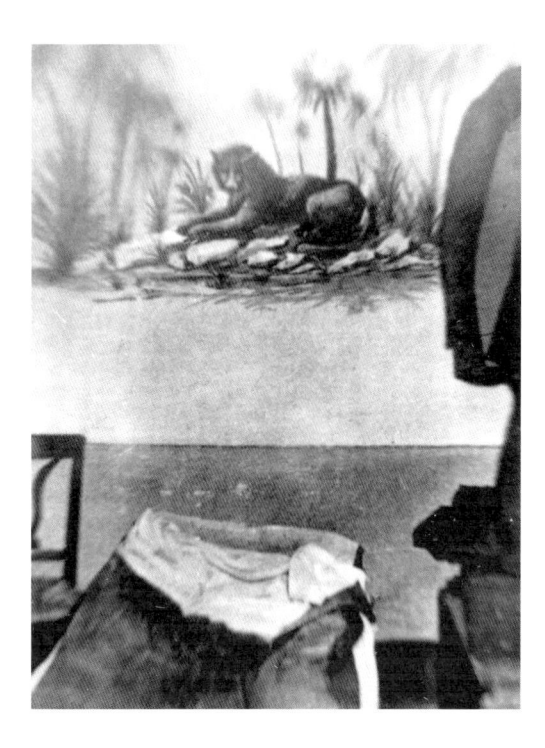

Turiddu's room occupied by a Carabinieri officer.

Giuliano's house is now a station.

## Chapter XIX

# A LONG CHAIN OF BETRAYALS

Since Col. Ugo Luca was assigned the command of the C.F.R.B. living conditions had worsened even more in Montelepre. His men were spread in town and in the countryside. They perpetrated actions that were far from being a part of the tasks that they were paid for and sullied the honor of the uniforms they wore.

During those terrible days, the inhabitants of Montelepre experienced hours of fear. They were forced to stay closed in their homes without being able to satisfy their most basic needs. You could not even open window that the home would become the target of their fire. For those who lived on the outskirts, the things were even worse. The Carabinieri, those who had presented themselves as the champions of justice, stained themselves with cruel actions against the civilian population. Not even the outlaws they were searching for committed similar actions.

Turiddu would boil with anger as he heard what was happening. His mind was full of shock, bewilderment and anger. He sent a letter of protest to Col. Luca. He wrote:

**"You have no idea that there are people that can testify that you were about to die, if they hadn't stopped my fury... So please don't bother these people anymore.... These people that you maltreat, because your hopes are vain.... You can be sure that whatever happens, I will never finish in your hands, while, if I wish, I can get rid of you whenever I want. If I haven't done so, it is because I wanted to avoid spilling more blood. But if I see that you're double-crossing me, I'll show you that I know how to punish you and all those with you. I'll prove it to you and it won't take long.**

**GIULIANO"**

In the meantime Frank Mannino and Rosario Candela, two of those who had joined the Foreign Legion, had deserted. They were literally terrified by that life. They had to face sufferings and dangers even greater than those they faced with my brother.

They landed secretly in Castellammare del Golfo on June 12, 1949. Since the town was a safe place, they stayed there for several months. At the end of October, they were tired of lazing around and they tried to contact Turiddu. Without his guide they felt like fish out of water. They were informed of what had happened during the period they were away. Many things had changed in the meantime! Finding Turiddu for a meeting was difficult even for them, who knew the right people and the situation.

After an unsuccessful round of attempts, they were informed that they were to get in touch with two brothers from Monreale, Nino and Ignazio Miceli. They sent them their letters for Turiddu, but some time went by before they received an answer.

He was still resentful for their having abandoned him and for the long time that went by without sending him any news. In the meantime a reporter arrived in Palermo from Sweden. She had a strange name for a Swede: Maria Tecla Cyliakus and Tecla was name of Greek origin.

She was not very beautiful. She seemed to be quite a normal looking woman. But the fact that she wore pants, which were a typically male garment, aroused the curiosity and the attraction of those who looked at her.

In those days the newspapers of half the globe were talking about Turiddu with great admiration and sympathy. He would receive letters from women from all over the world. They invited him to reach them in their countries. His pictures were on the front page of the most famous and prestigious newspapers of the world revealing his masculine beauty.

An aura of legend surrounded his figure and women were captivated by his charm. They sent him pictures of themselves wearing bathing suits and in seducing poses. They made him all kinds of proposals.

But Turiddu was well aware of the fact that he could never have a family of his own in his conditions. He preferred being honest with them so he would not even answer. One of the few exceptions was his long exchange of letters with Carmencita Franco, the daughter of Francisco Franco, the Spanish Caudillo. There was a friendly exchange of tenderness between the two. In one of her letters she offered him political asylum and the position of Minister of War, if he managed to reach her.

The Swedish reporter was fascinated by him. She had crossed all Europe with the intention of meeting him. She had asked for information in the police station. It was obviously the worst place to look for news or information that could help her. But this thin woman with red hair was very resolute.

She was ready to do anything to reach her target. She left for Montelepre. Once she reached the town, the first thing she did was to go to the Carabinieri station. She asked the Marshal advice on how to reach Turiddu.

He started to laugh loudly:

"Dear lady, if we knew how to reach him by now. . . ."

"But don't you have anything that could help me?" she insisted.

"The only thing I know is that his favorite hiding place is the Sagana estate. . . but when we go to look for him, either there is no trace of him or he appears in other places or in the most unthinkable areas!"

In that moment the reporter remembered that a year before Giuseppe Passatempo was killed near Giardinello. So she put two plus two together: she thought that Turiddu could have been in that area.

The marshal showed her where the town was to get rid of her. Maria Tecla was disappointed.

She tried to find out as much as possible from other relatives who had not been arrested, but that hope too soon vanished.

The inhabitants who were usually very hospitable with foreigners would suddenly change completely their behavior if someone started to ask indiscreet questions on Turiddu. It was not strange that people would suddenly turn their backs on the interlocutor. The redhead Swede soon was tired by all that wandering. All the patrols she had met along the road would ask first for her documents and then for her autograph.

She left Montelepre and went to Giardinello. She started to climb the hill to the west of that town. She was lucky that three of Turiddu's men were in that area that day. They saw her and they started to follow her with their binoculars.

They soon realized that she was a woman although she dressed like a man. They had no idea of what to do, so they called my brother with the walky-talkies that my husband had sent him from the United States.

Turiddu was on Mount "Saraceno" located at about a kilometer away. He told them to keep watching her until he arrived. The woman continued to climb towards the top of the hill. Every now and then she would stop to rest or to look at a map of the area.

Turiddu reached his men about a half an hour later. They all came out into the clear to attract her attention. A few minutes went by be-

Mass arrests in Montelepre: two thirds of the population was taken away to jail or interned.

fore she noticed them. When she finally did, she went towards them.

First my brother wanted to make sure that she was not a spy. He pushed his cap over his eyes and he walked in the midst of his men. He behaved like a soldier in disguise:

"Good morning!"

"Your documents please! Good morning!"

She answered in Italian with a bit of a strange accent.

"With whom. . . ."

Turiddu preceded her question and answered promptly:

"We're carabinieri in disguise! And you?"

"I'm a reporter!"

"What are you doing here?"

"I'm looking for Salvatore Giuliano."

Turiddu started to laugh. The others did the same.

"Ha! Ha! Ha! That's a nice one! We've been looking for him for years and we can't find him! How do you hope to find him? Do you know him? Have you ever seen him?"

"No! No" answered the reporter ingenuously.

"Then how do you hope to recognize him?"

"I only know that he has a scar here!" answered Tecla as she touched her front near her temple with a finger.

Turiddu lifted his cap and showed her the scar that was barely visible. She froze from the surprise, but she recovered promptly and shouted:

"You're Giuliano!"

Her surprise convinced my brother of her good faith and decided to reward her for her decision and courage. He led her to their camp. He arranged her lodging and he ordered his men that no one was to bother her or to look at her.

In the afternoon, after she had eaten and rested, he granted an interview. He went to a private place among the boulders and answered frankly to all her questions. He described his ideals, the reasons for his fight and his reactions. Maria Tecla was hanging on his lips and stared at him full of amazement.

She had identified herself completely with him. Listening to his story made her weep. She too saw that tears were rolling down Turiddu's face when he spoke of our family and our persecuted people.

Those tears, that emotion, that sharing of problems, anxieties and fears set their senses on fire: they hugged each affectionately.

The next day, as they spoke, Tecla saw that Turiddu wore a golden necklace with a small cross. She took it in her hands and asked curiously:

"What is this amulet?"
"It's no amulet! It's a cross!"
"What is a cross?" she asked sincerely and full of curiosity.
"What? You've never heard of Jesus Christ? Really? You're not joking?"

But looking into his eyes, he understood that she was not lying. Maria Tecla was an atheist. Turiddu, on the contrary, was deeply religious. During those three days spent in the mountains, they spoke a lot about God, until she converted to Catholicism.

He wrote the following verses for her:

> "Vinisti di la nivi a lu me suli
> sula cu lu curuzza 'ntra li mani
> comu la madonnuzza a lu figghiuzzu
> lu ciuri volli, nun volli lu pani".

> "You came from the snow to me, the Sun,
> Alone with your heart in your hands
> Like the Madonna came to her Son
> She wanted a flower, not bread."

When she returned to her newspaper, she published a long special that shocked public opinion. She wrote what she had seen: the government forces that behaved like an invading army in Montelepre. In doing so, she sided against the government forces.

The titles of her articles revealed her feelings for Turiddu:
"My beloved outlaw".
"The three most beautiful days of my life".

Many thought that she had fallen in love and that she had experienced three days of passion with my brother. But those titles had a different meaning. During those three days, Maria Tecla Cyliakus had discovered the existence of GOD.

Before returning to her country, she stopped in Paris and there she was baptized. A few months later she returned to Italy.

The courageous reporter wanted to meet Turiddu again, but her articles contrasted with those of the "regime's" press. She was arrested and maltreated. The diplomacy of her country had to intervene to have her freed. She was expelled from Italy and she was branded as an "undesired" person.

In the meantime the squads of the C.F.R.B. had intensified their raids all around Montelepre. Turiddu realized that each of his attacks worsened the retaliation against the town. He decided to leave the area to avoid further suffering.

He moved his camp to the hills around Salemi, a few kilometers away from Castelvetrano in the province of Trapani. He abstained from carrying out operations, but he kept in touch with some friends in Monreale (the Miceli brothers) and Borgetto (Domenico Albano). Thanks to them he always knew what was happening in Montelepre.

He spent his time studying English and writing letters to our family members. Despite we were being held prisoner in different places, he managed to keep in touch with us. In his letters to our mother he would always write:

**"Be strong and courageous. Don't be disheartened! I think of you in every moment of the day. The sadness I have in my heart is great, as I see you suffer because of human evilness. Be good to the poor."**

Even in prison or in the internment camps our family was always united. We would write to each other daily and exchange the information we managed to find out. This letter dated October 17, 1949, was sent by my brother to the Sicilian regional government:

**"If you would stop to reflect for a moment you would realize what mistake it is to consider me as a petty criminal. You would also feel regret for this son or brother of yours who is being insulted in so many ways, while you should be grateful to him instead for being where you are, because it is thanks to him and his desire for a free Sicily that the Autonomous Sicilian Government was created. The failure to acknowledge this means failing to acknowledge yourselves and the government. You still hope in the megalomania of few men who are trying to eliminate me, but, if you still believe this lie, then you can be sure that this conviction will destroy you in a delirium of shame because I will always be free.**

**GIULIANO"**

A reporter, a photographer and a cameraman were staying at the "Sole" Hotel in Palermo. After many failed attempts, they had found one of Turiddu's informers. Thanks to him they managed to set a meeting for an interview with him.

They had been waiting with suspense for a month, but their perseverance was rewarded. The meeting was set for December 10, 1949 at three in the morning along the road to Salemi. The three envoys were: Jacopo Rizza, Ivo Mendolesi and Italo D'Ambrosio. They rented a Fiat 500 "Topolino" and they went to the meeting point.

They waited for an hour driving back and forth until a man came out from behind a bush and stopped them. The three stopped the car next to him. They hoped that their waiting was over, but it was not so.

They spent yet another hour waiting. Finally an old truck came with five armed men on board. The vehicle stopped next to their car. The man told them to follow him. They drove for 20 kilometers and then stopped. They left the vehicles and continued on foot. They walked for half an hour along wet and muddy ground. Finally they reached an abandoned shack.

My brother and Gaspare Pisciotta were smiling on the threshold. Since 1948, when seven of his men emigrated to Tunisia, Pisciotta had become his right hand. Turiddu welcomed them with a little bow, introduced himself and shook their hands. He then looked towards the five men that had accompanied them, nodded to them and they left.

The three envoys spent six hours with Turiddu: Ivo Mendolesi had the chance of photographing him in many different poses, the cameraman D'Ambrosio filmed him and shot two hundred meters of tape, Jacopo Rizza gathered a lot of information on his life, his fight for independence, his discontent with politics and especially politicians, and on his "perpetual motion" machine.

In Italy the interview was published in three episodes in the weekly *"Oggi"* and in the United States in the *"New York Times"*. It was a world exclusive. These interviews shocked the public opinion and Col. Luca and all his men were angry.

It was said that the reporters had been better than them in finding him. They had uselessly searched for him for six long years.

Many reporters dreamed of that scoop, but those three only had the luck of meeting of my brother. Of course, there is always the other side of the coin. They were accused of criminal sympathies. But they were doing their job. Their acquittal put an end to the story, which was called the "treaded tail".

In the meantime the friendly contacts between my brother and Inspector Ciro Verdiani continued. Since he had been "ousted" by Luca, he was assigned a position in Border Services Inspector's Office. If my brother was to try to expatriate, Verdiani was the right man in the right place.

As Christmas approached, Turiddu obtained an appointment with the investigating magistrate in Palermo thanks to Verdiani. During the meeting he had the chance of interceding with Emanuele Pili in favor of our mother and all those in prison or interned. In exchange for this favor, he would renounce armed resistance against the police. The magistrate promised only to release our mother. For the others he said he would see what he could do, even though he then did nothing.

Turiddu returned to the Trapani area. With his few men he went to Marsala. On December 27, 1949 he met Inspector Verdiani in this city. He had been accompanied by the intermediaries, Ignazio and Nino Miceli, while Turiddu had come with his "faithful" companion Gaspare Pisciotta.

The inspector had come to inform him of the imminent release of our mother. That news had to be celebrated. They all ate together at lunch. They finished their meal with the traditional panettone and a toast with spumante.

About 20 days later our mother was acquitted and freed. After 18 months, she went back to Montelepre, but she could not return to our home. More than a year before it was occupied by the Carabinieri and transformed into a station. They had ruined it. There were no doors or windows. The wine casks were empty. They emptied what remained in them as a last slap in the face. The oil jars, which we had left full, were all broken. All the furniture was gone. Some pieces were antique and cost a lot. All the other objects in the house had vanished too as the wheat and the supplies. This was the desolation that my mother found when she went home. She was forced to go and stay in the house of my sister Giuseppina. Luckily, although it too was abandoned, it had not been sacked. My sister and her husband were interned on the island of Ustica.

My mother was to be watched: she was not truly free. Two carabinieri would take turns guarding the door of the house night and day. It was as if she was in house arrest. She had to ask the permission to talk to her neighbors: she had no money, no food, with only the clothes she was wearing. That poor woman ate nothing for the first three days at home.

For many days she managed to survive thanks to the generosity of her neighbors. In those days there was running water in very few homes and that was one of the few.

To avoid that the carabinieri found out about it, they would stick cooked pasta in the galvanized steel sheet containers, known as "bummula" and they would go in to get water.

Despite these measures against my mother, she managed to keep in touch with Turiddu anyway. He informed her of his agreement with Inspector Verdiani on shooting the movie of his life. He told her that the movie was almost finished and explained to her how it was to finish.

Once he had paid Verdiani, with his part of the money earned with the movie, he wanted to open a factory in Montelepre. All the heads of the poorest and most needy families, the unemployed and those who had been damaged because of this story would be hired.

Our mother told him to think for himself first, because, if one day they captured him, he would need the money to pay a good lawyer.

His answer was always the same:

"As long as I am alive, they will never catch me! Should they come one day to tell you that I am dead, don't believe them and don't go for the identification!"

For some time now the newspapers wrote that the trial on the massacre in Portella was about to start. In the meantime the exchange of letters between my brother and Inspector Verdiani had intensified. Here is an interesting one:

"**Dear Commendatore,**

**I read in the newspapers that the trial will start soon against those accused of the massacre in Portella delle Ginestre.**

**Please help them because all those boys are innocent and they confessed all the same. You know what methods they used. Only I know the truth, but it isn't my fault. What happened was a mistake, because the target was not that of killing the innocent victims, but another one.**

**All this was self-inflicted by the Communists. They forced us to do what we did. For the time being I will say no more, but, if you think that it is necessary, I am willing to speak to Judge Pili. If he wishes to speak to me again, I am ready to meet him. I would be pleased to do so, because it would be a great comfort.**

**Please take care of my sister Marianna and my sister Giuseppina. My mother told me that she is pregnant. Please care even of my father. He is now an old man. Send all my love to my family. My best regards also to Judge Pili.**

**Yours truly,<br>GIULIANO"**

In that same period my mother received news from Ustica: my sister Giuseppina was very ill. The pregnancy and the little and inadequate food had caused a great increase in the albumin content of our blood. Her whole body was swollen.

On that island she could not get all the assistance and care she needed. My mother asked the two soldiers guarding her house to have the permission to go to Palermo and to talk with the head of the police.

She was granted permission, as long as she was accompanied by her two "guardian angels". She went to speak to the head of the police escorted by the two men. His name was Marzano. She explained to him my sister's conditions and asked him to send her home. He was very kind and respectful with her. He granted her the permission to go and get her personally.

My mother was a strong woman. Turiddu had inherited his strength from her. She landed with the first boat to Ustica. She found my sister in very serious conditions. As soon as she returned to Palermo, she took her immediately to the hospital. A few days later in that same clinic she gave birth to a child that died immediately after its birth.

Meanwhile Inspector Verdiani received a letter from my brother a few days later. He sent him a message. He invited him to come and explain what happened in Portella because the trial in Viterbo was going to start on June 12, 1950.

If he wanted to help those accused of that crime, he had to explain how things went. Turiddu wrote a letter to the judges in Viterbo explaining the incident. Verdiani sent the letter to Judge Pili. He gave it privately to the lawyer, Romano Battaglia. He defended both Turiddu and many of his men. Thanks to him, the letter reached its destination.

In the letter Turiddu denied that those accused of the crime were the instigators, as stated by others, and he also denied the premeditation of the crime.

**"During the questioning of the defendants I have noted that those who retract their confessions are looked upon with diffidence. Does it mean that they were honest only when they confessed?**

**For this reason, I have felt the need to illustrate my considerations. If all those accused of the crime in Portella have declared to be guilty without being brutally tortured, why then should they not confirm what they said to the Carabinieri when they are standing before you? It is all too clear and obvious that they were tortured and it is also true that the whole world today is looking at Italy and at its judiciary system, which is founded on the low and vile mentality of an executioner (Brigadier Nicola Sganga, alias Don Pasquale). I don't want to believe it, because I would feel sorry for the whole of Italy, which feels to be democratic and civil, but, if the model is the method used by Don Pasquale and if the false inventions they were forced to sign are confirmed once again, our only hope is to appeal to Italian women and mothers to give birth to children made of iron capable of resisting to torture.**

**So the only way to be innocent and honest in Italy is to**

know how to resist torture? And if you cannot resist then you are a criminal and guilty?

All those the defendants, who have been defined as the bandits of Portella, are all INNOCENT, and if after all the evidence that I will present you, they will still be found guilty all the same, then I must protest, because it will be an unjustified crime committed to cover the wrongdoings of the police.

In Portella, together with 12 men, my idea was to scare the crowd with the shootout. The crowd would be dispersed and it would not have to listen to the falsities of Communist propaganda. After devising the plan, I decided to put it into action. I ordered my men to empty 3 chargers and to shoot about 20 meters above the crowd, so that, when they heard the gunfire, it get scared and leave the celebration.

We did as planned and we watched the people rushing here and there. After ten minutes we left thinking that everything had gone according to plan, but the next day we read in the newspapers about the terrible mistake. That news filled us with anguish. We tried to comfort each other trying to understand if someone had dared to shoot against the crowd, but we were all sure that we hadn't.

The terrible regret for those poor victims who had lost their lives because of the vile feeling and avidity of power of those who wish to reach power exploiting the misfortune of others led me to prepare a attack on Li Causi. Luckily for him, it too failed because when I went to his house he had already left.

These are the reasons that led me to carry out my plan in Portella. More than the material responsibility, I care about the moral responsibility. I could never have opened fire on those poor and defenseless workers on purpose.

1) Because I have never reached the point of being so vile as to do harm against defenseless people. Proof of this is that not only have I faced entire armies, but I have also behaved honorably by warning my opponents before launching an attack.

2) I could never have opened fire on purpose against people of my same social class. I have always lived in the midst of these people and I have helped them as best as I could.

3) I am no rich landowner, I do not belong to those who enjoy keeping in slavery the lower classes. I have never been at their service. I can even consider myself as being their enemy.

I am the son of a worker who created a family with his sacrifices. Since I was thirteen, I started to work hard to help my family. Anyone in Montelepre can confirm it. Furthermore, maybe for the abuses suffered at work, it is known to all the situation that led me to this adventurous life. It is impossible for me to have forgotten the sacrifice made by poor workers.

The arrest of my mother too can prove that I am no coward. I have faced entire convoys of armored vehicles with hundreds of carabinieri, while I could have fought the enemy with the same means. With a stick of dynamite I could have blown up an entire family, because after all I am considered an outlaw and I would be paying them back in their own. Why haven't I done it? Because I have a heart, too, unlike others and I have a brain that keeps me on the right path."

Since December, that is when my brother met with Judge Pili, he had stopped all actions. No one heard of him anymore nor was his presence signaled anywhere. Many thought that he had emigrated. Even Col. Luca and his men had no idea of what was happening. They even lifted the curfew in Montelepre. They finally understood that the massive operations with thousands of men were useless. All they had done was to attract the attention of the press.

In the meantime Frank Mannino and Rosario Candela had sent a letter to Turiddu and they received an answer. They were told where they could meet him. They were to contact Domenico Albano in Borgetto. He would have helped them to get in touch with the Miceli brothers. Once they had contacted them, they could have set a date for a meeting.

The two followed the instructions in the letter. They went to Monreale, where they found a nephew of the Miceli brothers. He was their intermediary. After a few hours he returned with the answer. If they wanted to meet Turiddu they were to come back fifteen days later on March 15, 1950.

The two went back to Montelepre and they found refuge in the Sagana estate in contrada "Tirone". But during those days many things had changed. The rivalry between the carabinieri and the police worsened. They refused to cooperate with each other and even tried to cheat one another.Col. Luca and Capt. Perenze had found out that the Miceli brothers, with the help of a man named Benedetto Minasola, were Inspector Verdiani's informers and that Verdiani was in touch with Turiddu. He considered all this an obstacle to their work. They were informed that the Inspector was authorized both to negotiate and to capture Turiddu.

They felt to have been bypassed. Salvatore Giuliano's arrest was exclusively up to the C.F.R.B. They decided to arrest all his informers to checkmate their antagonist. But the three men from Monreale said to be ready to help the carabinieri at specific conditions thus avoiding to be arrested.

Prove of this was that they said to be ready to help to capture some of Turiddu's men. They made the deal. First they signaled the presence of Frank Mannino and Rosario Candela in the Sagana area. Men of their gang managed to separate the two with an excuse.

On the morning of March 12, 1950, Rosario Candela was eliminated. To cover the responsibility of the Monreale Mafia gang, they put on a fake shootout with a C.F.R.B. squad. Unaware of what had happened Frank Mannino went to the appointment that the Miceli brothers said to have organized with Turiddu.

The appointment was in a house in the countryside. It was owned by two foremen: the Pecoraro brothers. It was located halfway between Pioppo and Monreale. It had been pompously called "Villa Carolina".

Mannino knew the place very well. It was one of the places where his squad had kept some hostages. He waited there anxiously and for a long time. He waited there until the early afternoon. Finally Nino Miceli's nephew came. Mannino went towards him and asked of his uncle. He said that he did not anything of that appointment.

Mannino begged him to go back to Monreale to tell his uncle that he was waiting for him. Two hours went by until the young man came back. The answer was that he had to wait until late into the evening. He was getting more nervous and nervous. He was tempted to leave, but he stayed. Around 11 o'clock in the evening he saw a truck coming. It was driven by Nino Miceli.

The two men embraced like brothers. Miceli then spoke:

"I have come to tell you that I did not manage today to get in touch with Turiddu! Don't worry! Tomorrow you'll see him!"

The two spent about an hour together. Then Nino Miceli left. They had agreed to meet again in the afternoon of the day after. Mannino went away to look for a safe place where he could spend the night.

The next day Miceli came with Benedetto "Nittu" Minasola. Both greeted each other and then Nino Miceli told Mannino:

"Ciccio, Turiddu is in Monreale! He can't come immediately because there are too many carabinieri around!"

He noticed the suspicious look on his face and added:

"Don't worry, he'll come tonight! He'll be here tonight!"

The little voice of his animal instinct developed in so many years on the run told him to get away, but the rational side of him had the best. It was a just a matter of waiting a few hours.

He waited patiently. Time seemed to have stopped. The hours seemed never-ending. This time Nino Miceli and Benedetto Minasola were punctual. He found them in front of the house. After the usual greetings, they told him that Turiddu and his men were waiting for him in the house. Reassured by their words, he followed them into the house. In the clearing outside the house Miceli's truck and black car were parked there. There was silence everywhere.

Frank Mannino followed them inside and lit them from behind with his flashlight. In the dark he noticed a group of men and he thought that they were my brother and his men. He went towards them with his hand outstretched to shake the hand that one of the men had stretched out:

"Hello to our friends!"

But when he was close enough, he felt his arm being grabbed, while all the others jumped on him and blocked him. The men he had exchanged for Turiddu and his men were Col. Paolantonio, Capt. Perenze, Marshal Lo Bianco and another five soldiers in disguise.

It was too late when Mannino realized that he had been betrayed. His arrest was part of the plan to capture the men closest to Turiddu. So the news was kept secret.

In the meantime my mother in Montelepre was visited by a stranger. She said to be the Princess of Ganci and that she wanted to donate 5 million Lire to Turiddu. My mother did not trust that woman. She feared that it was another trick of the Carabinieri so that they could arrest her again. She treated the person with respect, but refused the money. She wrote to Turiddu to inform him of the visit. She received his reply from Domenico Albano from Borgetto:

**"Dear Mother,**

**You did the right thing when you did not accept the Princess's money. As you know, I have decided to give up my fight and to avoid any other operation.**

**I depend on the generosity of the few financiers who are still helping me. If the money is really from the Princess, I'll send someone to go and get it. I need it to buy some things I need.**

**Turiddu"**

For some time now my mother was very worried. She had a strange feeling of danger. She could feel something strange in the air. Turiddu was at the top of list of her fears. She was not the only one to have this feeling: I felt them too and more intensely than her.

What was even stranger was that other friends of ours could feel the same premonition. There was betrayal in the air. There were strange rumors, strange conversations and vague warnings:

"Tell Turiddu to watch out!"

But no one knew anything precise. No one could explain this feeling. Yet there were many people who confirmed those omens.

In the meantime Frank Mannino was taken to Palermo to the Calatafimi station. He was closed in of the special cells underground. He was kept the whole time sitting on a chair with his hands and feet tied. They told him to cooperate but he refused angrily. They kept him in that position to convince him to accept those luring promises. They hoped he would give in sooner or later. But the days went by and he held on.

Col. Luca and Marshal Lo Bianco tired soon. They needed to capture someone important to put on trial in Viterbo. How could they start a "historical" trial with those beardless boys. They returned to Monreale to meet the Miceli brothers and Benedetto Minasola. They asked for their cooperation again to capture some other of Turiddu's men. Their real target was my brother, but they knew that it was impossible without the help of people close to him to avoid suspects.

But the Miceli brothers and "Nittu" Minasola had no intention of doing it, although they had betrayed other times as well. They explained clearly why they were hesitant: they had made a deal with Inspector Verdiani. He had promised them the 50 million Lire of the reward for his capture. They also feared for their lives, because if he found out he would have killed them.

The two officers threatened them to convince them to cooperate. They would have arrested them and interned them. Benedetto Minasola tried to calm them all down:

"You can't do this to us! We're cooperating already! Verdiani has already promised us that money!"

Marshal Lo Bianco tried to cut it short and said:

"We'll give you the reward, so that there won't be any problems with the money!"

Once they had reached the agreement, they started to discuss how to arrest Turiddu's other men. The Miceli brothers revealed that Nunzio Badalamenti and Castrenze Madonia wanted to meet my brother, too. With the usual system of the intermediaries, they had managed to get in touch with them. All they had to do was to plan a trap.

Their arrest was almost like that of Frank Mannino. They set an appointment on the outskirts of Monreale. The meeting point was the same as always: "Villa Carolina". They made them wait for the whole day of April 12, 1950 (it was Easter Monday). At 10 o'clock in the evening Benedetto Minasola reached them. Nino Miceli was waiting close by with his truck. It was loaded with baskets.

Minasola said he had been sent by Turiddu to take them to him. They followed him trustingly and they climbed in the back. Minasola told them they risked being seen. It was better if they entered two empty baskets on the truck. The others were filled with lemons and oranges. This way there was no risk of being caught along the way.

They obeyed hesitantly. They squatted in the basket with their arms ready in case of danger. Their short and uncomfortable voyage started. After about ten minutes the truck stopped shortly so that Minasola and Miceli could get off. Marshal Lo Bianco and two soldiers took their place. The truck then started off again on its night voyage towards Palermo. About a quarter of an hour later it stopped. The men suddenly heard Marshal Lo Bianco's voice break the silence of the night:

"You can get off! The trip is over!"

Slowly and with their muscles aching for the uncomfortable position, Nunzio Badalamenti and Castrenze Madonia came out of the baskets. They were dismayed when they saw that they were surrounded by a myriad of soldiers with their guns pointed against them.

Instead of being taken to Turiddu, they were in Palermo inside the courtyard of the station in Corso Calatafimi.

Col. Luca kept their arrest secret. They were not prisoners: they were kidnapped. They were sent into the "special" cells. They were reserved the same treatment suffered by Mannino. The only difference was that one of them fell into their trap.

Rizza Mendolesi and D'Ambrosio together with Turiddu and Pisciotta.

*My Brother, Salvatore Giuliano*

Gaspare Pisciotta and Salvatore Giuliano inside a hideout.

Salvatore Giuliano in 1949.

Chapter XX

# THE MAN DIES. . .
# THE LEGEND LIVES ON

Turiddu's feats were just a faraway memory. He had abandoned the Montelepre area at the end of November 1949. At first he had moved to the mountains around Salemi and Calatafimi. Finally he found refuge in the home of Giuseppe Marotta in Castelvetrano.

Experience had taught him that he could not have a fixed abode. But despite everything he would sleep often in that home and in that of Gregorio Di Maria, a lawyer. His meetings with Inspector Verdiani were held in that town. They would spend their talking on how to proceed with the movie.

It was almost finished: only the last scene had to be shot. It was the scene of his death. As explained previously, it was supposed to be only a stage illusion. Since Turiddu was the movie's cameraman, Verdiani said that he had found three people perfect for the job. All he had to do was to find the one that looked the most like him for that scene.

After years of battles and struggles he had ended up accepting Verdiani's proposal to leave the country. He had been given all the necessary guarantees that he could trust him. Very few of his men were still free. The others were either in jail or interned. Others were dead.

Ciro Verdiani had given his word: he would have done everything possible to help those who were in jail. In a few years time, all his men would be free again. Although Turiddu was convinced of his good faith, Turiddu told him:

"If it doesn't happen, I'll come back to Sicily and there will be no peace for you!"

Two months had gone by since Nunzio Badalamenti and Castrenze Madonia's capture. There was a rumor in Montelepre that three "picciotti" had disappeared and there was no trace of them. My mother was scared by the rumor. She had not received any news from Turiddu for weeks.

She tried to get in touch with him to warn him to watch out, but each day that went by seemed to widen the abyss between

The arrest of the journalist Maria Tecla Cyliakus.

them. However, the news of the disappearance of the three men reached Turiddu too. He decided to investigate on the case. He left from Castelvetrano with Gaspare Pisciotta and he went first to Borgetto. Domenico Albano confirmed the rumor and told him to go to Monreale to find out what had happened.

The next day, at dawn, they walked to Monreale following the trails they knew so well. They reached the town at 7 o'clock in the morning and they went to speak to an uncle of Castrenze Madonia. He welcomed them warmly, but he was shocked by their questions:

"From what I know, my nephew and another man had come to look for you. I even know that they contacted Don Nittu Minasola! Since then I have received no news from him. I thought that you were together!"

The situation was too obscure, but Turiddu had guessed what had happened. Staying in town was too dangerous. They went to the outskirts with "Aspanu". They decided to wait for nightfall amongst the thick bushes covering the nearby hills.

Late that night they went to the homes of Nino Miceli and Minasola. They pointed their guns against them and forced them to follow them. They took them into the countryside. In a clearing in the middle of a thick patch of olive trees there was an abandoned shack. They tossed them to the ground and Turiddu started to interrogate them:

"So? What have you done to my men?"

"What men are you talking about? We haven't seen anyone!" answered promptly Don Nittu. They still had not finished talking when Turiddu slapped them in their face.

"I want the truth!" replied Turiddu. "Don't try fooling me or I'm gonna kill you like dogs!" As he said this, he loaded his gun.

"I didn't do anything, he arranged everything!" stuttered Nino Miceli.

"It's not true!" replied immediately Minasola.

"You made the deal with Luca and Marshal Lo Bianco!"

Turiddu looked at them with disgust.

"What a nice pair of cowards and traitors!"

"And I even trusted you!"

Minasola tried to calm him down:

"Turiddu, we've always been loyal to you! If we co-operated with the police, it was because we were forced to! Otherwise they were going to arrest us!"

My brother had no intention of listening to their excuses and he continued to interrogate them:

"Where are my men now?"

"They must be in some station in Palermo" answered Miceli.

Turiddu turned to Pisciotta:

"Gaspare, stay with these two traitors! Watch them and, if they try to escape, kill them!"

He explained to Aspanu that he was going to try to propose Col. Luca an exchange of prisoners. He wrote him the following message:

**"I have no informers, you have my men. If they are still alive, free them! And I won't kill Minasola and Miceli".**

He waited a few days for his reply. But it was clear that Luca did not care whether they were spared or not. Turiddu returned to Castelvetrano. He had to define the last details of his agreement with Verdiani with regard to the end of the movie and his departure.

Gaspare Pisciotta was left to guard the prisoners. From the very moment Turiddu left, they tried to corrupt him. Benedetto Minasola was very clever for being a man without any school education. He knew how to talk convincingly.

He told how they had captured his friends. He reminded him of their friendship, but he invited him to look at the new situation. He said that Turiddu's days were counted. Sooner or later they would have captured him or killed him.

First Pisciotta was amused by what they said, but soon he started to worry. There was no need to know psychology to understand him. Minasola, that old fox, knew that he had him in his power. He told Pisciotta to cooperate with the police.

Gaspare was confused.

How could he betray the man that saved his life? They were blood brothers! Nino Miceli put an end to his perplexities like a tempting devil.

"And you have all these scruples, while Turiddu has made a deal with Verdiani to leave the country! He'll leave you here like a poor fool! The carabinieri will kill you!"

"It's not true! He says he will take me with him!" answered Pisciotta.

"If you join us, you have nothing to lose! You'll be a free man again! You'll have a part of the reward! Luca has raised it to 80 million Lire!"

"All I want is to be free!" answered Pisciotta faintly.

Both men said together:

"Free us and you'll get what you want!"

Gaspare was convinced and he accepted their offer. He freed

them and made a deal to meet Col. Luca. The Colonel wanted to avoid running risks, so he sent Col. Paolantonio because he still did not know well enough the last traitor.

And if Pisciotta captured him? What a dishonor for the Corps!

On the evening of June 19, 1950 Col. Paolantonio, Marshal Lo Bianco, Benedetto Minasola and Gaspare Pisciotta met in a house in Monreale. There they set the price for his betrayal: a pass with Pisciotta's photo on it with the name Giuseppe Faraci signed by Minister Scelba, a false passport and 25 million Lire (about one third of the reward).

After selling his friend, Pisciotta reached him in Castelvetrano. Turiddu was surprised to seem him.

"What are you doing here? Where are Minasola and Miceli?"

Gaspare Pisciotta staged the farce. Not even a professional actor could have done as well. He put his hands in his hair to show that he was desperate.

"It's a miracle I'm alive! I could barely keep my eyes open when those two men jumped at me!"

"Good job! You let them go like a beginner. Now rest! Tomorrow we'll decide what to do!"

In the meantime in Palermo one of the three men in isolation decided to cooperate with the Carabinieri. He too joined the long list of traitors teamed against Turiddu. He was lured by the promise of freedom and the money of the reward. He was ready to do anything.

Col. Giacinto Paolantonio, together with Marshal Lo Bianco and Calandra had succeeded in their plan. From that moment the "faithful" picciotto was no longer treated like a prisoner. He was a guest in the station.

He could go around freely and with the necessary precautions and an escort he could even go outside whenever he pleased.

Col. Ugo Luca was satisfied: his plan to defeat Turiddu was working. He knew he could never have succeeded in capturing my brother with the ordinary and extraordinary means he had. Only by resorting to the deception and betrayal of those closest to him, could he hope to succeed. Now thanks to this man helping Gaspare Pisciotta, he had an ace up his sleeve. His chances of winning were much better now.

Aspanu and Turiddu stayed together for three days in Castelvetrano, but my brother wanted to punish Miceli and Minasola: they deserved a severe punishment. He sent Pisciotta to Monreale to find them. If he succeeded, he would have then come to join him.

Gaspare arrived in Monreale on June 24, 1950. He knew where to go look for his accomplices. He told them the farce he had staged to convince Turiddu of their escape. They ate and drank together as they laughed of the ingenuousness of my brother who had believed his lies. He even told them of the task that Turiddu had assigned him.

Benedetto Minasola realized that the time had come to put the Colonel's plan into action. He informed the Colonel and he arranged a meeting between him and Gaspare Pisciotta.

Their first meeting was held in Monreale on June 26, 1950. Luca had come together with Capt. Perenze for the occasion. The two officers confirmed the terms of the deal made with Col. Paolantonio. They said that he was now one of their men.

They even gave him a special pass authorizing him to go around armed.

There is irrefutable evidence of the contacts between Pisciotta and Luca. The following letter from Gaspare was sent to the colonel. It was published in the newspaper *"L'Ora"* on June 5, 1972.

**"Dear Col. Luca,**

**Thank you for your letter. I am glad to hear that you will keep your promise especially in the light of those feelings of trust and frankness that have been established between us. As I wrote to you, I believe that the place we chose for the meeting with our friend is not indicated for the purpose, especially since it is very delicate and secret. You can trust no one. With regard to the meeting, I think that the Montelepre area would be fine, as long as you promise that all your men in town and the surrounding area will be sent away. Only if you keep your promise can we bring peace to Sicily and Italy and free them from this torment and the Communist threat. I cannot reveal anything now in this letter. I will tell you when we meet. If you satisfy my request, I promise you that I will be at your complete disposal and I guarantee that I will be useful to the poor, to the Government, and especially to Christian Democrat party. If you want the plan to work, tell our friend not to say anything to anyone even at the cost of dying. Don't make any move before talking to me. Avoid going out at night and change your car continuously to avoid being identified. Keep the Archbishop of Monreale, Giacalone, under surveillance. After it is all over, I will wait for what you promised.**

**Yours truly,**
**Gaspare"**

After that meeting, Pisciotta and Capt. Perenze became great friends. The next day the officer invited him to his house in Palermo. He took him to the Military Hospital for a check-up with Dr. Fici. Gaspare was happy. He could walk around the city together with the Captain and his gun well in sight.

The last link of the chain of betrayals had now been bonded. Only if Turiddu anticipated his departure could he hope to save himself.

In those days all the leading figures of Italian politics were in Sicily for the Fair of the Mediterranean. They had discussed the possibility of capturing my brother. The decision was unanimous. He was sentenced to death. Turiddu knew too much. He had had direct contacts with politicians, magistrates, prelates, generals of all corps, police officers and Carabinieri. He was a threat for their careers. They had to shut his mouth for good. Turiddu had to die.

With his revelations Turiddu could have caused a scandal of such dimensions that not only the regional government was at risk, but also the Italian State.

In the meantime Gaspare Pisciotta was staying at the house of Captain Perenze. On June 30, 1950, together with him and Col. Luca, he went to the Carabinieri station in Corso Calatafimi. They had to discuss the last details with the other traitor.

Probably it was an idea of the officers, but all the soldiers would salute Pisciotta as if he were an officer. Pisciotta was in ecstasy. In less than a month he passed from being an outlaw to an officer of the Corps of the Carabinieri. But his change was too great to be held a secret. He was too happy of his new position. He spoke of it to a girl he knew.

As soon as he left the girl sent a message to Turiddu. He addressed it to Giuseppe Marotta in Castelvetrano. The message said:

**"Beware of Pisciotta and take action immediately!"**

Marotta rushed worryingly to Turiddu. He found him in the house of the lawyer, Gregorio Di Maria. He was frantic:

"Turiddu! Turiddu! Look here! He too has betrayed you!" he said as he handed him the message.

"Leave this house! Anticipate your departure! Leave! I will find you a safer place for tonight! You must escape!"

Turiddu did not pay attention. That message could have been a trick to damage his friend. He answered dryly to Marotta's exhortations:

"If I have to beware of Pisciotta, then I must beware of you too! No! It can't be true! Gaspare is like a brother for me!"

Inspector Verdiani too had discovered the betrayals. At the risk of his life and career he wrote a letter to Turiddu using the stationary of the Border authorities.

The message arrived the day after that of Pisciotta's friend at the home of Di Maria. He said:

**"Beware of Pisciotta. He is in contact with the Carabinieri. Beware, the carabinieri and police are ready to get you!"**

This time Turiddu could not discard the warning. He decided to go once again to Monreale to see what was happening. Before leaving, he called a taxi driver in that town. He was a friend that had helped him other times. He asked him to tell Pisciotta that he was coming and he set an appointment in "Villa Carolina", which was half way between Monreale and Pioppo.

It was July 3, 1950.

Gaspare was informed of the message around noon and he left for Palermo with a black Fiat 1100 that the carabinieri had given him to use. He contacted Luca and Perenze. They then informed the others that the time had come.

Once again, the two officers showed Pisciotta that they trusted him. They gave him the picciotto "living" in isolation cell in the station in Corso Calatafimi. He was given a sachet with a white powder in it. There was message in it wrapped with an elastic band:

"You can sleep 24 hours with this." Gaspare took his "colleague" and they returned to Monreale.

It was almost dark when Turiddu arrived. He found Pisciotta smiling outside the door. Before answering he said:

"Why haven't you kept in touch?"

"Finding them isn't that easy! I still haven't found out anything!" answered Pisciotta promptly.

Turiddu looked straight into his eyes, but he turned away.

"You're lying!"

"What are you saying? How can you have doubts about me?"

He sounded sincere although he seemed a bit insecure. Behind him he could see a table with some bread and a bottle of wine. Turiddu went in and sat down. He pulled out some fresh cheese. Gaspare sat down in front of him. He was waiting for Turiddu to take off his gun to eat, but this time he did not.

His accomplice was hidden, ready to intervene once he received the signal. They both hoped to catch him by surprise, but they did not have the chance. If Gaspare tried to pull out his gun, Turiddu could have preceded him. He had only one hope: the sleeping powder sent to him by new friends. He managed to put it into the wine.

He filled the glasses and made believe that he was drinking too. Turiddu never drank wine, except for a glass every now and then during meals.

He looked at Gaspare with his piercing eyes to watch every move of his. He was insecure. Finally he was starting to realize everything. Maybe he was feeling like Caesar: he was ready to die, when he saw the conspirators headed by Brutus. His eyelids were heavy. The drug was starting to work.

He left his weapons and bags. He went into the other room. He took off his clothes and went to bed. He was fast asleep after a few minutes. Pisciotta waited half an hour before going in. They silently went in. They tied Turiddu's wrist to the bed with iron wire and his feet.

It was too easy! Too easy!

Now all they had to do was inform Minasola and Miceli. They would have informed the others. It was about midnight when Pisciotta left Turiddu with the other man. Up to when they were in company they had encouraged each other. But when Nunzio Badalamenti was left alone with Turiddu, he started to feel scared. He had received clear orders. There could be no hesitation. He had killed other times during shootings, but never in cold blood. It was different. Even if he was sleeping and tied up, the victim still scared him. He was sweating cold, his hands trembled as he looked at Turiddu while he slept. He looked at the gun in his hand and then at Turiddu. The idea of the reward and liberty made him more resolute. He pointed the gun against Turiddu's body. He closed his eyes and shot three times. Turiddu did not move. No sound came out of his mouth. He passed from sleep to death instantly. His relaxed expression did not change. He looked as if he were smiling. It was as if death had freed him.

He had been betrayed by those who he considered as his most loyal friends. He was sold like Jesus Christ. The comparison is not farfetched: Christ was betrayed for 33 pieces of silver, my brother for 80 million lire. The difference is not that great if you consider 2000 years of inflation.

With his premature death, he abandoned the scene of life like a redeemed man: he was purified by his good faith and by his betrayed friendship. His body now immobile laid there: the blood started to pour abundantly out of the wounds and down his neck. It started to form a pool near his shoulders.

His assassin was overwhelmed by the horror and remorse for what he had done. But there was already someone outside ready to take him back to his cell. Gaspare, Miceli and Minasola arrived in "Villa Carolina" on July 4, 1950 at dawn. When they found the body they were started to panic. Turiddu's killing was not part of the deal with Luca.

They were all dismayed: Pisciotta feared the retaliation of those still loyal to Turiddu. If they found out that he had betrayed, his life was in danger. He could no longer walk around freely. Someday, somewhere there would be a bullet waiting to kill him.

Minasola and Miceli knew that they had broken specific rules. If someone found Turiddu's body in their territory, they would have been sentenced to death and sooner or later they would have been executed.

They were all afraid for their lives so they decided to wait for Col. Luca and Capt. Perenze. Then they would decide what to do. At seven o'clock the officers arrived. They were not surprised at all by the news of Turiddu's death. They already knew how the story was to finish. The problem was the complaints and worries of the three traitors.

Capt. Perenze was a very imaginative man. In a few minutes he came up with a solution. He explained his idea to those present. Everyone knew that Turiddu had spent the last six months in the province of Trapani. Gaspare Pisciotta knew his hiding places. All they had to do was to leave the body there and stage a shootout.

The three killers would be safe thanks to this good idea and the Carabinieri would be attributed the merit of the killing of my brother. The idea was perfect: it was accepted unanimously. The three traitors were to guard the area around "Villa Carolina". They had to keep people away to avoid that the body be discovered.

Luca and Perenze returned to Palermo to organize the farce, but before leaving they split the spoils with the traitors. Luca took Turiddu's diary with the names of all the people he had been in touch with and with all the truth about the massacre in Portella. Capt. Perenze took his watch. He then gave it to Col. Paolantonio. The three jackals split the money that Turiddu saved for his departure.

As soon as Luca and Perenze returned to Palermo, they sent a massive force of carabinieri to Castelvetrano. They ordered that they leave already early in the afternoon. Luca went to meet Judge Emanuele Pili and informed him of the news.

Captain Perenze prepared everything to move the body without attracting attention. His men camouflaged a vehicle of the C.F.R.B. with newspaper posters. They had the time to arrange everything. Then they wrote the report on the false shootout.

The two officers returned to "Villa Carolina" at about 10 o'clock in the evening. They were on board the camouflaged truck driven by a carabiniere named Renzi. Pisciotta was the only one left to guard the house. Minasola and Miceli had run off after taking their part of the money.

First of all, they had to dress the body. It was very difficult owing to the rigor mortis. They put on his pants and sandals. They did not even notice that the belt was passed through all the loops. They did not put on his shirt because his undershirt was soaked with blood. They risked leaving compromising traces on the body. Probably for the same reason or because of the weight of the body, they did not even put the body into the vehicle: they dragged it on the ground.

After taking away his weapons, his belongings and clothing, all the traces left in the house were eliminated with care. Then Roberto Renzi, Capt. Perenze and Col. Luca headed to Castelvetrano with the truck.

Gaspare Pisciotta arrived there a few minutes before with his black Fiat 1100. His job was to "convince" Gregorio Di Maria to cooperate. The beginning of the operation to stage the false shootout started in Castelvetrano after midnight. Two carabinieri in disguise passed through via Serafino Mannone ordering people who were still outside to return to their homes and shut themselves in. But they met with resistance: due men working for the local bakery owned by a man named Lo Bello were sitting on the sidewalk waiting for the bread to rise. They had no intention of closing themselves in owing to the heat but they had to surrender to the orders of the law enforcement agents. It took more than half an hour before this operation was finished.

Once he had received the signal that the coast was clear, Gaspare Pisciotta passed with his car. He stopped in front of Di Maria's house. The lawyer knew him well and let him in. He had given them refuge many times.

Pisciotta went straight to the point and aimed his gun against him. The lawyer was trembling with fear and he listened in silence to Gaspare. He did not dare to oppose any resistance even when he was informed of what was going to happen in his courtyard.

The same treatment was reserved for the lawyer's mother and his maid, Nedda Frosina, who lived with her. Pisciotta threatened that he would kill them if they refused to cooperate and if they ever revealed what was happening.

Luca and Perenze arrived at the lawyer's home at two o'clock at night. They left the truck parked near the war memorial. They went there on foot to check the place: they went around the courtyard many times to determine the exact place where to put the body. Finally they knocked at the door to see if Pisciotta had done his part of the job. Once he confirmed that everything was fine, the two officers went outside again.

All around the house there were many soldiers hidden. Perenze called Brigadier Catalano and ordered him to go to the square and to get the truck. The brigadier took another man, Pietro Giuffrida, with him. He went to carry out the order he had received. It was almost 3 o'clock of July 5, 1950, when the truck drove without headlights down Via Serafino Mannone and went into the courtyard.

Perenze arranged the body on the ground: he laid it on the ground with its head bent to the left, with the left arm still close to the body, while the right one was stretched out. A gun was placed a few centimeters away from his hand. His right leg was slightly bent, while the other one was stretched out. All around they scattered some of Turiddu's belongings. Then they walked around his body a few times. When everything seemed ready, they pulled a gun and shot three times in the air. It was the signal for the start of the operation: the truck went away followed by Pisciotta's black 1100.

The moment had come for the farce. Captain Perenze took Turiddu's machinegun and shot into the air and then put it down next to the body. He took another machinegun and opened fire on the body. Capt. Perenze "courageously" killed a man already dead for 24 hours during a "shootout".

On July 5, 1950, the *"Giornale di Sicilia"* and *"La Sicilia"* informed the Sicilian people of the incident: a special edition was published immediately: "SALVATORE GIULIANO KILLED BY THE MEN OF THE C.F.R.B." "Operation headed by Col. Luca".

This was the official version for the people.

When it all happened I was still in jail in Termini Imerese when I heard the news. I felt like dying but I recovered immediately.

Turiddu had warned me.

I started to doubt: everything in the newspapers could not be true. These doubts have accompanied me for my whole life. These doubts have been fueled also by the fact that a few days earlier a young man who looked very much like Turiddu from Altofonte disappeared the day before the "official death" and there has been no news of him ever since.

That morning a petty officer of the Carabinieri went to knock at our door in Montelepre. He seemed satisfied, almost provocative. He said triumphantly to my mother:

"Do want to see your son for one last time? If so, come with us to Castelvetrano!" said the officer as he pointed to a car parked outside. My mother remained calm, but her heart was full of contrasting feelings. She told the officer to wait a few minutes. She went out and walked down the main road. She went to the house of Lillo Maggiore, the family's doctor, and asked him whether he could come with her. From the look on her face, the people understood that the long-feared day had come.

She remembered the message she had received a few days before:

"If they come one day to call you to say that I am dead, don't believe them!" But was he dead or alive? Turiddu was really dead? Or was someone else killed instead of him as Inspector Ciro Verdiani had been planning to do for some time now?

These atrocious doubts were pounding in her head. Deep down in her heart she hoped that he was alive. She went to Castelvetrano for the identification. She was accompanied by the family doctor, my sister Giuseppina and her husband who had recently been released from Ustica.

Along the road the doctor informed my mother of what he read in the newspapers. Her doubts kept growing and growing in her mind. It was impossible that Turiddu had died without defending himself. If there really were a shootout he would not have died alone.

In the meantime the authorities were carrying out the routine formalities. A report was written on the position of the body and it listed all his belongings. The reporters and the special envoys kept arriving from everywhere. Col. Luca was surrounded by the journalists as he showed off telling the details of the operation. But one of them asked:

"And for you this is a body that was killed last night at 3.30? How do you explain the dry blood on his neck where there are no wounds and the fresh blood under the body? How do you explain this stain here that does not run downwards but upwards? How do you explain these abrasions on his arms and face and these signs of tying around his wrists?"

That reporter was Tommaso Besozzi: Luca's bluff had been discovered. He stood up suddenly and sent everyone away. He ordered that the body be taken away to the morgue and put in some ice.

Why the ice if he had been killed a few hours earlier?

When my family reached Castelvetrano, his body had already been taken away. They made their way amongst the carabinieri, the police and the reporters. The latter were blinding them with the flashes of their cameras. The morgue was a long hallway with three rooms arranged longitudinally. The body was in the room at the end of the hallway.

Our mother advanced slowly looking straight ahead until she reached the second room. Before seeing his face, he seemed to recognize his body. She screamed desperately and fell to the ground. The doctor helped her immediately.

My sister Giuseppina was behind them, with her eyes veiled with tears and she saw our mother fall. She understood that it was our brother. She too fainted. Her husband managed to catch her before she fell. She tried to comfort her as best as he could, while the Dr. Maggiore was assisting our mother.

It took several minutes before she regained conscience. When they had recovered, the carabinieri led them out. The fainting was proof enough that the body was our brother's. For them the identification was over.

These are the facts.

Of all the versions on Turiddu's death, this is the one that we, the members of the Giuliano family, believe or that at least is the most likely.

Over all these years, it has been corroborated by many spontaneous testimonies: former carabinieri and police officers who were there in Castelvetrano that night, the Monreale taxi driver who received the message for Pisciotta, the testimonies of the farmers who saw Turiddu in Sagana on July 3, 1950 and the confession of Nunzio Badalamenti to his cellmates.

In conclusion, since no member of our family was allowed to see the body to search for some distinguishing sign, someone may ask whether is he really dead.

I have been asked this question hundreds of times. The answer to this question could be given by Inspector Ciro Verdiani, Judge Emanuele Pili, Col. Luca and all those who were in power at the time in Sicily and in Rome, if they were still alive. Maybe the truth is in those papers that the Anti-Mafia Committee cautiously ordered to keep secret until the year 2016. Those who will live to see that date will know.

The only fact was that body lying in the morgue in Castelvetrano. But if his body is really dead, his name and his legendary feats are still alive. The adventurous life of this extraordinary man who was a giant compared to the men of the Sicily of his days will never be forgotten. He was already a legend when he was still alive.

Turiddu is immortal.

Those who have fought for a sacred ideal is worthy of the admiration and the respect of the whole world. Those who suffer and die for it will live forever in the memory of their descendents, in the hearts of those who met him, loved him and know the truth.

They still speak of him and his feats with great respect. They speak as if it all happened yesterday, as if all these years had not gone by. For them, and for every Sicilian who is worthy to be called so anywhere in the world. Turiddu Giuliano was Sicily's Robin Hood, a superb warrior and fervent patriot, the symbol of the rebellion of the South against its oppression and slavery, A TRUE HERO.

Turiddu at his desk in De Maria's home in Castelvetrano.

*My Brother, Salvatore Giuliano*

Turiddu is ready to abandon the scene.

Nunzio Badalamenti and Frank Mannino.

Police Inspector Ciro Verdiani.

*My Brother, Salvatore Giuliano*

The macabre farce.

*My Brother, Salvatore Giuliano*

*My Brother, Salvatore Giuliano*

*My Brother, Salvatore Giuliano*

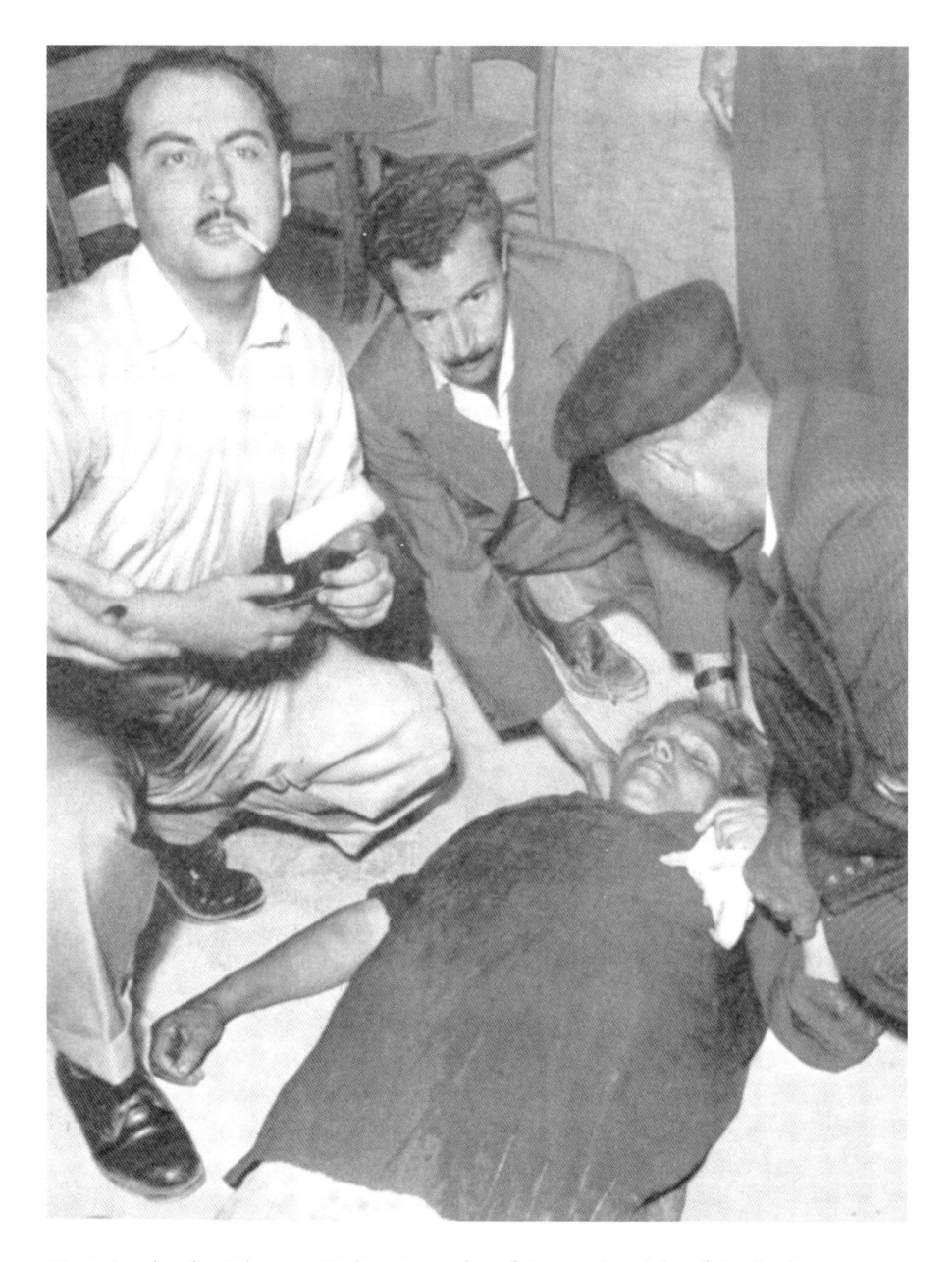

Maria Lombardo, Salvatore Giuliano's mother, faints at the sight of the body.

*My Brother, Salvatore Giuliano*

Luca tells the press his "story".

Carabinieri Colonel Paolantoni as he comments the news of Giuliano's death.

*My Brother, Salvatore Giuliano*

Marianna Giuliano shows the shirt of her summer uniform a few years before her death on May 10, 1986.

# WHAT REMAINS TODAY
IN MONTELEPRE

My Brother, Salvatore Giuliano

The house where Salvatore Giuliano was born.

The entrance to the cemetery in Montelepre.

Salvatore Giuliano's tomb.

Giuliano's Castle. The entrance to the restaurant and hotel.

A lateral view of Giuliano's Castle.

*My Brother, Salvatore Giuliano*

The entrance of the Castle's party hall.

Front view of Giuliano's Castle.

With cleverness (the eagle), strength and courage (the lion) I shall conquer Sicily (Trinacria). This was the coat of arms created by Salvatore Giuliano and carved into the golden buckle of his belt.

TABLE OF CONTENTS

Introduction ................................................................................. 5

CHAPTER I        - We Were Peaceful Farmers ........................................ 11
CHAPTER II       - The Man ................................................................ 17
CHAPTER III      - Human Folly Prevails. . . War Breaks Out! ............. 27
CHAPTER IV       - For a Handful of Wheat ........................................... 41
CHAPTER V        - Retaliation ............................................................. 53
CHAPTER VI       - Solitude ................................................................. 59
CHAPTER VII      - The Escape ............................................................ 67
CHAPTER VIII     - The Law of the Jungle ............................................ 73
CHAPTER IX       - The E.V.I.S. (Voluntary Army for
                   Sicilian Independence) Is Born .............................. 87
CHAPTER X        - The Two Colonels ................................................... 105
CHAPTER XI       - The War for Independence ..................................... 117
CHAPTER XII      - Checkmate! ........................................................... 137
CHAPTER XIII     - The Cease-Fire is Over! ......................................... 151
CHAPTER XIV      - Hurray for the Bride and the Groom! ..................... 167
CHAPTER XV       - My Brother and Portella delle Ginestre .................. 177
CHAPTER XVI      - The Ordeal of a Family .......................................... 195
CHAPTER XVII     - Illusions and Disappointments ............................. 209
CHAPTER XVIII    - Destruction all around Turiddu ............................. 221
CHAPTER XIX      - A Long Chain of Betrayals ..................................... 233
CHAPTER XX       - The Man Dies. . . The Legend Lives On .................. 253

What Remains Today in Montelepre ................................................. 279

Printed by Officine Grafiche Riunite - Palermo (Italy)
February 2000